Revising
A Level Accounting
By June Baptista M.Ed, M.Com

Welcome to Revising A Level Accounting. This book will be an invaluable tool to students who wish to gain mastery of the syllabus, as well as to teachers as a resource to set homework and class work to supplement those available in the student book. The question and answer format is intended to help both teachers and students write better answers.

Contact the author for answers at: junebaptista@hotmail.com

A catalogue record for this title is available from the National Library of New Zealand.
ISBN 978-0-473-15093-8
Photocopying prohibited

TABLE OF CONTENTS

CHAPTER 1
REVISION OF FUNDAMENTAL PRINCIPLES AND TECHNIQUES

Q **What does the double entry method of bookkeeping mean?**

Ans. For every business transaction, two entries are required: a debit and a credit.

Accounts debited are: Cash, goods or services received, assets, expenses and loses.

Accounts credited are: Cash, goods or services given, liabilities, revenue, income and profits.

Q **Where are accounts located?**

Ans. Accounts are located in Ledgers: The Sales ledger, the Purchases ledger and the Nominal ledger. Cash and cheque transactions are entered in the Cash book.

Q. **What are the different types of accounts?**

Ans. There are three types of accounts:

- a.   Personal accounts – accounts of people or businesses e.g. Jack's Account
- b.   Real accounts – account of tangibles e.g. Machinery account
- c.   Nominal accounts – accounts of intangibles e.g. Rent account

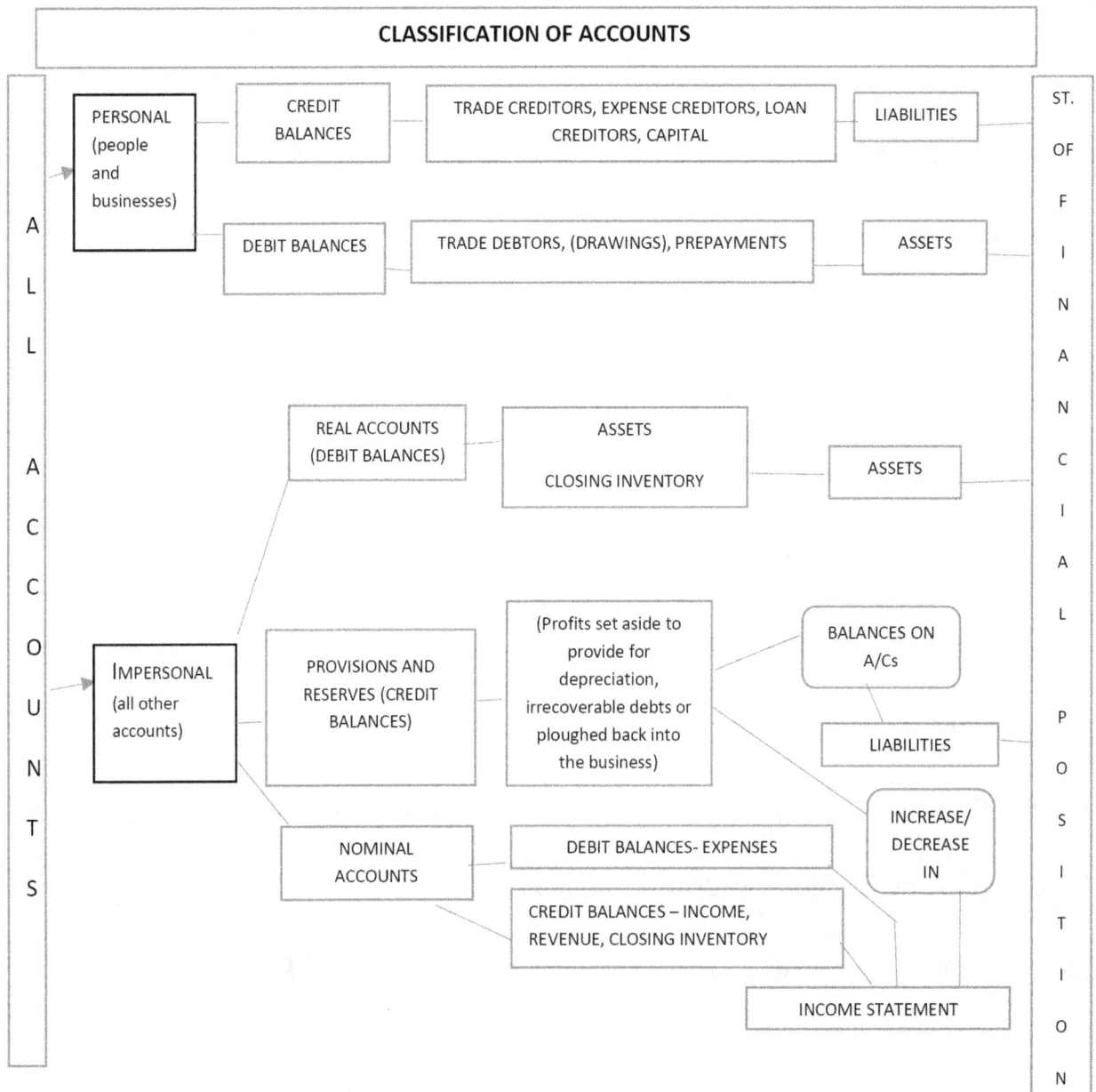

CLASSIFICATION OF ACCOUNTS

ALL ACCOUNTS

- PERSONAL (people and businesses)
  - CREDIT BALANCES → TRADE CREDITORS, EXPENSE CREDITORS, LOAN CREDITORS, CAPITAL → LIABILITIES
  - DEBIT BALANCES → TRADE DEBTORS, (DRAWINGS), PREPAYMENTS → ASSETS
- IMPERSONAL (all other accounts)
  - REAL ACCOUNTS (DEBIT BALANCES) → ASSETS / CLOSING INVENTORY → ASSETS
  - PROVISIONS AND RESERVES (CREDIT BALANCES) → (Profits set aside to provide for depreciation, irrecoverable debts or ploughed back into the business) → BALANCES ON A/Cs / LIABILITIES
  - NOMINAL ACCOUNTS
    - DEBIT BALANCES- EXPENSES → INCREASE/ DECREASE IN
    - CREDIT BALANCES – INCOME, REVENUE, CLOSING INVENTORY
    - INCOME STATEMENT

ST. OF FINANCIAL POSITION

THE TRIAL BALANCE AND ERRORS

Q. What is a Trial balance?

Ans. A Trial balance is a list of all balances in ledger accounts and the cash book at a given date. The debit balances are listed in the debit column and the credit balances in the credit account. If the totals of the two columns are equal, the ledger accounts, on the face of it, are arithmetically correct.

Q. Which errors are not disclosed by the Trial balance?

Ans. Errors that are not disclosed by the Trial balance are:
1. **Errors of omission.** Transactions omitted completely from the books of account.
2. **Errors of commission.** These errors occur when a posting is made to a wrong account of the same type.
3. **Errors of principle.** These occur when a posting is made to a wrong account of a different type, e.g. an item of capital expenditure is posted to a nominal account instead of being posted to a real account.
4. **Complete reversal of entries.** This arises when a posting is made to the wrong side of an account. An error twice its own size is caused.
5. **Errors of original entry.** These errors occur when postings are made to the right account on the right side of the account but with the wrong figures.
6. **Compensating errors.** These are errors which cancel each other out.

Q. Which errors are disclosed by the Trial balance?

Ans. The following errors are disclosed by the Trial balance:
a. Arithmetic errors
b. When only one of two postings is made
c. When two postings are made but with different figures.

Q. When is a suspense account opened?

Ans. A Suspense account is opened when the trial balance does not balance. (See Chapter 4)

Exercise 1.1

Decide whether the following items will appear in the debit or credit column of the Trial Balance (the first one is done for you):

Purchases -Debit
Sales revenue
Return outwards
Cash
Drawings
Capital
Trade receivables
Trade payables
Motor Van
Rent
Discounts allowed
Return inwards
Carriage outwards
Rent receivable
Carriage inwards

Bank overdraft
Stationery
Opening Inventory

DEPRECIATION

Q. What is meant by the term 'depreciation'?
Ans. Depreciation is the fall in the value of an asset due to factors such as wear and tear, obsolescence, depletion or time.

Q. What is the reason for making a provision for depreciation?
Ans. A provision is made for depreciation of an asset in order to spread the amount of depreciation over the useful life of that asset. This is done due to the matching principle. The cost of using the asset is matched to the revenue earned by it.

Q. What are the methods of calculating the annual provision for depreciation?
Ans. The three methods are:

a. The straight line method: The provision is a fixed charge calculated as a percentage or by using the following formula.

$$\text{Annual provision for depreciation} = \frac{\text{cost of asset} - \text{residual value}}{\text{estimated useful life (in years)}}$$

b. The reducing balance method: Depreciation is calculated as a fixed percentage of a written down value of the asset at the beginning of the year.

c. The revaluation method: This method is used for assets for which detailed records cannot be conveniently maintained e.g. loose tools. It is calculated by using the following formula.

Provision for depreciation = value of asset at start of year + additions during the year – value of asset at the end of the year.

EXERCISE 1.2

Depreciate a computer which cost $5000 for three years:
a) Using the Straight Line method @ 10%
b) Using the Reducing Balance Method @ 25 %.

EXERCISE 1.3

A firm provides for depreciation on its machinery at 10% of the cost of the machinery in existence at the end of the financial year. They find that they have charged machinery repairs $ 450 to the machinery account.
Required:
a. How would such an error have affected their profits of $3500?
b. Does it have any other effect on the financial statements of the company?

Q. Give the accounting entry to record the provision for depreciation of an asset.
Ans. *Debit:* the Income Statement
Credit: Provision for Depreciation of the asset account with the annual charge for depreciation.

Q. Does the annual charge for deprecation involve any payment?

Ans. No. It is a bookkeeping entry to match the cost of using the asset to the revenue earned by it during a year. It is a non-monetary item in the Profit and Loss section of the Income Statement.

Q. How is the provision for depreciation treated in the Statement of financial position?
Ans. The accumulated provisions for depreciation is deducted from the relevant asset to arrive at the net book value (or written down value) of the asset. The net book value is the balance of the original cost of the non-current asset not yet written off against revenue. It does not represent what the asset is worth and is not a statement of selling price of the asset.

Q. How is profit or loss on disposal of an asset calculated?
Ans. The following formula is used:
Profit/(loss) = proceeds of disposal – (original cost – accumulated depreciation to date of disposal)
OR
Profit/(loss) = proceeds of disposal – net book value at the date of the sale.

Q. What is meant by the term 'exceptional depreciation'?
Ans. When an event occurs that significantly reduces the value of a non-current asset as a result of which the asset's Net Book Value is more than the disposal value of the asset, then the asset is said to be 'impaired'. The procedure to follow in such an event is to reduce the Net Book Value immediately to its recoverable value. This is also called the 'carrying amount'. The reduction is treated as loss which is charged to the Income Statement. This is termed 'Exceptional Depreciation'.

EXERCISE 1.4
A Machine was purchased in 2000 at a cost of $100,000. It was presumed to have a useful life of 10 years with a residual value of $5,000. Depreciation was to be provided in the year the car was bought but not in the year of disposal. In 2005 it was found that the machine had a recoverable value of only $40,000
Required:
a) Find the Net Book Value of the machine at 31st December 2004.
b) What is the amount debited to the Income Statement on 31st December 2005?
c) If the machine now has a useful life of 4 years with no residual value, what should the Annual Depreciation be for the next 4 years?

EXERCISE 1.5
A car was purchased in 2001 at a cost of $35,000. It was presumed to have a useful life of 8 years with a residual value of $3,000. Depreciation was to be provided in the year the car was bought but not in the year of disposal. In 2003 it was found that the car had a recoverable value of only $20,000.
Required:
 a. **Find the Net book Value of the car at 31st December 2002.**
 b. **What is the amount debited to the profit and loss account section of the Income Statement on 31st December 2003?**
 c. **If the car now has a useful life of 5 years with a residual value of $500, what should be the annual depreciation for the next 5 years?**

EXERCISE 1.6
Machinery was bought for $6000 on July 5th 20x0. Depreciation is calculated using the straight line method @15% p.a. on machinery in use at 31st December. On 10th October 20x2 the machinery was sold for $1200 cash.

You are required to show:
a) Machinery a/c
b) Provision for depreciation a/c
c) Disposal of machinery a/c

EXERCISE 1.7
A firm bought two Motor Vehicles for $5000 each paying by cheque on 3rd January 20x1. Their policy was to depreciate their vehicles using the straight line method @ 10% on the basis of 'one month's ownership equals one month's depreciation'. On July 1st 20x2 one of the Motor Vehicles was sold for $4500 cash.
You are required to show for the period up to December 31 20x2
a) The Motor Vehicles A/c
b) The Provision for Depreciation – M.V. a/c
c) The Disposal of Motor Vehicle a/c

Q. What is meant by the term 'part exchange'?
Ans. When a new asset is acquired, it may be acquired in part exchange of a used asset being disposed of.

Q. What is the journal entry passed in such a case?
Ans. The part exchange value of the asset being disposed of is debited to the Non-current Asset Account and credited to the Disposals Account as the proceeds of disposal.

EXERCISE 1.8
A tractor was purchased for $35,000 on Jan 10, 20x4. The cost was settled by a cheque payment of $28,000 and the part exchange of a Motor Vehicle for the balance. The Motor Vehicle had cost $24,000 and had accumulated depreciation of $17,000 at Jan 10, 20x4. Depreciation is charged in the year of purchase and not in the year of disposal.
You are required to draw up the following accounts to show all the above transactions:
a) Tractor at cost
b) Provision for depreciation of Motor Vehicle
c) Motor Vehicle disposal

EXERCISE 1.9
Mallama's transactions in the year ended 31st December 20x5 included the following:
January 1 Machinery at cost $10,000; Provision for depreciation of machinery$5,900
August 8 Sold machine No 2x45 for $ 2,300. This machine had cost $4,500 when purchased in 20x3.
October10 Purchased machine No 4x34 which was priced at$2,700. The cost was settled by a cheque payment of $1,900 and the part exchange of machine No5x34. Machine No 5x34 had cost $1,320 when purchased in 20x2.
Mallama depreciates her machinery at 10% using the straight line method. She provides a full year's depreciation in the year of purchase, but none in the year of disposal.
Required: Prepare the following accounts to show the transactions on August 8 and October 10:
a) Machinery at Cost
b) Provision for Depreciation of Machinery
c) Machinery Disposal

PROVISION FOR IRRECOVERABLE DEBTS

Q. What are the different types of provision for irrecoverable debts?
Ans. The provision for irrecoverable debts may be:
  a. Specific – against identified debts

b. General – based on a percentage of debtors
c. A combination of both methods.

Q. What is the accounting entry to record a new provision for irrecoverable debts?

Ans. The accounting entry to record a new provision for irrecoverable debts is:

Debit Income Statement

Credit Provision for irrecoverable debts account

Q. What is the accounting entry to record an increase in an existing provision for irrecoverable debts?

Ans. The accounting entry to record an increase in an existing provision for irrecoverable debts is:

Debit: Income Statement

Credit: Provision for irrecoverable debts account

Q. What is the accounting entry to record a decrease in an existing provision for irrecoverable debts?

Ans. The accounting entry to record a decrease in an existing provision for irrecoverable debts is:

Debit Provision for irrecoverable debts account

Credit Income Statement.

EXERCISE 1.10

Josh maintains a provision for irrecoverable debts which is made up of a specific provision for irrecoverable debts and a general provision equal to 4% of the remaining debtors. The following information is available from Josh's books:

At 31 December

	Total debtors/ Trade receivables	Irrecoverable debts (included in total debtors)
	$	$
20x2	35,000	2,500
20x3	41,000	7,300
20x4	54,000	4,600
20x5	29,000	8,700

Required:

Calculate the total Provision for Irrecoverable Debts for each of the above years.

EXERCISE 1.11

Prepare:

a) The provision for irrecoverable debts account

b) The Income statement (extract)

c) The Statement of financial position (extract) to show the effect of each of the following:

1. On 30th June 200X the trade receivables were $24,000. Irrecoverable debts for the year were $3500. Irrecoverable debts which were not included in total trade receivables were found to be $1,200. It was decided to make a general provision for irrecoverable debts at 2%.

2. On 31st July 200x the trade receivables were $12,000, irrecoverable debts were $3200 and it was decided to provide for irrecoverable debts at 2.5% of remaining debtors/trade receivables.

3. On 30th June 200X the trade receivables were $20,000. Irrecoverable debts for the year were $1000. It was decided to provide for irrecoverable debts at 1.5% of debtors/trade receivables.

4. On 31st July 200x the trade receivables were $10,000, irrecoverable debts were $3000 and it was decided to provide for irrecoverable debts at 2.5% of remaining trade receivables.

EXERCISE 1.12

Jason has the following balances:

At 31st December 20x1: trade receivables $3000

At 31st December 20x2: trade receivables $5000

He maintains a provision for Irrecoverable Debts at 6% of closing trade receivables.

Required as at 31st December 20x2:

a) Provision for Irrecoverable Debts A/c

b) The Income statement (extract)

c) The statement of financial position (extract)

√ *Tip: The opening balance of the provision = 6% x 3000*

The closing balance of the provision = 6% x 5000

EXERCISE 1.13

Mary has debtors amounting to $3000 at 31st December 20x2. Her provision for irrecoverable debts account has a balance of $400. She wishes to provide for debtors at 10% of closing debtors.

Required:

a) Provision for Irrecoverable Debts a/c

b) Extract of the Income statement

c) Extract of statement of financial position

EXERCISE 1.14

Joey started business on January 1st 20x0. He adjusted his provision for irrecoverable debts at the end of each year on a percentage basis, in accordance with the current 'economic climate'. The following details are available for the three years ended 20x0, 20x1 and 20x2:

Year	Irrecoverable debts written off year to Dec. 31st	Trade receivables at Dec 31	% Provision for irrecoverable debts
20x0	147	4000	6
20x1	300	5000	7
20x2	400	4500	4

Required for each of the three years:

a) Irrecoverable Debts accounts

b) Provision for irrecoverable debts accounts

c) Extracts from the statement of financial position

FINANCIAL STATEMENTS

These are made up of: The income statement or the statement of financial performance

The statement of financial position (The balance sheet)

INCOME STATEMENTS

Q. Define:

a. The trading account

b. The profit and loss account

Ans. a. The Trading account is a section of the income statement wherein the gross profit is calculated. Gross profit = Sales revenue – (opening inventory + purchases – closing inventory)

b. The profit and loss account is a section of the income statement wherein the profit for the year is calculated. Profit for the year = Gross profit + income – expenses.

STATEMENT OF FINANCIAL POSITION
Q. Define: A statement of financial position

Ans. As the name suggests, a statement of financial position shows the financial position of a business. It lists the non-current assets, current assets, non-current liabilities, current liabilities and capital of a business.

EXERCISE 1.15
Sam is a sole trader. The following trail balance was taken from his books on 31st December, 20x1.

	Dr	Cr
	$	$
Furniture	47,000	
Capital		64,500
Sales revenue		102,000
Salaries	10,000	
Inventory at 1st Jan. 20x1	11,000	
Purchases	58,800	
Carriage inwards	1,000	
Insurance	2,000	
Electricity	1,600	
Irrecoverable debts	500	
Other operating expenses	2,300	
Motor expenses	1,500	
Advertising	1,600	
Discounts received		2,700
Provision for depreciation–Motor Van		500
Motor Van at cost	10,500	
Cash at bank	2,600	
Trade payables		2,500
Trade receivables	7,000	
Drawings	14,800	
	172,200	172,200

Sam gives you the following information:

1) He purchased goods worth $4500 in November 20x1. The invoice for these goods was not received until 3rd January 20x2. There are no entries in Sam's books regarding this transaction.

2) Depreciation for the year is as follows: Furniture @10% Straight Line; Motor van @ 10% Reducing Balance.

3) On 31st December 20x1: Insurance prepaid was $300; Electricity expenses accrued was $350

4) Inventory at 31st December 20x1 was $12000.

5) A provision for irrecoverable debts is to be made @ 5% of trade receivables

Prepare:

a) Sam's Income statement for the year ended 31st December 20x1

b) Sam's Statement of financial position as at 31st December 20x1.

BOOKS OF PRIME ENTRY

Q. What is meant by the term: books of prime entry?
Ans. These are books into which the first entries are made immediately after transactions have taken place and before they are entered in the ledger. They are also known as 'books of original entry' or 'subsidiary books'. There are separate books for different kinds of transactions. e.g. credit sales will be entered into the sales journal, a book of prime entry.

Q. Name the different books of prime entry.
Ans. The Books of Prime entry are:
a) The Sales Journal
b) The Purchases Journal
c) The Sales Returns Journal
d) The Purchases Returns Journal
e) The Cash Book
f) The General Journal.
g) The Petty Cash Book

Q. Outline two uses of the books of prime entry.
Ans. The uses of Subsidiary books are:
a) They are used to enter transactions that occur very often during the course of a business day. Hence, the ledgers are saved from being cluttered with too many insignificant details. Only the totals are posted into the Nominal ledger at the end of the month.
b) They save frequent trips to the ledger.

EXERCISE 1.16
Enter up the Purchases Journal and the Purchases Returns Journal from the following details. Then post to the Suppliers' accounts and show the transfers to the General ledger.
20x8
January 1   Credit purchases: Kombe $350, Sellaway $670
January 4   Credit purchases: Mallasa $270, Kellagary $500.
January 8   Goods returned by us to the following: Kombe $60, Mallasa $70.
January 11   Credit purchases: Phillipe $680, Kombe $300.
January 27   Goods returned by us: Phillipe $70.
January 30   Credit purchases : Phillipe $370.

EXERCISE 1.17
Sambo is a sole trader who buys and sells on credit. His transactions for the month of August 20x7 include the following:
August 3   Inventory sold to Ace & co. for $1000
August 7   Inventory sold to Ali & Sons for $450
August 14   Inventory returned to Ali & sons $50
August 25   Inventory sold to M. Ebrahim $2,000
August 29   Inventory returned to M. Ebrahim $300

Required:
a) Enter the transactions in Sambo's Sales Journal and Sales Return Journal and show the totals for the month.
b) Make the necessary entries in the ledger accounts.

BANK RECONCILIATION STATEMENT

Q. What is a Bank Reconciliation Statement?
Ans. A Bank reconciliation statement is a statement that reconciles the closing balance at the bank according to the business cash book and that of the bank statement, when they are different.

Q. Outline the steps to reconcile the differences between the closing balances in the cash book and the bank statement.
Ans. Steps to reconcile the differences between the closing balances in the Cash Book and the Bank Statement:
1) Mark with a tick the items in both the cash book and the bank statement that are similar
2) Circle the ones that are not ticked. Draw up an updated cash book incorporating the circled items from the bank statement. (Remember, items on the credit side of the Bank Statement will be entered on the debit side of the Cash Book and vice versa).
3) Update the cash book using items circled in the Bank Statement).
3) Draw up a Bank Reconciliation Statement using the items circled in the Cash Book.

EXERCISE 1.18

The following are extracts from the cash book and the bank statement of Jason.
You are required to:
a. **write up the cash book up to date**
b. **state the new balance as on 31st December 20x2.**

Cash Book

20x2		$			$
Dec 1	Bal b/d	1650	Dec 5	Nina	350
Dec 6	M. Mistry	300	Dec 16	Vivek	140
Dec 18	J. Wood	450	Dec 20	S. Big	250
Dec 24	M, Baron	120	Dec 31	Bal c/d	1780
		2520			2520

Bank Statement

20x2		Dr	Cr	Balance
Dec 1	Bal b/d			1650
Dec 6	3408	350		1300
Dec 8	Deposit		300	1600
Dec 20	Vivek	140		1460
Dec 21	Wood		450	1910
Dec 23	S. Big	250		1660
Dec 27	Deposit		120	1780
Dec 28	Credit transfer		200	1980
Dec 31	Bank Charges	60		1920

TEST YOURSELF

1.1. Multiple Choice questions
i) Which of the following accounts will normally have a credit balance?
a) Trade payables

b) Stationery
c) Drawings
d) Purchases

ii) Which of the following accounts will normally have a debit balance?
a) Capital
b) Rent
c) Rent receivables
d) Purchases returns

iii) Which of the following errors do NOT affect the Trial Balance?
a) An error in calculation.
b) Recording a debit entry and not recording the corresponding credit entry.
c) Recording one figure in the debit entry and a different one in the credit entry.
d) An account that should have been debited has been credited and the account that should have been credited has been debited.

iv) John sold inventory to Gayatri $450 on credit. He debited Gaya's account incorrectly but credited Sales correctly. Which journal entry should be passed to correct this error?

Account to be debited	Account to be credited
A) John $450	Gayatri $450
B) Gayatri $450	Gaya $450
C) Gayatri $900	Gaya $900
D) Gaya $450	Gayatri $450

v) Ebrahim received $345 cash in full settlement of a debt owing to him by Hussein of $350. How should this be recorded in Ebrahim's books?

Account/s to be debited	Account/s to be credited
A) Cash $345	Hussein $345
B) Cash $345	Discounts Allowed $5; Hussein $345
C) Hussein $345	Cash $345
D) Hussein $350	Cash $345; Discounts Received $5

vi) Mogambo paid Agatha $350 by cheque. Agatha debited Mogambo's Account $350 and credited her bank account with $350 in error. Which of the following entries will correct this error?

Account debited	Account credited
A) Mogambo $350	Bank $350
B) Mogambo $700	Bank $700
C) Bank $700	Mogambo $700
D) Bank $350	Mogambo $350

vii) Sheriff discovered that he had totalled his Sales Invoice to Malini incorrectly as $321 instead of $231. Which of the following entries should he pass to correct this error?

Account to be debited	Account to be credited
A) Malini $90	Sales $90
B) Malini $231	Sales $231
C) Sales $90	Malini $90
D) Sales $ 231	Malini $231

viii) Interest received amounted to $12,700 and interest paid amounted to $8,000. The interest paid has been credited to the Income Statement and the interest received has been debited to the Income Statement.
What is the resulting effect on the profit for the year of the business?
A) Profit for the year overstated by $4,700

B) Profit for the year understated by $4,700
C) Profit for the year overstated by $20,700
D) Profit for the year understated by $20,700

ix) The following are the balances on Jan 1 20x5 concerning leasehold premises:

	$
Historic cost	40,000
Provision for depreciation	8,000

The financial year end is 31st December and leasehold premises are to be amortised over the term of the lease of 20 years on a straight-line basis.
What is the provision for depreciation for the year ended December 31 20x5?
a) $1,600
b) $2,000
c) $400
d) $3,200

1.2. An inexperienced bookkeeper has extracted a Trial Balance at 31st December 20x2 from Eric's books.
It contains some errors and does not balance

	Dr	Cr
	$	$
Purchases		45,000
Sales revenue	34,000	
Trade payable	32,000	
Trade receivable		54,000
Sales returns	1,560	
Purchases returns	670	
Salaries		1,200
Rent receivable	3,400	
Advertising		14,000
Rent	22,000	
Postage and Stationery		2,140
Discounts allowed	220	
Discounts received	400	
Fixtures and fittings		50,000
Machinery	34,000	
Bank overdraft	12,000	
Drawings		19,000
Land and Buildings	84,000	
Delivery Van		25,500
Inventory at1st December 20x4	20,000	
Inventory at 31st December 20x4	35,000	
Capital	290,150	
	569,400	210,840

Required
Re-write the Trial Balance and correct the errors so that it balances.

1.3. You are given the following information:

	$
N.B.V. of non-current assets on January1, 20x3	27,900
N.B.V. of non-current assets on December 31, 20x3	13,500
N.B.V of non-current assets disposed of during the year ended December 31, 20x3	9,300
Cost of non-current assets purchased during the year ended December 31, 20x3	7,000

Depreciation is calculated at 10% using the straight line method of depreciation.

What is the amount charged to the Income statement for the year ended December 31 20x3 as depreciation?

1.4 You are given the following information relating to the non-current assets of a business:

	$
Net book value at the start of the year	27,000
Net book value at the end of the year	32,800
Depreciation charge for the year	3,200
Disposals at net book value	1,400

Required:
Calculate the value of non-current assets bought during the year.

1.5. A trial balance at 31 December 20x1, before making end-of-year adjustments, showed:

	$
Trade receivables	20,000 (Dr)
Provision for irrecoverable debts	700 (Cr)

At 31 December 20x1, it was decided to write off an irrecoverable debt of $1,000 and to make a provision for irrecoverable debts of 2% of trade receivables. During the year an amount of $300 was received from a customer relating to a debt that was written off in the year ended 31 December20x0.

Required:
Calculate the total irrecoverable debts expense for the year ended 31 December 20x1.

1.6. Seema's bank statement shows a credit balance of $5,890. A comparison with the cash book reveals the following:
  i)   Cheques totalling $16,780, sent to suppliers, have not been presented.
  ii)   Cheques totalling $13,560, received from customers, have not been credited by the bank.
  iii)   Bank charges of $130 have not been entered in the cash book.

Required:
What is the correct cash book balance?

1.7. The following draft statement of financial position as at 31 March 20x7 of Chung Lui, retail trader, was prepared.

		$	$
Non-current assets:			
Freehold property – at cost		24,000	
	- provision for depreciation	4,800	19,200
Motor vehicles	- at cost	18,000	
	- provision for depreciation	9,000	9,000
			28,200
Current assets:			
Inventory		13,000	
Trade receivables		9,000	
Bank		1,600	23,600
			51,800

Current liabilities:
Trade payables and accruals   3,800

Capital – at 1 April 20x6   50,000
Add profit for the year ended 31 March 20x7 10,000
                                                 60,000
Less drawings   12,000   48,000
                                                           51,800

After the draft balance sheet had been prepared, the following discoveries were made:

1.   A quantity of goods sent to M. Chow on a sale or return basis remained unsold on 31 March 20x7. These goods had cost Chung Lui $600 and were expected to sell for $1,000.   In preparing the draft accounts for the year ended 31 March 20x7, it was assumed that all the goods had been sold on credit by M. Chow as planned. M. Chow is to be paid a commission of 2% on the gross proceeds of all sales made for Chung Lui.

2.   Trade receivables include $200 due from L Lingham who has now been declared bankrupt. It is unlikely that any money will be received for this debt.

3.   A provision for irrecoverable debts at 31 March 20x7 of 2% of trade receivables at that date is to be created.

4.   Provision is to be made for electricity charges of $700 accrued due at 31 March 20x7.

5.   On 1 October 20x6, Chung Lui hired (leased) a motor van for one year from Ace Vehicles Ltd. The hire charge of $3,000 was paid in advance. However, in preparing the draft accounts above, it was assumed that the motor van had been purchased for $3,000.

6.   Chung Lui depreciates freehold property @10% per annum on cost and Motor vehicles @ 25% per annum on cost.

Required:
A corrected statement of financial position as at 31 March 20x7.

CHAPTER 2
ACCOUNTING POLICIES, PRINCIPLES AND STANDARDS

Q. What are accounting policies?

Ans. IAS 8 defines accounting policies as 'the specific principles, bases, conventions, rules and practices applied by an entity in preparing and presenting financial statements'.

Q. List the two factors that should be borne in mind when selecting policies.

Ans. The two factors that should be borne in mind are:
a. Where an accounting policy is given in an accounting standard then that policy must apply.
b. Where there is no accounting policy provided to give guidance then the directors of the entity must use their judgement to give information that is relevant and reliable. They must refer to any other standards or interpretations or to other standard setting bodies to assist them. However, they must ensure that their subsequent interpretation or recommended method of treatment for the transaction does not result in conflict with international standards or interpretations.

Q. What are accounting principles?

Ans. Accounting principles can be defined as the broad concepts that apply to almost all financial statements. These would include such things as going concern, materiality, prudence and consistency.

Q. What are accounting bases?

Ans. The methods developed for applying the accounting principles to financial statements. They are intended to reduce subjectivity by identifying and applying acceptable methods.

Q. What are Accounting objectives?

Ans. The objective of:
1. The Statements of comprehensive income is to provide a 'true and fair view' of the profit or loss made by a company for the year.
2. The Statement of financial position is to give a true and fair view of the state of affairs of a company at the date of publication of the statement.

Q. Define the term 'true and fair view'.

Ans. The word 'true' means that the information contained in the statements are an indication that they are based on transactions that have in fact taken place. E.g. the figure for sales revenue recorded in the income statement represents the actual sales made during the period. The word 'fair' implies that assets or transactions shown are in keeping with accepted accounting rules of valuation and cost.

Q. Who are the users of accounting information?

Ans. The users of accounting information are:

Suppliers – to ensure that performance ensures payment of their dues.

Government - to assess performance in relation to tax liabilities

Investors – they use past performance as a basis for future investment.

Lenders – to ensure that performance ensures payment of their dues.

Employees - to assess performance as a basis of future wage and salary negotiations and to gauge continuity of employment.

Customers - to ensure performance in relation to the likelihood of continuity of trading

The general public - to ensure ethical trading.

Q. Define the Historic cost principle.

Ans. This principle requires that all assets are normally shown at cost price. It is the cost price that is used as a basis of valuation of an asset. This is done to avoid subjectivity when valuing an asset.

Q. Define the Business entity principle.

Ans. This principle implies that the affairs of the business are treated as being separate from the non-business activities of its owner/s.

Q. Define the dual aspect principle.

Ans. This principle states that there are two aspects to every transaction. One account is always debited and another is credited. These two aspects are always equal to each other. The name given to this method of recording transactions is: The double entry method.

Q. Define the money measurement principle.

Ans. Accounting information is concerned with facts that: 1) can be measured in money 2) most people will agree to that money value.

Q. Explain the substance over form principle.

Ans. This is when the practical aspect (substance) is preferred to the legal aspect (the form) of a business transaction. For example, a car bought for business purposes on hire purchase remains the property of the seller, legally, until the final instalment has been paid. This is the legal view (the form). However, the car is being used by the purchaser for business purposes and this is the practical aspect (substance). The accounting view is that the car is no different from other cars that have not been bought on hire purchase.

Q. Define the accruals principle.

Ans. This Principle states that all expenses and income relating to the financial period to which the accounts relate should be taken into account without regard to the date of payment or receipt, respectively.

Q. Define the prudence principle.

Ans. There are two aspects to this principle:
1) All assets should be understated rather than overstated and all liabilities should be overstated rather than understated. The accountant should choose the figure that will cause the capital of the firm to be shown at a lower amount rather than at a higher one. This ensures 'a true and fair view' of the statement of financial position.
2) Profits should not be anticipated and all losses should be recorded. This ensures 'a true and fair view' of the Income statement.

Q. Define the realisation principle.

Ans. Profits should be realized on a sale when the title has passed. Profits should be treated as realized only when realized in the form of cash or of other assets (e.g. trade receivables). When a trader sends goods to a potential customer on 'Sale or return', for instance, the sale has not taken place until the customer informs the trader that she has decided to buy the goods.

Q. Define the going concern principle.

Ans. This principle implies that the business will continue to operate for the foreseeable future.

Q. Define the consistency principle.

Ans. Once a firm has fixed a method for the accounting treatment of an item, it will enter all similar items that follow in the same way. If the firm does change the method, it should be after a lot of consideration. If profits are affected by a material amount due to a change then, either in the Income Statement itself or in the reports accompanying it, the effect of the change should be stated.

Q. Mention the circumstances when changes in accounting policies may occur.

Ans. Changes in accounting policies can only occur:

a. if the change is required by a standard or interpretation.

b. if the change results in the financial statements providing more reliable and relevant information. Once any changes are adopted then they must be applied retrospectively to financial statements. Thus, the previous figure for equity and other figures in the income statement and statement of financial position must be altered, subject to the practicalities of calculating the relevant amounts.

Q. Define the concept of Materiality and aggregation.

Ans. This concept states that classes of similar items are to be presented separately in the financial statements. This would apply to a grouping such as current assets.

Q. What are the uses of an IAS (International Accounting Standard)?

Ans. The objectives of the standard are:
- To ensure that appropriate recognition criteria and measurement bases are applied. E.g. to provisions, contingent liabilities and contingent assets
- That sufficient information is disclosed in the notes.

Q. Enumerate the topics covered by the IAS as required by CIE.

Ans. The topics are:

IAS1 Presentation of financial statements

IAS2 Inventories

IAS7 Statement of cash flows

IAS8 Accounting policies

IAS10 Events after the statement of financial position date

IAS16 Property, plant and equipment

IAS18 Revenue

IAS23 Borrowing costs

IAS33 Earnings per share

IAS36 Impairment of assets

IAS37 Provisions, contingent liabilities and contingent assets

IAS38 Intangible assets

Q. What does IAS1 say about offsetting?

Ans. Offsetting is generally not permitted for both assets and liabilities and income and expenditure. For example it is not permitted to offset a bank overdraft with another bank account not in overdraft.

Q. What does IAS 1 say about comparative information?

Ans. There is a requirement to show the figures from the previous periods for all the amounts shown in the financial statements. This is designed to help users of them to make relevant comparisons.

Q. List the four qualitative factors of financial statements.

Ans. The factors are:

a) **Understandability** – the information is readily understandable by users.

b) **Relevance** – the information may be used to influence economic decisions of users.

c) **Reliability** – the information is free from material error and bias.

d) **Comparability** – the information enables comparisons over time to identify and evaluate trends.

Q. What does IAS1 say about the components of financial statements?
Ans. A complete set of financial statements comprises of:

a. The income statement or a statement of comprehensive income
b. A statement of changes in equity
c. Accounting policies and explanatory notes.
d. The statement of financial position or a statement of financial information/position
e. A statement of cash flow

Exhibit

ABC Limited		
Income Statement/Statement of comprehensive income for the year ended	This year $000	Last year $000
Revenue	100,000	80,000
Cost of Sales	(60,000)	(45,000)
Gross Profit	40,000	35,000
Distribution Costs	(8,000)	(7,000)
Administration Expenses	(11,000)	(10,000)
Profit/(Loss) from Operations	21,000	18,000
Finance Costs	(3,000)	(2,000)
Profit/(Loss) Before Tax	19,000	16,000
Tax	(4,500)	(4,000)
Profit/(Loss)for the year attributable to Equity Holders	14,500	12,000
Other income and revaluation gains can be shown after the profit or loss attributable to equity holders		

Exercise 2.1
You are given the following information by Carousel Ltd:

	20x2 $	20x1 $
Revenue	200,000	120,000
Cost of sales	130,000	90,000
Distribution costs	7,000	6,500
Administration expenses	3,000	5,000
Finance costs	2,500	1,500
Tax	1,500	1,000

Required:
Draw up an income statement for the year ended 20x2 in proper form.

Exhibit		
Statement of Changes in Equity		
Retained Earnings		
	This year $000	Last year $000
Balance at start of year	43,000	35,000
Profit for the year	14,500	12,000
Transfers for other reserves (Revaluation Reserves, Share Premium, Revenue Reserves, etc.)	-	-
	57,500	47,000
Dividends (Ordinary) paid	(5,000)	(4,000)
Transfers to other reserves	-	-
Balance at end of year	52,500	43,000

Template for alternative presentation
Statement of changes of equity for the year ended..................

	Share capital and reserves	Retained earnings	Revaluation reserve	Total equity
Balance at start of the year				
Total profit (comprehensive income) for the year				
Dividends paid				
New share capital				
Balance at the end of the year				

Exercise 2.2
Mohanlal Ltd gives you the following information:

	20x2 $	20x1 $
Retained earnings b/f	80,000	75,000
Profit for the year	16,000	14,000
Ordinary dividends paid	6,000	4,000
Transfer to general reserve	6,000	5,000

Required:
Draw up a statement of changes in equity in proper form.

Exhibit of an explanatory note: Ordinary Dividends

	This year $000	Last year $000
Amounts recognised as distributions to equity holders during the year:		
Final dividend for last year of $0.075 per share	3,000	2,200
Interim dividend for this year of $0.050 per share	2,000	1,800
	5,000	4,000
Proposed final dividend for this year of $0.095 per share	3,800	3,000

Note:
1. *Only ordinary dividends paid during the year are now included in the financial statements.*
2. *The proposed final ordinary dividend is subject to approval of the shareholders at the Annual General Meeting. It is only included by way of a note to the financial statements.*
   No liability is included in the financial statements in respect of the proposed final ordinary dividend.

Exercise 2.3
Kale Ltd's equity share capital is made up of 100,000 ordinary shares of $1 each.
You are given the following information:
Final dividend for the year ended 20x2 was $5000
Final dividend for the year ended 20x0 was @6%

Interim dividend paid for the year 20x2 was $3,000
Interim dividend paid for the year 20x1 was $1,000
Proposed dividend for the year ended 20x2 was @4.5%
Proposed final dividend for the year ended 20x1 was $5000

Required:
Draw up a dividend note for the company for the year ended 20x2

Exhibit of Statement of financial position (This format is not currently preferred)

XYZ Limited
Statement of Financial Position at ....

	This year $000	Last year $000
Non – current Assets		
Goodwill	7,700	8,000
Property, Plant & Equipment	100,000	92,100
	107,700	100,100
Current Assets		
Inventories	1,000	800
Trade and other receivables	5,000	4,000
Cash and cash equivalents	500	300
	6,500	5,100
Current Liabilities		
Trade and other payables	1,200	1,000
Tax liabilities	3,500	4,000
	4,700	5,000
Net Current Assets	1,800	100
Non – Current Liabilities		
Bank Loan	(5,000)	(5,200)
	104,500	95,000
Equity		
Share Capital	40,000	40,000
Share Premium	2,000	2,000
General Reserve	10,000	10,000
Retained Earnings	52,500	43,000
	104,500	95,000

Alternative template (currently preferred):

XYZ Limited
Statement of financial position/Statement of Financial Position at ....

	This year $000	Last year $000
Non – current Assets		
Goodwill	7,700	8,000
Property, Plant & Equipment	100,000	92,100
	107,700	100,100
Current Assets		
Inventories	1,000	800
Trade and other receivables	5,000	4,000
Cash and cash equivalents	500	300
	6,500	5,100
Total Assets	114,200	105,200
Equity and Liabilities:		
Equity		
Share Capital	40,000	40,000
Share Premium	2,000	2,000
General Reserve	10,000	10,000
Retained Earnings	52,500	43,000
	104,500	95,000
Non – Current Liabilities		
Bank Loan	5,000	5,200
Current Liabilities		
Trade and other payables	1,200	1,000
Tax liabilities	3,500	4,000
	4,700	5,000
Total Equity and Liabilities	114,200	105,200

Q. Define: window dressing
Ans. Directors of companies are known to inflate profits and understate loses in an attempt to portray the financial position of a company to be better than it really is. For example, cheques to creditors may be drawn on the last day of the financial year but sent only at the start of the next financial year. The liabilities of the company would thus be artificially deflated in the Statement of Financial position. However, it is not a true and fair view as the creditors have not, in fact, been paid.

Q. What does IAS 2 deal with?
Ans. IAS 2 deals with inventory valuation.

Q. Define: Inventory
Ans. IAS 2 defines inventory as the stock of goods which the business holds in a variety of forms:
1. Raw materials for use in a subsequent manufacturing process.

2. Work in progress, partly manufactured goods.

3. Finished goods, completed goods ready for sale to customers.

4. Finished goods which the business has bought for resale to customers.

Q. List possible costs of purchase.
Ans. Purchase price, transport costs, import duty, other direct handling costs are included in cost of purchase.

Q. List possible costs of Conversion
Ans. Direct labour, direct materials and cost of production are known as costs of conversion.

Q. How should inventory be valued?
Ans. Inventory should be valued at the lower of cost and net realisable value.

Exhibit
The Amina Stationery Company bought 20 boxes of photocopier paper at $4 per box. Following a fire in their stockroom 4 of the boxes were damaged. They were offered for sale at $2 per box. All were unsold at the end of the company's financial year.
Required:
At what price will they be valued in the annual accounts?

Solution:
16 boxes will be valued at their cost of $4 per box, a total of $64.
4 boxes will be valued at $2 per box, a total of $8.
The total stock value will be $72.

Q. How are groups of similar items of inventory valued?
Ans. Each item in the group should be considered separately when deciding whether they should be valued at cost or net realisable value. This is to ensure that there are no hidden losses.

Exhibit
Mally sells five different grades of products. The following are the costs and net realisable value of these grades:

	Cost	NRV
	$	$
Grade 1	400	350
Grade 2	1,000	980
Grade 3	600	640

Grade 4	570	600
Grade 5	1500	2,000
	4,070	4,570

Required: Calculate the value to be used for inventory valuation.

Solution:	$
Grade 1	350
Grade 2	980
Grade 3	600
Grade 4	570
Grade 5	1,500
Inventory Value	4,000

Exercise 2.4

Selma sells six different grades of a product. The following are the costs and net realisable value of these grades:

	Cost	NRV
	$	$
Grade 1	300	450
Grade 2	900	990
Grade 3	500	570
Grade 4	300	360
Grade 5	700	670
Grade 6	1,400	1,000
	4,100	4,040

Required:
Calculate the value to be used for inventory valuation.

Q. What does IAS 2 say about the different methods to be used for valuing inventory?

Ans. IAS 2 allows two different methods for valuing inventory:

1. First in, first out (FIFO). This assumes that the first items to be bought will be the first to be used, although this may not be the physical distribution of the goods. Thus, remaining inventory valuation will always be the value of the most recently purchased items.

2. Average cost (AVCO). Under this method a new average value (usually the weighted average using the number of items bought) is calculated each time a new delivery of inventory is acquired.

IAS does not allow for inventory to be valued using the Last in, first out (LIFO) method.

Similarly, inventories which are similar in nature and use to the company will use the same valuation method. Only where inventories are different in nature or use can a different valuation method be used.

Once a suitable method of valuation has been adopted by a company then it should continue to use that method unless there are good reasons why a change should be made. This is in line with the **Consistency** principle.

Q. What are the different types of inventory held by a manufacturing company?
Ans. A manufacturer may hold three categories of inventory:
   a. Raw materials
   b. Work in progress
   c. Finished goods

Q. How should raw materials be valued?

Ans. Raw materials are valued at the lower of the cost of the raw materials (applying either FIFO or AVCO) and their realisable value.

Q. How should work in progress and finished goods be valued?
Ans. IAS 2 requires that the valuation of these two items includes not only their raw or direct material content, but also includes an element for direct labour, direct expenses and production overheads. The cost of these two items therefore consists of:

    a. Direct materials
    b. Direct labour
    c. Direct expenses
    d. Production overheads – costs to bring the product to its present location and condition
    e. Other overheads which may be applicable to bring the product to its present location and condition.

Q. What is excluded from the cost of these work in progress and finished goods?
Ans. The cost of work in progress and finished goods excludes:

    a. Abnormal waste in the production process
    b. Storage costs
    c. Selling costs
    d. Administration costs not related to production.

Exhibit:
The XYZ Manufacturing Company manufactures wooden doors for the building trade. For the period under review it manufactured and sold 8,000 doors. At the end of the trading period there were 2,000 completed doors ready for despatch to customers and 200 doors which were half completed as regards direct material, direct labour and production overheads.
Cost for the period under review were

	$
Direct material used	10,000
Direct labour	6,000
Production overheads	4,200
Non-production overheads	10,000
Total Costs for the period	30,200

Required:
Calculate the value of work in progress and finished goods.

Solution

Total units sold	8,000
Finished goods units	2,000
Half completed units (200 x 0.5)	100
Production for the period	10,100
Attributable costs	$20,200

Cost per unit = 20,200 / 10,100 = $2
Value of work in progress:
200 x 0.5 x $2 = $200
Value of finished goods:
2,000 x 2 = $4000
(Adapted from the IAS booklet published by The University of Cambridge International Examinations)
Note: Overheads are excluded from the calculations.
The value of finished goods will be compared with their net realisable value when preparing the final accounts.

Exercise 2.5

Thematic Manufacturing Company manufactures Chairs for schools. For the period under review it manufactured and sold 10,000 chairs. At the end of the trading period there were 5,000 completed chairs ready for despatch to customers and 150 chairs which were one third completed as regards direct material, direct labour and production overheads.

Cost for the period under review were

	$
Direct material used	15,000
Direct labour	9,000
Production overheads	1,500
Non-production overheads	5,000
Total Costs for the period	30,500

Required:

Calculate the value of work in progress and finished goods.

Q. What does IAS 7 deal with?

Ans. IAS 7 deals with cash flow statements. This topic is covered in chapter 15.

Q. How does IAS 8 define errors?

Ans. Errors are defined as: 'omissions from, and misstatements in, the entity's financial statements for one or more prior periods arising from a failure to use, or misuse of, reliable information that:

    a. was available when those financial statements for those periods were authorised for issue; and

    b. could reasonably be expected to have been obtained and taken into account in the preparation and presentation of those financial statements'

Errors in this context could be mathematical mistakes, mistakes in applying policies and oversights or misinterpretation of the facts. It also includes fraud.

Q. What is the general principle to be followed when an error is made?

Ans. The general principle is that the entity must correct material errors from prior periods in the next set of financial statements. Thus, comparative amounts from prior periods must be restated, subject to the practicalities of calculating the relevant amounts.

Q. Explain: Events after the statement of financial position date.

Ans. These are events which occur between the statement of financial position date and the date on which the financial statements are authorised for issue. They can be favourable or unfavourable. Such items may occur as a result of information which becomes available after the end of the year and, therefore, need to be disclosed in the accounts.

The key is the point in time at which changes to the financial statements can be made. Once the financial statements have been approved for issue by the board of directors they cannot be altered. For example, the accounts are prepared up to 31 December. They are approved for issue by the board of directors on 30 April in the following year. Between these two dates, changes resulting from events after the 31 December can be disclosed in the accounts.

Q. List the two events that could occur after the statement of financial position date.

Ans. There are two types of events:

    a. Adjusting

    b. Non – adjusting

Q. Write a short note on adjusting events.

Ans. If, at the date of the statement of financial position, evidence of conditions existed that would materially affect the financial statements then the financial statements should be changed to reflect these conditions.

Examples of adjusting events could include:

a. The settlement after the statement of financial position date of a court case which confirms that a present obligation existed at the date of the statement of financial position.
b. The determination after the date of the statement of financial position of the purchase price or sale price of a non-current asset bought or sold before the year end.
c. Inventories where the net realisable value falls below the cost price.
d. Assets where a valuation shows that impairment is required.
e. Trade receivables where a customer has become insolvent.
f. The discovery of fraud or errors which show the financial statements to be incorrect.

Q. Write a short note on non-adjusting events.
Ans. No adjustment is made to the financial statements for such events. If material, they are disclosed by way of notes to the financial statements. Examples include:
a. Losses of production capacity caused by fire, floods or strike action by employees.
b. Announcement or commencement of a major reconstruction of the business.
c. Changes in tax rates.
d. Entering into significant commitments or contingent liabilities.
e. Commencing litigation based on events arising after the date of the statement of financial position.
f. Major share transactions.
g. Major purchase of assets.

Q. What does IAS 10 say about ordinary dividends declared or proposed after the statement of financial position date?
Ans. Dividends (ordinary) declared or proposed after the statement of financial position date are no longer recognised as a liability in the statement of financial position. They are non–adjusting events and are now to be shown by way of a note to the accounts.

Q. What does IAS 10 say about liquidation of a business after the statement of financial position date?
Ans. If, after the statement of financial position date, the directors determine that the business intends to liquidate or cease trading and that there is no alternative to this course of action, then the financial statements cannot be prepared on a going concern basis.

Q. Define, Using IAS 16:
a. Property, plant and equipment
b. Depreciation
c. Depreciable amount
d. Useful life
e. Fair value
f. Residual value
g. Carrying amount
Ans.
a. Property, plant and equipment are defined as tangible assets:
i. held for use in the production or supply of goods and services
ii. for rental to others
iii. for administrative purposes
iv. which are expected to be used for more than a period of one year.
b. Depreciation can be defined as the systematic allocation of the depreciable amount of an asset over its useful life.
c. Depreciable amount is defined as the cost or valuation of the asset, less any residual amount.
d. Useful life is defined as the length of time, or number of units of production, for which an asset is expected to be used.
e. Fair value is defined as the amount for which an asset could be exchanged between knowledgeable, willing parties in an arm's length transaction.

f. Residual value is the net amount the entity expects to obtain for an asset at the end of its useful life, after deducting the expected costs of disposal.

g. Carrying amount is defined as the amount at which an asset is recognised in the statement of financial position, after deducting any accumulated depreciation and impairment loss.

Q. When is an asset recognised by the entity?

Ans. The statement provides that an item of property, plant and equipment is to be brought into the financial statements when:

1. it is probable that future economic benefits will flow to the entity; and
2. the cost of the asset can be reliably measured.

Q. How are day to day costs of servicing or repairing the asset to be treated?

Ans. Day to day costs of servicing or repairing the asset should be charged as expenditure in the income statement.

Q. How are costs of frequent replacement of parts of the assets to be treated?

Ans. Where parts require frequent replacement then these costs can be recognised as part of the carrying amount of the asset – subject to the rules of recognition. e.g. seats in an aeroplane

Q. How are the costs of regular inspection of an asset to be treated?

Ans. Where the asset requires regular inspections in order for the asset to continue operating then the costs of such inspections can also be recognised in the carrying amount, subject to the rules of recognition.

Q. Which costs, at the time of purchase of an asset, are permitted by IAS 16 to be included in the statement of financial position as the cost of the asset?

Ans. The statement provides that the following can be included as part of the cost in the statement of financial position:

1. the initial purchase price
2. any import duties, taxes directly attributable to bring the asset to its present location and condition
3. the costs of site preparation
4. initial delivery and handling costs
5. installation and assembly costs
6. cost of testing the asset
7. professional fees: architects' or legal fees

Q. Which costs should be excluded from the cost of an asset?

Ans. The following costs should be excluded:

1. any general overhead costs
2. the start-up costs of a new business or section of the business
3. the costs of introducing a new product or service, such as advertising

Q. What does IAS 16 have to say about valuation of an asset, once it is acquired?

Ans. Once the asset is acquired the entity must adopt one of two models for its valuation:

1. Cost model – cost less accumulated depreciation
2. Revaluation model – the asset is included (carried) at a revalued amount. This is taken as its fair value less any subsequent depreciation and impairment losses. Revaluations are to be made regularly to ensure that the carrying amount does not differ significantly from the fair value of the asset at the statement of financial position date.

Q. What guidance does IAS 16 provide about the fair value in the revaluation of
a. land and buildings

b. plant and equipment?

Ans. a. The revaluation of land and buildings is usually determined from a valuation by professional valuers

b. Plant and equipment is revalued at market value.

**Q. Plant and equipment is included as part of a company's non-current assets. It decides to revalue its plant and equipment and finds that some is worth more and some worth less than the values on the statement of financial position.
What does it need to do?**

Ans: The Company must revalue all its plant and equipment.

Q. What guidance does IAS 16 provide about the frequency of the revaluations?

Ans. IAS 16 has this to say:

1. if the changes are frequent then annual revaluations must be made
2. where changes are insignificant then revaluations can be made every three to five years

Q. How is the surplus on revaluation to be treated?

Ans. Any surplus on revaluation is transferred to the equity section of the statement of financial position.

Q. How is loss on revaluation to be treated?

Ans. Any loss on revaluation is recognised as an expense in the income statement.

Q. Should depreciation be charged if the fair value of an asset exceeds its carrying amount?
Ans. Yes.

Q. Should depreciation be charged when the residual value is greater than the carrying amount?
Ans. No.

Q. List the four factors to be taken into account when considering the useful life of an asset?

Ans. When considering the useful life of an asset the following should be considered:

1. expected usage of the asset, its capacity or output
2. expected physical wear and tear
3. technical or commercial obsolescence
4. legal or other limits imposed on the use of the asset

Q. How is freehold land depreciated?

Ans. Freehold land is not to be depreciated, other than in the case of a mine or quarry. It is carried in the statement of financial position at cost.

Q. Are land and buildings to be depreciated together?

Ans. No. Land and buildings are to be separated out. The element of land is not depreciated but the buildings are.

Q. When is an asset derecognised?

Ans. This occurs when the asset is sold or no further future economic benefits are expected from its use. Any profit or loss on disposal is shown in the income statement.

Q. Define: a. Revenue

b. Fair value

Ans. a. Revenue

IAS 18 defines revenue as 'The gross inflow of economic benefits arising from the ordinary activities of an entity.' This means sales, either of goods or services. It also includes income from interest, say bank interest, dividends received and royalties received. The definition can also be widened to include revenue and gains from non – revenue activities, such as the disposal of non – current assets or the revaluation of assets.

b. Fair value:

It is defined as 'The amount for which an asset could be exchanged, or a liability settled between knowledgeable, willing parties in an arm's length transaction.' Revenue is to be measured at the fair value of the consideration received or receivable.

Q. List the three types of income recognised by IAS 18.

Ans. The three types of income are:
1. Sale of goods
2. Rendering of services
3. Interest, dividends and royalties

Q. When can income from sale of goods be recognised?

Ans. This is to be recognised when all of the following criteria have been met:
a) the seller of the goods has transferred to the buyer the significant rewards of ownership.
b) the seller retains no continual managerial involvement in and no effective control over the goods.
c) the amount of revenue can be reliably measured.
d) it is probable that the economic benefits will now flow to the seller.
e) the costs incurred, or to be incurred in respect of the transaction can be reliably measured.

Q. When can income from rendering services be recognised?

Ans. The sale or rendering of services is to be recognised in the seller's books by reference to the stage of completion of the transaction at the statement of financial position date. This is usually regarded as a percentage of completion. Again, in order for recognition to take place, the following criteria have to be met:
a) the amount of revenue can be reliably measured.
b) it is probable that the economic benefits will now flow to the seller.
c) at the statement of financial position date the stage of completion can be reliably measured.
d) the costs incurred in and the costs to complete the transaction can be reliably measured.

Q. When can income from interest, dividends and royalties be recognised?

Ans. In each case it is necessary to consider whether it is probable that the economic benefits will flow to the entity and that the amount of revenue can be reliably measured. Provided these two conditions are met, then the amount is to be recognised as follows:
1. for interest – using a time basis to calculate the interest.
2. for dividends – when the shareholder's right to receive payment is established.
3. for royalties - on an accruals basis in line with the royalty agreement.

Q. What does IAS 23 deal with?

Ans. IAS 23 deals with borrowing costs.

Q. Define: Borrowing costs

Ans. Borrowing cost is interest and other costs incurred in connection with the borrowing of funds. They include interest on bank overdrafts and borrowings, amortisation of discounts or premiums on borrowings and amortisation of ancillary costs incurred in the arrangement of borrowings.

Q. What is a qualifying asset?

Ans. A qualifying assets is an asset that takes a substantial period of time to get ready for its intended use. E.g. property, plant and equipment and investment property during the construction period.

Q. What does IAS 23 say about the treatment of borrowing costs for a qualifying asset?

Ans. Borrowing costs in relation to the acquisition, construction and production of a qualifying asset should be treated as part of the cost of the relevant asset.

Q. How much of the borrowing costs are eligible for capitalisation?

Ans. Where funds are borrowed specifically, costs eligible for capitalisation are the actual costs incurred less any income earned on the temporary investment of such borrowings.

Q. What does the standard say about disclosure?

Ans. IAS 23 states that the following should be disclosed:
1. The accounting policy adopted
2. The amount of borrowing cost capitalised during the period
3. The capitalisation rate used.

Q. What is the basic method of calculating earnings per share as set out by IAS 33?

Ans. Earnings per share (EPS) = $\dfrac{\text{Profit for the year after tax and dividends on preference shares}}{\text{Number of ordinary shares issued}}$

Two earnings per share calculations are to be given:
1. using the profit or loss attributable to ordinary equity holders
2. using the profit or loss from continuing operations

Both of these are to be presented on the face of the income statement. This is usually done at the foot of the statement.

Exhibit:

For the year ended 31 December the income statement of a company shows the following:

	$000
Continuing operations	
Profit before tax	1 500
Tax	(500)
	1 000
Preference dividend	(200)
Profit for the year from continuing operations	800
Discontinued operations	
Profit for the year from discontinued operations	400
Profit for the year attributable to equity holders	**1 200**

At the start of the year the entity had 2 million ordinary shares of $1 each.

Required:
   a. **Earnings per share attributable to equitable shareholders**
   b. **Earnings per share from continuing operations attributable to equity shareholders**

Solution:

a. earnings per share attributable to equity holders = $\dfrac{\$1,200,000}{2,000,000}$ =$0.60 per share

b. Earnings per share from continuing operations attributable to equity holders = $\dfrac{\$800,000}{2,000,000}$

= $0.40 per share

Both of these figures are to be shown on the face of the income statement.

Exercise 2.6
For the year ended 31 December the income statement of MAXX Plc shows the following:

	$000
Continuing operations	
Profit before tax	2 000
Tax	(1 000)
	1 000
Preference dividend	(400)
Profit for the year from continuing operations	600
Discontinued operations	
Profit for the year from discontinued operations	100
Profit for the year attributable to equity holders	**700**

At the start of the year the entity had 1 million ordinary shares of $1 each.
Required:
   a.   **Earnings per share attributable to equitable shareholders**
   b.   **Earnings per share from continuing operations attributable to equity shareholders**

Exercise 2.7
For the year ended 31 December the income statement of a company shows the following:
$000

Continuing operations	
Profit before tax	1000
Tax	(300)
	700
Preference dividend	(250)
Profit for the year from continuing operations	450
Discontinued operations	
Profit for the year from discontinued operations	150
Profit for the year attributable to equity holders	**600**

At the start of the year the company had 1 million ordinary shares of $1 each. On 1st July the company issued a further 1 million shares of $1 each at full market value.
Required:
   a.   **Earnings per share attributable to equitable shareholders**
   b.   **Earnings per share from continuing operations attributable to equity shareholders**

Q. How does IAS 35 identify discontinuing operations?
Ans. IAS 35 identifies this as a relatively large component of a business enterprise, for example a business or geographical segment that the entity is disposing of either by selling it or ceasing operations in respect of it (say, permanently closing it down).

Q. When is discontinuance deemed to have begun?
Ans. The discontinuance begins after the earlier of the following:
   • When the entity has entered into an agreement to sell all or substantially all of the assets of the discontinuing operation, **or**
   • The board of directors has approved and announced the planned discontinuance.

Q. What is to be disclosed?
Ans. The following must be disclosed
1. A description of the operation being discontinued
2. The business or geographical segments in which it is reported. This must be in accordance with IAS 14, a statement not required in the examination.
3. The date the plan for discontinuance was announced
4. The timing of expected completion, if this is known or can be determined

5. The carrying amounts of the total assets and total liabilities to be disposed of
6. The amounts of:
   a. revenue
   b. expenses
   c. and operating profit or loss attributable to the discontinued operation
7. The amount of gain or loss recognised on the disposal of assets or settlement of liabilities attributable to the discontinued operation
8. The net cash flows attributable to the operating activities of the discontinuing operation
9. The net selling prices received or expected to be received from the sale of those net assets for which the entity has entered into a binding agreement, together with the expected timing thereof and the carrying amount of those net assets.

Q. How is it disclosed?
Ans. Only the gain or loss on actual disposal of assets and settlement of liabilities must be shown on the face of the income statement. The IAS does not prescribe a particular way or format for the disclosure. Acceptable ways include:
1. Separate columns in the financial statements for continuing and discontinuing operations
2. One column, but with separate sections (with sub totals) for continuing and discontinuing operations
3. Separate line items for discontinuing operations on the face of the financial statements with detailed disclosures about discontinuing operations in the notes. It must be borne in mind that disclosure requirements of IAS 1 must still be met in this case.
In periods after the discontinuance is first approved and announced and before it is completed, the financial statements must update any prior disclosures relating to the assets and liabilities to be disposed of and changes in the amount or timing of cash flows.

Q. What is the purpose of IAS 36?
Ans. The purpose of this standard is to ensure that assets are carried in the statement of financial position (their carrying amount) at no more than their value or recoverable amount. If the recoverable amount is less than the carrying amount then the carrying amount must be reduced. This is an impairment loss and must be recognised in the income statement as an expense.

Q. What does IAS 36 apply to?
Ans. The standard applies to most non – current assets such as land and buildings, plant and machinery, motor vehicles and so on. It also applies to intangible assets such as goodwill and investments.

Q. Which assets does IAS 36 not apply to?
Ans. It does not apply to inventories, which are the subject of their own standard IAS 2.

Q. Define:
a. Impairment loss
b. Fair value less costs to sell
c. Recoverable amount
d. Value in use
e. Cash generating unit
f. The Impairment Review
Ans.
a. Impairment loss can be defined as 'The amount by which the carrying amount of an asset exceeds its recoverable amount.'
b. Fair value less costs to sell can be defined as 'The amount obtainable from the sale of an asset in an arm's length transaction between knowledgeable, willing parties, less the costs of the disposal.'
   1. The best evidence of fair value is a binding sale agreement less disposal costs.

2. If there is an active market as evidenced by buyers, sellers and readily available prices, then it is permissible to use the market price less disposal costs.
3. Where there is no active market then the entity can use an estimate based on the best information available of the selling price less the disposal costs.
4. Costs of disposal are direct costs only, for example legal or removal expenses.

c. Recoverable amount: In respect of the asset, 'the higher of its fair value less costs to sell and its value in use.'

d. Value in use: 'The present value of the future cash flows obtainable as a result of an asset's continued use, including cash from its ultimate disposal.'

This is usually calculated using discounted cash flow techniques. In considering this the entity should consider the following:

1. Estimated future cash flows from the asset.
2. Expectations of possible variations - either in amount or timing of the future cash flows.
3. Current interest rates.
4. The effect of uncertainty inherent in the asset.

e. Cash generating unit: 'the smallest identifiable group of assets that generates cash inflows that are largely independent of the cash inflows from other assets or group of assets'.

Note here the link back to IAS 16 in respect of these definitions.

The statement gives guidance on the sources or causes of impairment. It does so by looking at them:

Externally, for example:

1. A significant fall in the market price of the asset
2. Adverse effects caused by technology, markets, the economy and laws.
3. Increases in interest rates
4. Stock market valuations, where the stock market valuation of an entity is less than the carrying amount of its net assets.

Internally, for example:

1. Obsolescence or damage to the asset.
2. The economic performance of the asset is worse than expected.

f. The impairment Review: The impairment review involves comparing the asset's carrying amount with the recoverable amount. It is conducted in three stages:

1. Ascertain the asset's carrying amount – its net book value.
2. Compare this with the asset's recoverable amount. The recoverable amount will be the **higher** of:
   - the asset's fair value less costs to sell and
   - the asset's value in use.
3. If the carrying value is greater than the recoverable amount then the asset is impaired. It must be written down to its recoverable amount in the statement of financial position. The amount of the impairment is recognised as an expense in the statement of financial position

Exhibit:

An entity has three non – current assets in use at its statement of financial position date. Details of their carrying values and recoverable amounts are set out below:

Asset	Carrying amount $	Fair value less costs to sell $	Value in use $
1	30000	10000	50000
2	15000	12000	14000
3	20000	15000	9000

In the statement of financial position they should be shown at the following values:

Asset	Value in Statement of financial position $	Reason
1	30000	The carrying amount is less than the recoverable amount, its value in use.
2	14000	The carrying amount is greater than the recoverable amount, the highest of which is its value in use.
3	15000	The carrying amount is greater than the recoverable amount, the highest of which is its fair value less costs to sell.

Q Give an example of a material event, occurring shortly after the year end that should be disclosed <u>only</u> as a note to the accounts?
Ans. Loss of stock due to flood damage.

Q. Maniben Ltd suffered a substantial uninsured loss of $65,000 when stock was stolen from its premises. How will the loss be disclosed in the company's published accounts?
Ans. The loss will be disclosed as an exceptional item.

Q. Lamington & co.'s year end is 31 March 2006. On 15 April 2006 a major fire took place at the company's factory. On 25 April 2006 a major debtor at 31 March 2006 went into liquidation.
In accordance with IAS 10, *Events after statement of financial position date,* how should the two events be treated in the financial statements?
Ans. The fire should be disclosed in notes and the liquidation should accrue in accounts.

Exercise 2.8
The following information is available from the financial statements of LMS Ltd.

	$000
Premium received on the issue of shares	150
Profit on ordinary activities after taxation	600
Unrealised surplus on revaluation of assets	280

Required:
What should the company show as the net gain for the year?

Exercise 2.9

You are given the following information:	$000	$000
Net profit for the year		215
Preference dividends	15	
Ordinary divedends – Interim paid	25	
Final approved	75	115
Retained profit for the year		100

The final dividend, though approved by shareholders will be paid after one year.
Calculate the 'earnings' to be included in the earnings per share?

Q. Under the standard IAS 1 *'Presentation of financial statements'*, give an example of what need not be separately disclosed.
Ans. Profit or loss on overseas operations.

Q. Give an example of an item in the cash flow statement that gives an indication of the company's long-term capital investment policy (as required by IAS 7)
Ans. Capital expenditure.

Q. Give an examle of an event, occuring after the statement of financial position date, that should be adjusted in the statement of financial position.
Ans. A debtor in the statement of financial position subsequently becoming bankrupt.

Q. Why is it important for users of corporate reports that changes in the methods of providing for depreciation of non-current assets be disclosed?
Ans. It enables comparison with previous years' accounts.

Q. IAS 8 describes certain accounting polices including:
a. accruals
b. consistency
c. going concern
d. prudence
Which two accounting policies must be applied in the preparation of published accounts?
Ans. Accruals and going concern

Q. Which profit figure is used in the calculation of earnings per share?
Ans. Net profit for the year after interest.

Q. Give an examle of an adjusting event.
Ans. The insolvency of a major debtor.

Q. Name one non – adjusting event.
Ans. A fire at a warehouse.

Q. Give an example of an item to which the following rule does not apply: 'Certain information concerning non-current assets must be disclosed in the notes to the financial statements'.
Ans. Scrap value of an asset.

Q. Give an example of an adjustment that will result in an increase in a company's profit for the year.
Ans. The capitalisation of development costs.

Q. What does IAS 37 deal with?
Ans. IAS 37 deals with provisions, contingent liabilities and contingent assets.

Q. How is a provision defined under this standard?
Ans. A provision is a liability of uncertain timing or amount.

Q. When should a provision be recognised?
Ans. A provision is recognised when:
- An entity has a present obligation as a result of a past event
- It is probable that an outflow of resources embodying economic benefits will be required to settle the obligation
- A reliable estimate can be made of the amount of the obligation.

Q. Define: Contingent liability
Ans. A contingent liability is:
- a possible obligation that arises from past events and whose existence will be confirmed only by the occurrence or non-occurrence of one or more uncertain future events not wholly within the control of the entity
- a present obligation that arises from past events but is not recognised because either it is not probable that an outflow of resources embodying economic benefits will be required to settle the obligation or the amount of the obligation cannot be measure with sufficient reliability.

Q. Should a contingent liability be recognised?
Ans. No

Q. Should a contingent liability be disclosed?
Ans. Yes, unless the possibility of an outflow of resources embodying economic benefits is remote.

Q. Define: Contingent assets
Ans. A contingent asset is a possible asset that arises from past events and whose existence will be confirmed only by the occurrence or non-occurrence of one or more uncertain future events not wholly within the control of the entity.

Q.   Should a contingent asset be recognised?
Ans. No

Q. What does IAS 38 deal with?
Ans. The objective of IAS 38 is to prescribe the accounting treatment for intangible assets that are not dealt with specifically in another IAS.

Q. How is an intangible asset defined under IAS 38?
Ans. An intangible asset is an identifiable non-monetary asset without physical substance. E.g. patents, computer software, copyrights, motion picture films, customer lists, licenses, import quotas, customer and supplier relationships, marketing rights

Q. How can intangible assets be acquired?
Ans. Intangible assets can be acquired:
- by separate purchase
- as part of a business combination
- by a government grant
- by exchange of assets
- by self-creation (internal generation)

Q. When should an intangible asset be recognised?

Ans. An intangible asset (whether purchased or self-created – at cost) should be recognised if it is probable that the future economic benefits that are attributable to the asset will flow to the enterprise **and** the cost of the asset can be measured reliably.

Q. When should expenditure on an intangible asset be recognised as an expense?
Ans. If the asset does not meet both the definition of and the criteria for recognition as an intangible asset, the expenditure on this asset should be treated as an expense when it is incurred.

Q. What happens if the intangible item does not meet both the definition of and recognition criteria in the case of a business combination?
Ans. Any such expenditure included in the cost of acquisition should form part of the amount attributable to goodwill recognised at acquisition date.

Q. How are intangible assets to be measured?
Ans. Intangible assets (initial measurement) should be measured at cost.

Q. How are research costs treated?
Ans. All research costs are to be treated as an expense.

Q. Are development costs capitalised?
Ans. Yes, but only after the technical and commercial feasibility of the asset for sale or use have been established. This means that the entity must intend to and be able to complete the intangible asset and either use it or sell it or be able to demonstrate how the asset will generate future economic benefits.

Q. How should computer software that has been purchased be treated?
Ans. It should be capitalised.

Q. How should computer software be amortised?
Ans. Computer software should be amortised over the useful life (of not more than 20 years), based on the pattern of benefits. The straight-line method is the default.

Q. How should an intangible asset be amortised?
Ans. An intangible asset should be amortised over the best estimate of its useful life (not exceeding 20 years).

Q. What are the disclosure requirements prescribed by IAS 38?
Ans. For each class of intangible assets the following should be disclosed:
- useful life or amortisation rate
- amortisation method
- gross carrying amount
- accumulated amortisation
- explanation about any intangible assets being amortised over longer than 20 years
- intangible assets carried at revalued amounts
- the amount of research and development expenditure recognised as an expense in the current period.

Q. What is a directors' report?
Ans. According to the Companies Act 2006 the Directors' Report should be produced once a year. This report allows for greater transparency in corporate governance. It enables the shareholders to make informed decisions when casting their votes at annual or other meeting as it provides an essential minimum standard of information.

Q. List the information that a directors' report should contain.

Ans. The Directors' Report should contain:

1. The directors' names
2. The company's principal activities
3. A business review (for large companies)
4. An explanation from the directors of how their leadership has lived up to their duty to promote the success of the company with regards to all the company's stakeholders and to maintain the reputation of the business to a high standard
5. A fair review of the risks and uncertainties facing the company
6. A backward looking analysis of the business' development in the last year. The review required is a balanced and comprehensive analysis, consistent with the size and complexity of the business, of the development and performance of the business of the company during the financial year; and the position of the company at the end of that year.
7. The company's effect on the environment and its employees
8. The use of key performance indicators (Key performance indicators means: 'factors by reference to which the development, performance or position of the business of the company can be measured effectively')
9. An explanation of the accounts
10. A directors' remuneration report
11. The amount (if any) that the directors recommend should be paid by way of dividend

Exercise 2.10
A company's year-end is 31 March 2010. On 17 June 2010 a major fire took place at the company's factory. On 10 July 2010 a major debtor at 31 March 2010 went into liquidation.
Required:
In accordance with IAS 10, Accounting for post-statement of financial position events, how should the two events be treated in the financial statements?

Exercise 2.11
The table shows information extracted from the financial statements of a company for the year ended 31 March 2005.

	$000
Premium received on the issue of shares	200
Profit on ordinary activities after taxation	700
Unrealised surplus on the revaluation of property	280

Required:
What should the company show as the net gain for the year?

Exercise 2.12
A company has issued a debenture loan carrying interest at the rate of 8 % payable every 31 December. Also, each 31 December $20 000 of the debenture is redeemed. At 31 December 2005 the total debenture loan outstanding was $100 000.
Required:
Which amounts should be disclosed in the company's published Statement of financial position at 31 December 2006 for:
   a. **accrued interest**
   b. **current liabilities**
   c. **long-term loan?**

TEST YOURSELF

2.1. Choose the correct alternative:
i Which item is not required in the Report of Directors of a limited company?

A audit fee
B future developments for the business
C the names of the directors
D the proposed dividend details

ii. Which of these items must be disclosed, according to company law, in the notes to a Company's published Profit and Loss Account?
A vehicle running costs
B the remuneration of the auditors
C exceptional items
D details of research and development activities undertaken

iii. Which will show the lowest figure in the statement of financial position of a company?
A authorised share capital
B called-up share capital
C issued share capital
D paid up share capital

iv. IAS 35 requires a special format for the Profit and Loss Account. Under this standard which of the following need not be separately disclosed?
A profit or loss on continuing operations
B profit or loss on discontinued operations
C profit or loss on disposal of an operation
D profit or loss on overseas operations

v. IAS 8 is an accounting statement that describes certain accounting policies including
1. consistency
2. accruals
3. going concern
4. prudence.
Which two accounting policies must be applied in the preparation of published accounts?
A 1 and 2
B 1 and 3
C 2 and 3
D 2 and 4

2.2. The financial statements of Manik plc showed the following in respect of non-current assets:

	$000
Cost at 1 January 2012	2000
Less: accumulated depreciation	200
Net book value at 1 January 2012	1800

During the year ended 31 December 2012 the following took place.
New machinery costing $100,000 was purchased. This had been entered in the ledger.
Machinery which had cost $200,000 and had been depreciated by $50,000 was sold. The proceeds of the sale were $145,000 and this had been credited to the suspense account.
No depreciation has been charged on the plant and machinery for the year. Depreciation is charged at 10% on the net book value of plant and machinery at 31 December 2012. The charge is to be included in the Administrative expenses for the year.
Required:
   (a) **Prepare a statement suitable for inclusion in the published accounts to show the cost, accumulated depreciation and net book value of plant and machinery at 31 December 2012.**
The trainee accountant at Manik plc has provided the following financial information at 31 December 2012

	$000
Revenue	4000
Cost of sales	1000
Administrative expenses	1700
Distribution costs	450
Suspense account	145
Dividends paid and proposed	135
Inventory	400
Trade receivables	385
Trade payables	120
Cash and cash equivalents	170
Long term loan	300
Ordinary shares of $1 each	1250
Retained earnings at 1 January 2012	265

Additional information

1. No adjustments have been made in respect of distribution costs owing of $20,000 and administrative expenses prepaid of $15,000.
2. Interest on the long-term loan is chargeable at 10% per annum. Only the interest paid during the year of $20,000 has been included in administrative expenses.
3. The estimated tax charge for the year is $365,000.
4. The figure for dividends paid and proposed is made up as follows:

Final dividend for the year ended 31 December 2011 paid in 2012	$50,000
Interim dividend paid 30 September 2012	$25,000
Proposed final dividend to be paid in March 2013	$60,000

5. On 1 December 2012 the company issued a further 500,000 shares of $1 each at $1.50. These shares would qualify for the proposed final dividend to be paid in March 2013.

Required
(b) Prepare the company's income statement for the year ended 31 December 2012.
(c) Prepare a statement of changes in equity for the year ended 31 December 2012.
(d) Prepare the company's statement of financial position at 31 December 2012.
(e) Explain how proposed dividends are treated in the published accounts.
   (UCLES, 2013, AS/A Level Accounting, Syllabus 9706/41, May/June)

2.3. Asterix plc, a manufacturing company, has extracted the following balances from its books of account for the year ended 30 April 2012:

	$000
Revenues	6,500
Purchases of raw materials	1,450
Carriage inwards	130
Carriage outwards	75
Direct labour	1,675
Factory overheads	1,350
Office overheads	1,025

Inventories at 1 May 2011:

Raw materials	140
Work in progress	165
Finished goods (at transfer price)	330

Additional information:
1. Factory overheads of $70,000 are accrued at 30 April 2012.
2. Office overheads of $35,000 have been prepaid at 30 April 2012.
3. Depreciation for the year on the non-current assets totalled $150,000 and this is to be split between the factory and the office in the ratio 2:1.
4. Completed production is transferred at a mark-up on cost of 20%.
5. Inventories were valued on 30 April 2012 as follows:

	$000
Raw materials	235
Work in progress	320
Finished goods (at transfer price)	438

Required
(a) Prepare a manufacturing account and income statement for the year ended 30 April 2012.

(b) Prepare an extract from the statement of financial position at 31April 2012 to show all inventories.

IAS 23 sets out the required accounting treatment for borrowing costs.

(c) Explain how the directors should deal with the interest on a loan taken out to acquire a 'qualifying asset'.

IAS 36 sets out the accounting procedures to ensure that assets are carried on the statement of financial position at nor more than their recoverable amount.

Required
(d) Explain the accounting treatment to ensure that this is achieved.

(UCLES, 2012, AS/A Level Accounting, Syllabus 9706/42, May/June)

CHAPTER 3
CONTROL ACCOUNTS

Q. What are control accounts?

Ans. Control accounts are so called because they control a section of a ledger. Control accounts are also called 'total accounts'. This is because they are made up of the totals of various appropriate books of prime entry in order to check the arithmetical accuracy of ledgers in a company. A control account for a sales ledger is often known as a 'Sales ledger control account' or a 'Total trade receivables account'. It controls the sale ledger. A control account for a Purchases Ledger is often known as a 'Purchases ledger control account' or a 'Total trade payables account'. It controls the purchases ledger. If there is a difference in the trial balance, the control accounts will show whether or not any difference is in the sales or purchases ledger accounts. If the control accounts agree with the balances on the sales and purchases ledgers, the difference must lie in the nominal or general ledger.

Q. What are the purposes of control accounts?

Ans. The purposes of control accounts are:
1. Control accounts act as an independent internal check on the work of the purchases and sales ledger accountants, to detect errors and prevent fraud. These accountants should not have access to the control accounts and the person who draws up the control accounts should not have access to the sales and purchases ledger accounts. Hence, it is advisable that the control accounts are maintained in the general ledger, not in the purchases or sales ledgers.
2. Control accounts act as independent check on the arithmetical accuracy of the aggregate of the balances in the sales and purchases ledgers.
3. Control accounts help identify the ledger or ledgers in which errors have been made when there is a difference on the trial balance.
4. Control accounts can be used to provide totals of debtors (trade receivables) and creditors (trade payables) quickly.

Q. What are the limitations of control accounts?

Ans. Control Accounts have the following limitations:
   a. Control accounts may contain errors themselves.
   b. Control accounts cannot guarantee the accuracy of individual ledger accounts e.g. if compensating errors have been made in individual ledger accounts.

Q. Where is information for a sales ledger control account obtained from?

Ans. Opening Debtors/Trade receivables - from the list of debtors' balances drawn up at the end of the preceding period.
Credit sales - the total of the sales journal.
Return Inwards - the total of the sales returns journal
Cheques received - the bank column on the debit side of the cash book.
Cash received - the cash column on the debit side of the cash book.
Closing Debtors/Trade receivables - the list of debtors' balances drawn up at the end of the current period.

Q. Where is information for a purchases ledger control account obtained from?

Ans. Opening Creditors/Trade payables - the list of creditors' balances drawn up at the end of the preceding period.
Credit Purchases - the total of the purchases journal.
Return Outwards - the total of the purchases returns journal.
Cheques paid - the bank column on the credit side of the cash book.
Cash paid – the cash column on the credit side of the cash book.

Closing Creditors/Trade payables – the list of creditors' balances drawn up at the end of the current period.

Q. List the usual contents of the sales ledger control account.

Ans. The contents of the sales ledger are as follows:

Debit side	Credit side
Total of the sales ledger debit balance b/f	Total of the sales ledger credit balance b/f
Credit sales for the period (from the sales journal)	Sales returns for the period (Total of the sales returns journal)
Refunds to customers (cash book)	Cash received from debtors (cash book)
Dishonoured cheques (cash book)	Cash discounts allowed (discount column of cash book)
Interest charged to customers (journal)	Irrecoverable debts written off on overdue accounts (journal)
Cash received from irrecoverable debts recovered (cash book)	Irrecoverable debts recovered (journal)
	Offsets (journal)
Total of any sales ledger credit balances at end of period c/f	Total of sales ledger debit balances at end of period c/f

Note: *Cash sales and provision for irrecoverable debts are not recorded in the sales ledger control account.*

Q. List the usual contents of the purchases ledger control account.

Ans. Debit side	Credit side
Total of the purchases ledger debit balances b/f	Total of purchases ledger credit balances b/f
Total of purchases returns (purchases returns journal)	Total credit purchases (purchases journal)
Total of cash paid to suppliers (cash book)	Refunds from suppliers (cash book)
Cash discounts received (discount column of cash book)	Interest charged by suppliers on overdue invoices (purchases
Offsets (journal)	journal)
Total of credit balances at end of period c/f	Total of debit balances at end of period c/f

Exercise 3.1
From the following prepare the sales ledger control account and the purchases ledger control Account for the month of March 20x3.

20x3		$
March 1	Purchases ledger balances	3,400 (cr)
		20(dr)
	Sales ledger balances	5,200(dr)
		26(cr)
	Totals for the month:	$
	Purchases journal	34,700
	Sales journal	14,500
	Return inwards journal	1,250
	Return outwards journal	2,500
	Cheques paid to suppliers	20,000
	Cheques and cash received from customers	10,000
	Discounts received	500
	Discounts allowed	300
	Balances on the sales ledger set off against balances in the purchases ledger	1,200
	Decrease in provision for irrecoverable debts	30
March 31	Debit balance on purchases ledger accounts	400
	Credit balance on sales ledger accounts	120

RECONCILIATION OF CONTROL ACCOUNTS WITH LEDGERS

Q. What is meant by the term 'Reconciling the control accounts?
Ans. When the balance on the control account and the total of the balances in the ledger it controls differ, the cause or causes must be found and the necessary corrections made. This is known as 'Reconciling the control accounts'.

Q. What happens when an item is incorrectly posted from a book of prime entry to a personal account in the sales or purchases ledger?

Ans. The control account is not affected. However, a reconciliation, as mentioned above, should be made as the balance of the control account and the totals of the balances in the ledger it controls, will differ. The control account will reveal the error.

Exhibit:
A credit sale of $467 to Sam is correctly entered in the sales journal but is posted to Sam's account in the sales ledger as $764. The sales ledger balances totalled $45,000.
Required:
Calculate the revised sales ledger balance

Solution:
The difference = 764-467 = $297. The total of the sales ledger balance is overstated by $297. The revised sales ledger balance will now be: 45,000 – 297 = $44,703.

Q. What happens when a page of a book of prime entry has been wrongly totalled?
Ans. The Control Account will be incorrect but the ledger it controls will not be affected. The control account will reveal the error.

Exhibit:
The sales journal total for January has been overstated by $ 3,000. At 31 January the credit sales as per control account are: $23,000
Required:
Calculate the total of the balances as per the sales ledger at 31 January

Solution:
The correct balance as per the control account should be: $23,000 – 3,000 = $20,000. This will then match the total of the balances as per the sales ledger. Hence the total of the balances as per the sales ledger at 31 January is $20,000.

Q. What happens when a transaction is entered incorrectly in a book of prime entry?

Ans. When this happens, the error is repeated in the control account as well as in the personal account in the corresponding ledger. The control account will not reveal this error.

Exhibit:
A supplier's invoice for $650 has been entered in the purchases journal as $560. The total trade payables as per the purchases ledger was $7,800.
Required:
a) Calculate the revised figure for total trade payables
b) By how much would the control account be affected?

Solution:
a) The difference = 650-560 = $90
The revised total trade payables will now be $7,800 + 90 = $7,890.
b) The control account balance will also have to be increased by $90.

Q. What happens when a transaction is omitted from a book of prime entry?
Ans. The transaction will be omitted from the personal account in the appropriate ledger and from the control account. The control account will not reveal the error.
Exhibit:
A sales invoice for $600 has been omitted from the sales journal. The total trade receivables as per the control account is $2,300.

Required:

a) Calculate the revised figure for total trade receivables

b) By how much would the control account be affected?

Solution:

    a. The total trade receivables will now be $2,300 + $600 = $2,900

    b. The sales ledger control account balance will also have to be increased by $600.

Exercise 3.2

The following errors have been discovered:

a. A credit note for $50 has been entered as an invoice.

b. Purchases of $359 have been entered on the wrong side of a supplier's account in the purchases ledger.

c. No entry has been made to record an agreement to contra an amount owed to Mac of $780 against an amount owed by Mac of $380.

d. An invoice for $769 has been entered in the purchases journal as $697.

e. A cash discount of $50 from a trade payables (creditor) had been completely omitted from the accounting records.

Required: Draw a table with the following headings: Decrease; increase; no effect, to show the numerical effect of correcting each of these items on the total trade payables account.

Exercise 3.3

The following balances have been extracted from the books of Madonna at 31 December 20x7.

	$
Total of purchases ledger balances (cr)	3,980
Total of sales ledger balances (dr)	8,885
Total of sales ledger balances (cr)	79
Balance on total trade receivables' account(dr)	9,836
Balance on total trade payables' account(cr)	5,000

The following errors have been discovered:

1) A debit balance in the sales ledger $45 has been extracted as a credit balance in the list of sales ledger balances.

2) A purchases invoice of $140 has been omitted from the purchases day book.

3) Discounts received in December amounting to $340 have been credited to the total trade payables' account.

4) The sales day book has been overcast by $600.

5) A balance of $340 on a customer's account in the sales ledger has been set against the amount owing to her in the purchases ledger but no entries have been made for this in the total trade receivables' and total trade payables' accounts.

6) A supplier's invoice for $760 has been entered in the purchases journal as $670

Required:

1) Prepare the amended sales ledger and purchases ledger control accounts

2) Calculate the following as at 31 December 20x7:

    a) The revised sales ledger balances

    b) The revised purchases ledger balances.

3.1 Multiple-choice questions

i) The following information has been obtained from the books of Chenny Ltd.

	$
At Jan 1 20x5 the purchases ledger	
balances b/f (cr)	8,000
(dr)	25
In the month of January 20x5:	
Total invoices received from suppliers	45,000
Goods returned to suppliers	546
Discounts received	2,000
Cheques sent to suppliers	28,000
Cash paid to suppliers	1,200
At January 31 20x5 the purchases ledger	
balances c/f (dr)	300

What is the credit balance in the purchases ledger at January 31, 20x5?
A) $20,929   B) $22,729   C) $21,529   D) $ 22,429

ii) Which of the following items do not appear on the debit side of the Sales Ledger Control account?
A) Dishonoured cheques   B) Credit sales   C) Cash Sales   D) Irrecoverable debts recovered

iii) The following information is given to you: $
Total of sales ledger balances at 31 December 20x9 (debit) 23,000
(credit)   150

The following errors have been discovered:
1) A credit sale of $560 has been omitted from the journal
2) A page of the sales journal has been overstated by $2,000
What is the correct sales ledger debit balance?
A) $ 22,850   B) $ 23,560   C) $21,560   D) $21,410

iv) The balance on the purchases ledger control account is $45,000 (credit) at 31 March 20x5.
The following errors have been discovered:
1) A balance of $300 on a customer's account in the sales ledger has been set against the amount owing to him in the purchases ledger but no entry has been made for this in the Sales or Purchases ledger control accounts.
2) A supplier's invoice for $790 has been entered as $970 in the purchases journal.
What is the amended balance in the purchases ledger control account after the above errors have been corrected?
A) $44,700 B) $44,520 C) $44,320 D) $44,820

v) A sales ledger control account has been reconciled with the Sales Ledger Balances as shown.

	$
Balance as per Control Account	81,000
Total of Sales Journal for one month	
not included in the control account	2,000
Cash received from customers not	
included in the control account	1,400
Total of balances in the Sales Ledger	81,600

What is the correct figure for trade receivables to be shown in the Statement of financial position?

A) $81,000   B) $83,000   C) $81,600   D) $82,400

3.2 The books of Mary Rose gave the following information for the month ended 31 May 2003. All sales and purchases were on credit.

	$000
Sales ledger balance at 1 May 2003	5,627
Purchases ledger balance at 1 May 2003	4,388
Sales for the year	100,384
Purchases for the year	64,987
Sales returns	1,997
Purchases returns	864
Payments received from customers (all banked)	92,760
Payments made to suppliers	63,520
Debtor's dishonoured cheque	109
Discount allowed	4,082
Discount received	3,241
Irrecoverable debts written off	1,884
Debit balances transferred to purchases ledger control account	208

The total of Mary Rose's sales ledger balances is $9,387, which differs from the closing balance in the sales ledger control account.

Required: a) Extract the relevant information from the above and prepare the sales ledger control account for the month ended 31 May 20x3

The following errors have been discovered since the sales ledger control account was prepared.
i)   A sales invoice for $2001 had been completely omitted from the books.
ii)   A page of the sales day book with entries totalling $7820 had been omitted from the total sales but the individual entries had been posted to the debtors' accounts.
iii)   A debit balance of $4020 had been omitted from the list of debtors.
iv)   A sales ledger account has been understated by $220
v)   A purchases ledger account had been overstated by $350.
vi)   Discount allowed had been overstated by $620.
vii)   Discount received had been understated by $450.
viii)   An entry for $1620 in the sales day book had been omitted from the customer's account.
ix)   A contra entry had been made in the purchases ledger for a debit balance of $1412 in the sales ledger, but no entry had been made in the control accounts.
x)   A receipt of $1210 was debited to bank but not posted to the customer's account.
xi)   A credit note for $720, sent to a customer, had been entered in the sales day book and posted as a sale to both accounts.
xii)   A customer owing $1820 was declared bankrupt during May 2003. The debt was written off in the control account but no entry had been made in the customer's account.
Required:
b.1) Prepare an amended sales ledger control account, extracting the relevant information from the list of errors given above.
2) Prepare a statement altering the total of the sales ledger balance to agree with the new sales ledger control account balance.
[UCLES, 2004, AS/A Level Accounting, Syllabus 9706/2, Oct/Nov]

3.3 The following information was extracted from the books of William Noel for the year ended 30 April 2001.

	$
Purchases ledger balance at 1 May 2000	43,120
Credit purchases for the year	824,140
Credit purchase returns	12,400
Cheques paid to suppliers	745,980
Cash purchases	8,940
Discount received on credit purchases	31,400
Credit balances transferred to sales ledger accounts	5,210

Required:

a. **Draw up the purchases ledger control account for the year ended 30 April 2001.**

The total of the balances in William Noel's purchases ledger amounts to $67,660, which does not agree with the closing balance in the control account.
The following errors were then discovered:
1) Discount received had been overstated by $ 1,000.
2) A credit purchases invoice for $2,040 had been completely omitted from the books.
3) A purchases ledger account had been understated by $100.
4) A credit balance of $850 in the purchases ledger had been set off against a contra entry in the Sales Ledger but no entry had been made in either control account.
5) A payment of $1,450 had been debited to the supplier's account but was omitted from the bank account.
6) A credit balance of $3,210 had been omitted from the list of suppliers.

Required: b.

i.   Extract the necessary information from the above list and draw up an amended purchases ledger control account for the year ended 30 April 2001.

ii.   Beginning with the given total of $67,660, show the changes to be made in the purchases ledger to reconcile it with the new control account balance.

[UCLES,2001,AS/A Level Accounting, Syllabus 8706/2, October/November.]

3.4 The closing balance on a Purchases Ledger control Account is $ 143,000. The Purchases Journal has been undercast by $2,500.
What is the correct closing balance on the Purchases Ledger control Account?

3.5 The balance on a sales ledger control account is $50,000. The following items are then discovered:
i)   The total of the sales journal is understated by $400
ii) Discounts allowed $1,400 has not been entered in the sales ledger control account
iii) Irrecoverable debts written off $300 have not been recorded in the sales ledger control a/c.
iv) A provision for doubtful debts of $3,000.
What is the total of the balances in the sales ledger?

3.6 At 1 Janaury20x1 a business has a provision for doubtful debts of $3,100. At 31 December the provision is to be 5% of trade receivables. The balance on the Trade Receivables Control account at 31 December 20x1 is $48,900 before writing off a irrecoverable debt of $450. The business operates a separate Irrecoverable Debts account.
Required:
Calculate the entry in the income statement for the provision for doubtful debts, stating whether it is a debit or credit entry.

3.7 In a control account prepared by a business, trade receivable was $ 15,000. A customer, who owes the business $500, is also a supplier to whom the business owes $300 for inventory supplied.

   Required: What is the accurate trade receivables control account balance?

3.8 Balances from the sales ledger of Errol as at 31 July 20x1 totalled $17,200. The trial balance containing this figure as trade receivables does not balance. The schedule of debtors (trade receivables) does not agree with the balance on the sales ledger control account as well.

   The following errors are discovered:
1.   An invoice for $84 for a sale to Debbie has been completely omitted from the books of accounts.
2.   The discount allowed column in the cash book has been overcast by $200
3.   Goods with a selling price of $1,000 had been dispatched to Mason on a 'sale or return' basis. This transactions has been entered in the sales day book though Mason has not indicated his intention to purchase these goods.
4.   A irrecoverable debt of $50 was written off in the sales ledger. However, no entry was made in the journal.
5.   Goods returned by Samuel, which had been invoiced in the sum of $160, had been correctly entered in the sales returns book but debited to Samuel's account as $106.

   Required:
   a.   Draw up the sales ledger control account, showing clearly the original balance on the account at 31 July 20x1, and the entries required to adjust the account for the above items.
   b. Calculate Errol's corrected trade receivables figure at July 31 20x1.

CHAPTER 4
SUSPENSE ACCOUNTS

Q. When is a suspense account opened?
Ans. A suspense account is opened when the totals of the two sides of the trial balance differ. It is opened with the difference between these totals.

Q. When is a suspense account closed?
Ans. When the errors are subsequently discovered, they are corrected, using a journal entry. If all the errors are discovered, the suspense account will close when this journal entry is passed. E.g. if the sales account was undercast by $50.
> Debit the suspense account with $50
> Credit the sales account with $50.

Q. How can errors be classified?
Ans. Errors can be broadly classified as:
  i.   Errors that affect the trial balance.
  ii.   Errors that do not affect the trial balance

Q. Explain: errors that affect the trail balance
Ans. These are predominantly of three types and are shown up by differing totals in the trial balance. These would be the result of **errors in additions, using one figure for the debit entry and another figure for the credit entry,** entering only **one aspect of a transaction,** and so on.

Q. Name the errors that do not affect the trial balance
Ans. Errors that do not affect the trial balance are:
  a. Error of omission
  b. Error of commission
  c. Error of principle
  d. Error of complete reversal
  e. Error of original entry
  f. Compensating errors

Q. How will an entry posted to the wrong side of an account be corrected?
Ans. It will be corrected by an adjustment equal to twice the amount of the original error: once to cancel the error and once to place the item on the correct side of the account.

Q. How will errors that do not affect the double entry be corrected?
Ans. Such errors do not need to be corrected by debit and credit entries. E.g. a balance on a purchases ledger account was copied incorrectly onto a summary of balances for inclusion in the trial balance. The summary of balances should be amended and a one-sided entry in the journal prepared to correct the suspense account.

Exhibit:
The bookkeeper extracted a trial balance on 30th June 20XX which failed to agree by $550, a shortage on the credit side of the trial balance. A suspense account was opened for the difference. In the first week of July 20XX, the following errors made in the previous financial year were found:
a) Purchases book undercast by $70.
b) Sales of $350 to Manny had been debited in error to Mason's account.

c) Sales day book had been undercast by $670.
d) Rent account had been undercast by $100.
e) The sale of a machinery $1,500 had been credited in error to Sales account.
f) A credit balance of $50 in the purchases ledger had been omitted from the list of balances extracted from the ledger. The total of the list had been included in the trial balance.

Required:
1) Show the journal entries necessary to correct the errors (Narratives are required).
2) Draw up the suspense account after the errors described have been corrected.
3) If profit for the year had been calculated at $4500 for the year ended 30 June 20XX, show the calculations of the corrected profit for the year.
Solution:

1.   Journal entries:

	Dr $	Cr $
a) Purchases account	70	
Suspense account		70
(Correction of purchases account being undercast by $70)		
b) Manny's account	350	
Mason's account		350
(Error of commission, now corrected)		
c) Suspense account	670	
Sales account		670
(Correction of an undercast in the Sales account)		
d) Rent account	100	
Suspense account		100
(Correction of undercast in the Rent account)		
e) Sales account	1, 500	
Machinery account		1,500
(Error of principle, now corrected)		

f) **Note:** This is not a double-entry error. Nevertheless, it has affected the trial balance. The list of balances must be corrected and a one-sided entry in the Suspense account is required.   Dr
f) Suspense account $50

2.   Suspense account

	$		$
Sales	670	Difference on trial balance	550
Correction			
of trade payables	50	Purchases	70
		Rent	100
	720		720

3) Calculation of corrected profit for the year ended 30 June

	(+) $	(-) $	$
Profit for the year before corrections			4,500
a. Increase in purchases		70	
b. No effect on profit for the year			
c. Increase in sales	670		
d. Increase in rent		100	
e. Decrease in sales		1,500	
f. No effect on profit			
	670	(1670)	(1,000)
Corrected net profit for the year ended 30 June			3,500

*√ **Tip:** If the error has a name then the suspense account is not involved: example b, above is an error of commission, hence the suspense account is neither debited nor credited.*

Exercise 4.1
A bookkeeper extracted a trial balance on 30th June 20XX which failed to agree by $500, a shortage on the credit side of the trial balance. A suspense account was opened with the difference. In the first week of July 20XX, the following errors made in the previous financial year were found:
a.   Purchases book undercast by $70.
b.   Sales of $350 to Manny had been debited in error to Mason's account.
c.   Sales day book had been undercast by $670.
d.   Rent account had been undercast by $100.
e.   The sale of a machinery $500 had been credited in error to Sales account.
Required:
1) Show the journal entries necessary to correct the errors.
2) Draw up the suspense account after the errors described have been corrected.
3) If profit for the year had been calculated at $4500 before the errors were discovered, what is the corrected profit?

Exercise 4.2
Study the following information and answer the questions that follow:
The trial balance of Hakim as at 31 July 20XX showed a difference that was posted to a suspense account. Draft financial statements for the year ended 31 July 20XX were prepared showing a profit for the year of $3500. The following errors were subsequently discovered:
1.   Sales $560 to Malli had been debited to Mason's account
2.   A payment of $350 for rent had been entered on the debit side of the rent account as $340.
3.   The sales journal had been undercast by $450.
4.   Repairs to motor van $45 had been charged to the motor van account.
5.   A cheque for $445 being rent received from Bala, had only been entered in the cash book.
6.   A purchase of fittings $350 had been entered in the purchases account.
7.   A cheque for $56 received from a debtor had been correctly entered in the cash book but posted to the customer's account as $50.
   Required:
   a) Give the journal entries necessary to correct the above errors.
   b) Prepare Hakim's suspense account, showing clearly the difference on the trial balance at 31 July 20XX as the first entry and the entries required to adjust the errors.
   c) Show the effect of each of these adjustments on the profit for the year in the draft accounts and the correct profit for the year ended 31 July 20XX.

Exercise 4.3
Study the following information and answer the questions that follow:
The trial balance of Helen as at 31 December 20XX showed a difference that was posted to a suspense account. Draft financial statements for the year ended 31 December 20XX were prepared showing a profit for the year of $8900.
   The following errors were subsequently discovered:
   1) Sales $670 to Merci had been debited to Mern's account
   2) A payment of $560 for rent had been entered on the debit side of the rent account as $650.
   3) The sales journal had been overcast by $370.
   4) Repairs to motor van $56 had been charged to motor van account.

5) A cheque for $500 being rent received from Mala, had only been entered in the cash book.

6) A purchase of machinery $5000 had been entered in the purchases account.

7) A cheque for $69 received from a debtor had been correctly entered in the cash book but posted to the customer's account as $70.

Required:

a) Give the journal entries necessary to correct the above errors.

b) Prepare the suspense account in Helen's ledger showing clearly the difference on the trial balance at 31 December 20XX as the first entry and the entries required to adjust the errors.

c) Show the effect of each of these adjustments on the profit for the year in the draft accounts and the correct profit for the year ended 31 December 20XX.

Exercise 4.4

Show how each of the following errors would affect the agreement in the totals of a trial balance:

a) A sale of goods to Manning $350 was correctly entered in the sales book but was entered in Manning's account as $530.

b) $35 discounts received was debited to the discounts allowed account.

c) $45 taken for personal use was credited to the capital account.

d) Stock at close was overvalued by $500.

e) $45 rent received was debited to the sales account.

f) Cheque from Jules $450 was credited to Julia's account.

g) $53 cash received from the sale of a motor van was credited to the sales account and debited to cash account.

Solution:

Trans action	No effect	Debit side will exceed the credit side by amount shown	Credit side will exceed the debit side by the amount shown
a			
b			
c			
d			
e			
f			
g			

Exercise 4.5

The following is a trial balance incorrectly drawn up:

	$	$
Purchases		3500
Returns inwards	450	
Inventory 1st January 20XX		350
Sales revenue	3850	
Inventory 31st December 20XX		1000
Trade payables	1200	
Discounts received	450	
Telephone		50
Premises		3000
Trade receivables	350	
Discounts allowed		50
Furniture and fixtures		400

Capital	6000	
Suspense		3950
	12300	12300

Required:

a. **A corrected version of the trial balance dated 31st December 20XX based on the above information, but with an amended figure for the suspense account.**

The following errors were found after the corrected version of the trial balance, above, was prepared.

i.   The total of the sales journal was understated by $300.

ii.   A payment of $3800 to a supplier has not been posted from the cash book to the purchases ledger.

iii.   A cheque for $450 received from a debtor has been correctly entered in the cash book but has been entered in the debtor's personal account as $300.

iv.   A purchase of furniture $600 had been included in the purchases account.

v.   A sale of motor van for $600 cash has been completely omitted from the books of account.

Required:
1) Journal entries to correct each of these errors (narratives not required).
2) The suspense account, using the amount arrived at in the corrected version of the trial balance from (a), above.

Exercise 4.6

Manana's trial balance does not balance and she has opened a suspense account with the difference in the totals. The following errors have now been discovered:

1) Rent paid $450, had been credited to the rent receivable account.

2) Goods returned to Kala had been credited to Kala's account and debited to the purchases returns account. The goods had cost $690.

3) Discounts received, $70 had been posted to the debit of the discounts allowed account in error.

4) A debit balance of $60 in the sales ledger had been completely omitted from the list of balances extracted from the ledger. The total of the list had been included in the trial balance as trade receivables.

5) The debit side of the telephone charges account had been understated by$100.

Required
a)   Prepare Journal entries to correct the errors. (Narratives are required.)
b)   Prepare the suspense account showing the opening balance and the correcting entries.
c)   The draft income statement showed a profit for the year of $6,890 for the year ended June 30 20x8. Calculate the revised net profit for the year ended June 30, 20x8.

Exercise 4.7

The following errors in the accounting records of a business have been detected and corrected:

a)   A purchase invoice for $300 was omitted from the books of accounts.

b)   A sale for $250 to M was debited to the account of N.

c)   The sales journal was over-stated by $150.

The gross profit for the year before the errors were corrected was $56,900.

Required:
Calculate the correct gross profit for the year.

Exercise 4.8

A trial balance does not balance. The difference has been entered in a suspense account. Subsequent to that, the following errors were discovered:

1)   The provision for depreciation had been overcast by $1,000

2) The credit balance on the purchases ledger control account of $43,000 has been included as a debit balance.

3) A payment in cash of $450 for heating and lighting has been credited in the cash book and debited to the irrecoverable debts account.

Required:

Prepare the requisite credit entry to the suspense account.

Exercise 4.9

A company omitted discounts allowed of $500 from its trial balance. During the year a motor van had been sold for cash of $700 but the only accounting entry made was a debit in the bank account.

Required:

Calculate the balance on the suspense account stating whether it is a debit or credit balance.

TEST YOURSELF
4.1 MULTIPLE CHOICE QUESTIONS

i) The balance of closing stock $7,600 had been entered on the debit side of the trial balance is $6,700. What is the effect on the trial balance?

	Debit total	Credit total
A)	none	none
B)	Overstated by $6,700	none
C)	Overstated by $900	none
D)	none	Overstated by $900

ii.) Repairs to machinery $930 had been posted to the machinery at cost account as $390 in error. Which of the following entries are required to correct this error?

Debit	Credit
A) Machinery at cost account with $390 Suspense account with $540	Repairs to machinery account with $930
B) Repairs to machinery account with $930	Machinery at cost account with $390 Suspense account with $540
C) Machinery at cost account with $540	Repairs to machinery account with $540
D) Repairs to machinery account with $540	Machinery at cost account with $540

iii) A debt of $70 in the sales ledger had been written off as irrecoverable but no entry had been made in the irrecoverable debts account. What is the effect on the trial balance?

A) **The credit side is overstated by $70.**
B) **The credit side is understated by $70.**
C) **The debit side is overstated by $70.**
D) **The debit side is understated by $70.**

iv) A cheque for $23 from Chenai, a customer, had been credited to his account as $32. Which of the following entries will correct this error?

	Debit	Credit
A)	Chenai's account with $9	Suspense account with $9
B)	Suspense account with $9	Chenai's account with $9
C)	Chenai's account with $23	Suspense account with $23
D)	Suspense account with $23	Chenai's account with $23

v) An invoice for $135 for the purchase of inventory from Nancy had been completely omitted from the books. What is the effect on the Trial Balance?
A) **The credit side is understated by $135.**
B) **The debit side is understated by $135.**
C) **The credit side is overstated by $135.**
D) **No effect.**

4.2 The trial balance as at 30 June, 20x6 drawn up by Melissa does not balance. She has opened a suspense account with the difference in the totals of the trail balance. The draft income statement showed a net profit of $5,600 for the year ended 30 June, 20x6 and the statement of financial position at that date showed working capital of $4,560. The following errors were then discovered.
i) $300 inventory was taken for personal use without paying for them.
i) Repairs to machine $35 were debited to machinery account.
iii) A cheque $45 received from Ali was debited to Ali's account and credited to bank account.
iv) $566 goods purchased from Fatima were entered in the books as $560.
v) Sales on credit to Kyle $350 was entered in the account of Wyle.
vi) The sales account was undercast by $45 and the discounts received account was overcast by $45.
Required:
a) Pass Journal entries to correct these errors.   (Narratives are not required.)
b) Calculate the revised working capital at 30 June, 20x6.
c) Calculate the revised net profit for the year ended 30 June, 20x6.

4.3   Madeline Jones has discovered the following:
1) A machine was purchased from Jones &Co. for $4,600 but no entry has been made in Madeline's books.
2) $350 paid for motor van has been wrongly debited to the purchases account as $530.
3) A cheque for $2,600 received from Sami has been debited to Sami's account and entered on the credit side of the cash book, in error.
4)   A purchase of office stationery $ 350 had been debited to the purchases account as $530 in error.
5)   Goods have been sold to Harry on credit for $2,500 less 25% trade discount. Correct entries have been made in the sales journal but $2,000 has been posted to Harry's ledger account.
Required:
a) Prepare entries required in Madeline's journal regarding each of the above matters. (Narratives are required)
b) Prepare a suspense account starting with the difference on the trial balance.

4.4	Which of the following errors in the general ledger would cause the debits to exceed the credits in a trial balance?
i. A contra between the sales and purchases ledgers has been entered on credit side of both control accounts.
ii. A rental receipt has been entered twice in the rent receivable account.
iii. The closing inventory at the end of the previous period has not been entered in the inventory account.
iv. The opening electricity accrual has been brought forward on the wrong side of the ledger account.

4.5 A cheque for payment of wages of $214 has been debited to the purchases account as $241.
What are the correcting entries?

4.6 On 1 January Harry had prepaid rent of $65. During the year, four rent payments of $100 each were made. On 31 December, Harry owes $35. Harry has charged the rent payments made during the year in his income account.
What is the effect on profit for the year?

4.7 Rent accrued $670 was treated as a prepayment when preparing the income statement of Hyung Ho's sole trader business.
What was the effect on profit?

CHAPTER 5
INCOMPLETE RECORDS

Q. What are incomplete records?

Ans. Any method other than that of double entry used to maintain books of accounts will produce incomplete records. Very small businesses may often maintain only a cash book or records of debtors and creditors. In such a case, only one aspect of a transaction is recorded and this is termed single-entry bookkeeping. If a business does not maintain any books of accounts but retains source documents such as invoices, notes, cheque counterfoils and bank statements, then the final accounts cannot be prepared in the normal way and this is an incomplete record situation.

Q. What is a 'Statement of Affairs'?

Ans. A 'Statement of Affairs' is a statement from which the capital of the owner is deducted. It resembles a statement of financial position but is missing some information. It contains the assets, liabilities and capital of the owner.

Q. How can profit for the year of a sole trader be calculated without the aid of double entry records?

Ans. The capital shown in the opening statement of affairs is compared to that in the closing statement of affairs. Drawings and capital introduced by the owner is taken into consideration as well. The equation to be used is:

Profit for the year = Closing capital – Opening capital + Drawings – Capital introduced (if any).

Exhibit:

M. Mosambi started business on 1st January 20x1. He introduced $40,000 cash into the business and a motor van valued at $5,000. At 31st December 20x1 he has trade receivables of $3,500, a bank balance of $36,000, cash in hand $4,400, inventory $2,000 and trade payables $5,900. The motor van is to be depreciated by $500. His drawings were $5,000.

Required:

Statements to show the profit or loss for the year ended 31st December 20x1.

Solution:

M. Mosambi's Statement of Affairs as at 1st Jan. 20x1

	$
Non-current Assets: Motor Van	5000
Current Assets: Cash	40,000
	45,000
Represented by: Capital	45,000

M. Mosambi's Statement of Affairs as at 31st Dec. 20x1

	$	$
Non-current Assets:		
Motor van		5,000
Less Depreciation		500
		4,500
Current Assets:		
Inventory	2,000	
Trade receivables	3,500	
Cash at bank	46,000	
Cash in hand	4,400	55,900
Total assets		60,400
Current Liabilities:		
Trade payables		5,900

Capital:
Balance at 1st Jan. 20x1: 45,000
Add Profit for the year*   14,500
                            59,500
Less Drawings   5,000   54,500
Total liabilities and equity   60,400
Working:* Profit = Closing capital – Opening capital
                    + Drawings
                  = 54,500 – 45,000 + 5000
                  = $ 14,500

Exercise 5.1

Gauri does not keep a complete accounting system, but the following information is available from her records:

	At 31st Dec. 20x1	At 31st Dec. 20x2
	$	$
Inventory	4,200	4,600
Trade receivables	3,480	2,590
Trade payables	1,340	100
Shop fittings	7,400	7,100
Cash at bank	4,790	5,340

Gauri has drawn $50 per week from the business for personal expenses.

Required: Gauri's net profit for the year ended 31st December 20x2

Exercise 5.2

Kelly is a sole trader who does not keep full accounting records. She is able to provide the following information:

	At 31st August 20x2	At 31st August 20x3
Non-current assets		
At cost	$ 30,000	$ 26,000
Current assets	$ 10,000	$ 21,000
Current liabilities	$ 5,000	$ 1,000

Kelly' drawings for the year ended 31st August 20x3 was $3,000

Required:
a) Kelly's statement of affairs as at 31st August 20x2
b) Kelly's statement of affairs as at 31st August 20x3
c) Kelly's profit or loss for the year ended 31st August 20x3

Exercise 5.3

Karmi is a sole trader who does not keep full accounting records. She is able to provide the following information:

	At 31st August 20x2	At 31st August 20x3
Non-current Assets		
at cost	$ 30,000	$ 36,000
Current assets	$ 12,000	$ 34,000
Current liabilities	$ 3,000	$ 1,000

It is decided that the fixed assets held at 31st August 20x3 should be depreciated by 5% on cost.
Kami's drawings for the year ended 31st August 20x3 was $2,000

Required:

a) Kami's statement of affairs as at 31st August 20x2
b) Kami's statement of affairs as at 31st August 20x3
c) Kami's profit or loss for the year ended 31st August 20x3

Q. How are sales and purchases calculated using incomplete records?
Ans. The Total Trade Receivables Account (Sales Ledger Control Account) is used to calculate total credit sales and the Total Trade Payables Account (Purchases Ledger Control Account) is used to calculate total credit purchases.

Exhibit:
A & sons Traders had the following figures for the Years ended:

	31st December 20x3	31st December 20x4
	$	$
Trade receivables	34,500	53,600

For the year ended 31st December 20x4:
Cash sales: $1,500
Cash receipts from debtors: $1060
Discounts allowed: $45
Irrecoverable debts: $56

Required:
Calculate the sales for the year ended 31st December 20x4
Solution:

Total Trade receivables Account

20x4		$	20x4		$
Jan 1	Balance b/d	34,500	- Discounts allowed		45
-	Credit sales	20,261	- Cash received from customers		1060
			- Irrecoverable debt		56
			Dec 31 Balance c/d		53,600
		54,761			54,761

20x5
January 1 Balance b/d 53,600

Total sales for the year = Credit sales + Cash sales
$$=20,261+1,500$$
$$= \$21,761$$

Exercise 5.4
ACE Traders had the following figures for the Years ended:

	31st December 20x1	31st December 20x2
	$	$
Trade receivables	14,500	13,600

Cash sales: $2,500
Cash receipts from trade receivables: $560
Receipts by cheque from trade receivables: $ 360
Discounts allowed: $50
Irrecoverable Debts: $70
Required: Calculate the sales for the year ended 31st December 20x2

Exhibit:
Calculate the total purchases for the year ended 31st December 20x3 from the following information:
Trade payables at 1st Jan 20x3: $ 2,450
Trade payables at Dec 31st 20x3: $1,200

Payments to creditors during the year: Cash $3,609;
Cheque $2,870

Cash purchases for the year: $1,000
Discounts received: $35

Solution:

Total Trade payables Account

20x2		$	20x2		$
-	Cash	3,609	January 1 Bal b/d	2,450
-	Bank	2,870	-	Cr purchases	5,264
-	Discounts received	35			
Dec 31	Balance c/d	1,200			
		7,714			7,714
			20x3		
			Jan 1 Bal b/d	1,200

Total purchases for the year = 5,264+1,000 = $ 6,264

Exercise 5.5

Calculate the total purchases for the year ended 31st December 20x3 from the following information:

Trade payables at 1st Jan 20x3: $ 4,500

Trade payables at Dec 31st 20x3: $3,600
Payments to trade payables during the year:
Cash $3,500; Cheque $3,800
Discounts received $47

NOTE: *Using the total sales and purchases figure, it is possible to prepare the trading account section of the Income Statement.*

Exercise 5.6

Mason is a trader buying and selling entirely on credit terms. He does not keep complete accounting records but is able to provide the following information for the year ended 31st December 20x3:

	At 1st Jan 20x3	At 31st Dec 20x3
	$	$
Inventory of goods	4,000	3,000
Trade payables	1,500	2,000
Trade receivables	3,700	5,600

During the year cheques received from customers amounted to $3,700 and cheques paid to suppliers amounted to $2,500.

Required: Prepare Mason's trading account section of the Income Statement for the year ended 31st Dec. 20x3.

MARK UP AND MARGIN

Mark – up = $\frac{\text{Gross profit} \times 100}{\text{Cost of sales}}$

Margin = $\frac{\text{Gross profit} \times 100}{\text{Sales}}$

√ **Tips:**
1) If the mark – up is known, the margin can be found out using this method:
Take the same numerator to be the numerator of the margin; the denominator is the total of the mark- up's numerator and denominator.
e.g. if mark – up is 25% (¼) then the Margin is 1/5

2) *If the margin is known, the mark – up can be found out in the following way:*
Take the same numerator of the margin; the denominator is the difference of the denominator
and the numerator of the margin e.g. If the margin is 20% (1/5) then the mark-up is 1/4

Exhibit: Tom provides the following information for the year ended 31st December 20x3:
Margin = 25%

Sales	$20,000
Inventory at 1st January 20x3	$4,500
Inventory at 31st December 20x3	$4,800

Required:
Prepare a trading account to show the calculation of the purchases for the year.
Solution:

Tom's Income Statement for the year ended
31st Dec., 20x3

	$	$
Sales		20,000
Less Cost of Goods sold:		
Inventory at 1st Jan., 20x3	4,500	
Add Purchases	*15,300	
	19,800	
Less Inventory at		
31st Dec. 20x3	4,800	15,000
Gross Profit		**5,000

Working:

$$** \text{Margin} = \frac{\text{Gross Profit} \times 100}{\text{Sales}}$$

$$25 = \frac{\text{Gross profit} \times 100}{20,000}$$

$$\frac{25 \times 20,000}{100} = \text{Gross Profit}$$

$ 5,000 = Gross Profit

* Sales – (Opening Inventory + Purchases – Closing Inventory) = Gross Profit
20,000 – (4,500 + Purchases – 4,800) = 5000
20,000 + 300 – Purchases = 5000
20,300 – 5,000 = Purchases
$ 15,300 = Purchases

Exercise 5.7
The sales of a business were $40,000.
The cost of goods sold was $ 25,000.
Calculate:
a) The mark – up
b) The margin

Exercise 5.8
Malati's craft store caught fire on 12th June 20x3. The entire inventory was destroyed. On 1st January her inventory was valued at $500. From 1st January to 12th June 20x3, her sales were 5,000 and her purchases were $3,000. Her profit margin was 50%.
Calculate the cost of the inventory destroyed. Show your answer in the form of a trading account.

Exercise 5.9

The following are the figures for 20x2:

	$
Inventory 1st January 20x2	500
Inventory 31st Dec. 20x2	700
Purchases	5,000

A uniform rate of mark –up of 25% is applied.

Find the gross profit and sales figures.

Exhibit:

The following is a summary of Manoj's bank account for the year ended 31st December 20x4:

	$		$
Balance 1st Jan. 20x3	4,000	Payment to suppliers	36,000
Receipts from customers	45,000	Rent	1,000
Balance 31st Dec. 20x3	7,225	Insurance	500
		Office expenses	275
		Drawings	18,450
	56,225		56,225

All of the business takings have been paid into the bank with the exception of $8,700. Out of this, Manoj paid wages of $5,200, drawings of $1,100 and purchase of inventory $2,400.

Additional information available:

	Balances at 31st Dec 20x3	Balances at 31st Dec 20x4
	$	$
Inventory	12,000	14,000
Trade payables	5,400	6,500
Trade receivables	10,000	9,650
Rent prepaid	150	200
Insurance owing	50	100
Machinery at valuation	3,500	3,250

Required:

Draw up a set of final accounts for the year ended 31st December 20x4.

Solution:

Manoj's Income Statement for the year ended
31st Dec 20x4

	$	$
Sales		53,350
Less Cost of goods sold:		
Inventory at 1st January 20x4	12,000	
Add Purchases	39,500	
	51,500	
less inventory at 31st Dec. 20x4	14,000	37,500
Gross Profit		15,850
Less Expenses:		
Rent (1,000+ 150 – 200)	950	
Insurance (500 –50 + 100)	550	
Office expenses	275	
Wages	5,200	

| Depreciation (3,500 – 3,250) | 250 | 7,225 |
| Profit for the year | | 8,625 |

Manoj's Statement of Financial Position as at 31st Dec. 20x4

	$	$	$
Non-current Assets:	Cost	Depreciation	N.B.V .
Machinery	3,500	250	3,250
Current assets:			
Inventory		14,000	
Trade receivables		9,650	
Prepayments		200	23,850
Total assets			27,100
Current liabilities:			
Trade payables		6,500	
Accruals		100	
Overdraft		7,225	13,825
Capital:			
Balance at 1st Jan. 20x4		* 24,200	
Add Profit for the year		8,625	
		32,825	
Less Drawings (18,450 + 1,100)	19, 550		13,275
			27,100

Working: Capital at 1 Jan. 20x4 = Assets – liabilities

= (4,000+ 12,000+ 10,000+ 150 +3,500) – (5,400 + 50)

= *$ 24,200

√ *Tip: Always calculate the capital (using all the opening balances including the opening bank balance), the sales and purchases for the year before writing up the final accounts.*

Exercise 5.10

Mobin does not keep a complete accounting system, but he provides the following information:

	At 31st Mar 20x1	At 31st Mar 20x2
	$	$
Inventory	3,000	5,000
Trade payables	2,500	3,000
Trade receivables	3,500	4,000
Shop fittings	6,000	5,500
Balance at bank	2,100	2,000

Additional information:

a) Cheques received from trade debtors $30,000.

b) Cash sales banked $3,500.

c) Cheques paid to trade creditors $16,700.

d) Mobin's drawings for the year were $550 per month.

Required:

From the above information, calculate Mobin's

i)   **Purchases and sales**

ii)   **Capital at 31st March 20x1 and 31st March 20x2.**

iii)   **Net profit for the year ended 31st March 20x2.**

Exercise 5.11

Jeswant owns a retail business but he does not keep accounting records.
The table below shows his assets and liabilities at 31st December 20x2 and 20x3:

	At 31st Dec 20x2	At 31st Dec 20x3
	$	$
Inventory of goods	6,500	6,000
Trade receivables	2,500	3,000
Trade payables	1,500	2,100
Electricity accrued	150	170
Rent prepaid	1,400	1,700
Motor vans	3,500	4,600

All takings were banked and all payments were made by cheque. The receipts and payments for the year ended 31st December 20x3 were as follows:

Receipts		Payments	
	$		$
Takings from cash sales	28,000	Suppliers	20,000
Received from customers	12,000	Electricity	600
		Rent	2,500
		Insurance	150
		Office expenses	550
		Drawings	10,000
		Motor Van	1,500

Required:

a) **Prepare Jeswant's income statement for the year ended 31st December 20x3**

Exercise 5.12

Moby does not keep a complete accounting system, but he provides the following information:

	At 31st Mar 20x1	At 31st Mar 20x2
	$	$
Stock	4,000	6,000
Trade payables	2,000	3,500
Trade receivables	2,500	5,000
Shop fittings	6,560	6,000
Balance at bank	2,010	3,000

Additional information:
a) Cheques received from trade debtors $25,000.
b) Cash sales banked $3,000.
c) Cheques paid to trade creditors $10,000.
d) Moby's drawings for the year were $1550 .

Required:

From the above information, calculate Moby's

A   i)   Purchases and sales

ii)   Capital at 31st March 20x1 and 31st March 20x2.

iii)   Net profit for the year ended 31st March 20x2.

B   Draw up Moby's statement of financial position as at 31st March 20x2

Exercise 5.13

Fred Sinatra set up business on 1 April 2003 selling watches from a market stall.

Fred has asked you to calculate his profit for the year ended 31 March 2004 using the following information.

(i)   All sales were made for cash. Payments were made by cheque unless otherwise stated.

(ii)   Opening capital was $17,600 which was paid into a bank account opened on 1 April 2003.

(iii)   The bank balance on 31 Mar2004 was $2120dr

(iv)   Fred's purchases for the year totalled $33,120, but on analysing this figure it was found to include $2000 paid for secure display cabinets and $800 for petrol for Fred's motor car. The remainder was for the purchase of watches for resale.

(v)   Fred bought a motor car to be used in the business for $5750.

(vi)   Rent of $60 per month had been paid from cash sales.

(vii)   Drawings of $100 per week were taken from cash sales.

(viii) Motor car expenses for the year cost $515.

(ix)   Fred kept a petty cash float of $100.

(x)   Fred's pricing policy was cost plus 75%.

(xi)   The motor car and display units are both to be depreciated over five years on a straight line basis, with no residual value. A full year's depreciation is applied in the year of purchase.

Required:

(a) Prepare Fred's bank account for the year ended 31 March 2004.

(b) Calculate Fred's total sales for the year ended 31 March 2004.

(c) Calculate Fred's stock at 31 March 2004.

(d) Prepare Fred's income statement for the year ended 31 March 2004.

[UCLES, 2004, AS/A Level Accounting, Syllabus 9706/2, Oct/Nov]

Exercise 5.14

On 1 January 2009 Clara Coyle, a sole trader, had the following balances:

	$
Inventory	24,170
Premises	60,000
Fittings and fixtures (NBV)	28,000
Cash & cash equivalents (bank)	4,000
Rates prepaid	440
Trade receivables	3,810
Trade payables	3,420
Capital	117,000

There was no opening cash or cash equivalent.

Full accounting records were not kept, but the following information was available for the year ended 31 December 2009:

Bank account receipts:	$
Loan from uncle (interest free)	10,000
Receipts from trade receivables	163,100
Cash sales paid into bank	34,000
Bank account payments:	

Payments to trade payables   141,508
Ordinary goods purchased by cheque   6,300

Rates	$ 2,600
Drawings	$ 3,650
General expenses	$ 4,410
Wages	$ 21,300

Cash payments from cash sales:
| General expenses | 2,680 |
| Ordinary goods purchased | 1,200 |

Balances at 31 December 2009:
Trade receivables	4,100
Trade payables	11,850
Rates prepaid	240
General expenses owing	400
Wages owing	1,620
Cash and cash equivalents (cash)	515
Bank	?

Additional information:

1. The selling price on all goods is based on cost plus 25%
2. During the year Clara Coyle withdrew goods, costing $140, from the business, for her own use.
3. The business allowed discounts, $1,300, to its trade receivables.
4. The business received discounts, $1,600, from its trade payables.
5. No additions or disposals of non-current assets took place during the year.
6. Depreciation of $3,000 is to be provided on fixtures and fittings.
    Premises are not depreciated.

    Required:
    a. **Calculate the total sales for the year ended 31 December 2009.**
    b. **Calculate the total purchases for the year ended 31 December 2009.**
    c. **Prepare the income statement for Clara Coyle for the year ended 31 December 2009.**
    d. **Prepare the statement of financial position for Clara Coyle at 31 December 2009.**

    [UCLES, 2010, AS/A Level Accounting, Syllabus 9706/22, Oct/Nov]

TEST YOURSELF
5.1 MULTIPLE CHOICE QUESTIONS

i) A 1June 20x6 Kusum's trade receivables amounted to $13,000. In the year to 31 May 20x7 she received $78,000 from trade receivables and allowed them settlement discounts of $2,560. At 31 May 20x7 her trade receivables were $15,600. What were Kusum's sales for the year?

A) $83,160   B) $80,600   C) $77,960   D) $75,400

ii) Melanie's mark up on inventory is 25% to arrive at the selling price. All of her inventory was stolen on 5 July 20x3. Her inventory at 31 December 20x2 was $15,000. From 1 January to 5 July 20x3 sales totalled $36,000 and purchases were $18,000. What was the cost of the stolen inventory?

A) $18,000   B) $ 9,000   C) $4,200   D) $3,000

iii) At 1 January 20x8 Dudley's business assets were: Motor van $35,000 (cost $40,000), Furniture $1,500, Stock $500, trade receivables 3,500 (of which $550 were known to be irrecoverable), cash at bank $1,400. His trade payables totalled $2,300.
At 31 December 20x8 his assets were: Premises which had cost $1,00,000 and on which a mortgage of $80,000 was still outstanding, motor van $31,000, furniture $1,100, inventory $350, trade receivables $2,000, cash $2,900.
His trade payables amounted to $5,600 and he had a bank overdraft of $60. During the year Dudley's drawings amounted to $300 a month.
What was his profit for the year?

A)$8,940   B)$13,940   C) $12,640   D) $16,240

iv) Kacey's records showed the following: Opening inventory $5,600, closing inventory $3,400 and sales for the year $45,000. Kacey sells her goods to produce a gross margin of 25%. What were Kacey's purchases?

A) $ 31,550   B) $33,800   C) $42,800   D) $47,200

v) Mildred commenced business with $12,000 she had received as a gift from her grandmother and $5,000 she had received as a loan from her father. She used some of this money to purchase a motor van for $8,000. She obtained a mortgage for $50,000 to purchase a workshop. What was her capital?

A) $15,000   B) $12,000   C) $17,000   D) $67,000

5.2   On the night of 4 September 20x3, Bailey's warehouse was burned down and most of the inventory destroyed. The inventory salvaged was valued at cost in the sum of $3,400. Bailey claimed for compensation from his insurance company.
Additional information:
Statement of financial position as at 31 December 20x2 (extract)

	$
Inventory	27,000
Trade receivables	13,450
Trade payables	10,980

Further information for the period 1 Jan 20x3 – 4 September 20x3:

Receipts from trade receivables	37,800
Cash sales	14,500
Payments to Trade payables	30,700

At 4 September 20x3:

Trade receivables	20,560
Trade payables	18,730

Bailey achieves a margin of 30% on all sales.

Required: Using the information, calculate the amount of the claim.

5.3 Manish suspects a loss of cash has occurred. He provides the following data:

i) Cash balance at the start of the month $500.

ii) Cash balance at the end of the month $200.

iii) Cash banked $20,600.

iv) Cash sales for the month $ 30,000.

Calculate: How much cash has been lost?

5.3 Hassle Back started business on 1 May 2007. On that day:

i. Hassle Back brought in his personal car which was valued at $4,100 and cash $6,500, which was immediately banked.

ii. The business took a loan (repayable in 2015) from the bank on August 1 2007, of $5,300 @ 16% interest p.a. This amount was banked immediately.

Hassle Back provides the following details of his business' cash and bank transactions for the year ended 30 April 2008:

Cash transactions:	$
Wages to staff	3,200
General operating expenses	320
Heating and lighting	95
Car expenses	155
Cheque transactions:	
Lease payments for premises	4,800
Additional wages to staff	7,050
Redecoration of premises	1,235
Additional general operating expenses	1,375
Purchases	105,950
Additional lighting and heating	965
Fixtures and fittings	4,895
Interest on loan	424
Accountancy fees	355
Additional car expenses	1,050

Additional information:

i. All cash sales were banked after meeting cash payments.

ii. Hassle Back's drawing were $100 in cash per week.

iii. Hassle Back took inventory worth $335 (at cost price) for personal use.

iv. General operating expenses included a payment of $215 made out to an insurance company for Hassle Back's personal life insurance.

v.   One fifth of the car expenses were for private purposes.

vi.   Lease payments for premises were $960 per quarter payable in advance.

Assets and liabilities at 30 April 2008 were as follows:

	$
Inventory	14,500
Cash balance	125
Bank balance	8,150
Car	3,150
Fixtures & fittings	4,200
Creditors for purchases	10,950

There were no sales of non-current assets during the year ended 30 April 2008.

Required:

a.   Prepare a cash and bank account for the year ended 30 April 2008.

b.   Prepare the financial statements for the year ended 30 April 2008

CHAPTER 6
NON-PROFIT MAKING ORGANISATIONS

Q. What is the main purpose of Non-Profit Organisations?
Ans. These organisations, such as clubs and societies are run so that the members can participate in activities such as golf, swimming etc. They also provide facilities and services to their members. Their main aim is not profit making but to cater to the welfare of their members.

Q. Who normally maintains the accounting records of such an organisation?
Ans. The person who maintains accountant records of such an organisation is normally called a treasurer.

Q. What is the difference in the terms used by a profit making firm and a non- profit making firm?
Ans. The difference is outlined in the table below:

	Profit – making firm	Non-profit organisation
1.	Income statement	Income and expenditure account
2.	Profit for the year	Surplus of income over expenditure
3.	Net loss	Excess of expenditure over income
4.	Capital	Accumulated fund
5.	Cash book/account	Receipts and payments account

Q. A society's expenditure has exceeded its income in the past two years.
i. State why this should not be allowed to continue
ii. Suggest four actions that the society can take to improve the situation.
Ans. i. If the society continues in this way it will not have enough finance to run its business once all its creditors demand payment and it will have to close down eventually. Since the society is meeting the needs of its members or community, the closure of the society would not be a desirous outcome for everyone concerned.

ii) Ways the society can improve the situation are:
a) Hold some profit - making activity such as a dance or open a profit -making bar.
b) Rent out its equipment or fields etc. to increase income.
c) Increase the amount of subscriptions or recruit more members.
d) Organise charity drives and solicit donations.

Q. If a club is running a bar, which account will be used to calculate the profit made?
Ans. A 'Trading Account' will be used. The profit calculated in this account is then transferred to the income and expenditure account as income. The bar is an ancillary activity raising money to supplement income. A trading account is prepared as this is a trading activity.

Q. What are the other types of ancillary activities?
Ans. Non-trading activities may also be carried out which are incidental to a club's main purpose. Examples are socials, competitions, outings etc. These are dealt with in the income and expenditure account.

Q. What is meant by the term 'subscriptions'?
Ans. 'Subscriptions' is what the members of the non-profit organisations pay to the organisations as a kind of membership fee. It is treated as an income by the organisation.

Q. How is 'subscriptions prepaid' by members treated in the financial statements?
Ans. As subscriptions are treated as income, a subscription prepaid is income prepaid and as such is a liability. It is thus shown as a current liability in the statement of financial position of the organisation.

Q. How is 'subscriptions accrued' treated in the financial statements?
Ans. As subscriptions are treated as income, a subscription accrued is income accrued and as such is an asset. It is thus shown as a current asset in the statement of financial position of the organisation.

Q. Explain: The receipts and payments account
Ans. This is a summary of the cash book/account for the year. All money received is debited and money paid is credited. The book/account is then balanced at the end of the financial period. It must be remembered that non-monetary items should not be entered in this account. Hence, depreciation, accruals and prepayments do not affect this account.

Exhibit:

The Honest Golf club had $4,500 in the bank on 1st July 20x2. All receipts are paid into the bank and all payments are made by cheque. The following information is provided of all the money received and payments made during the year ended 30th June 20x3:

	$
Subscription received	3,560
Payment of golf competition fees	60
Ground rent received	400
Travelling expenses	179
Sundry expenses	2,000
Purchase of new equipment	1,000
Receipts from spectators	2,000
Net proceeds from annual ball	450

Required: Prepare the receipts and payments account for the year ended 30th June 20x3.

Solution:

Honest Golf Club receipts and payments account for the year ended 30th June 20x3

Receipts	$	Payments	$
Balance b/d	4,500	Golf competition fees	60
Subscriptions received	3,560	Travelling expenses	179
Receipts from spectators	2,000	Ground rent	400
		Sundry expenses	2,000
		Equipment	1,000
Receipts from ball	450	Balance c/d	7,671
	10,910		10,910

Exercise 6.1

The treasurer of Mainstream Football Club provides the following information of the receipts and payments during the year ended 31st December 20x4:

	$
Subscriptions received	3,600
Receipts from bar sale	4,500
Purchase of bar supplies	2,000
Purchase of new equipment	1,200
Wages of bar – tender	800
Wages of caretaker	600
Rates	500
Insurance	300

Receipts from spectators
of home matches   1,500
Rent received   700
The Club had $ 3,700 in the bank on 1st January 20x4.
Required
Prepare the Receipts and Payments Account for the period.

Exercise 6.2
Information about the Kosi Leisure club for the year ended 31st August 20x3 is given:

	$
Balance at bank at 1st September 20x2	200
Purchase of equipment	140
Collections at matches	2,000
Receipts from sale of snacks	400
Rent received	350
Administrative expenses	95
Sundry expenses	100
Wages of part – time staff	300

Required:
Prepare a Receipts & Payments Account for the year ended 31st August 20x3.

Q. What is the function of a trading account in a non-profit organization?
Ans. A trading account should be prepared if a non - profit organisation carries out a regular trading activity to supplement its income. This activity is incidental to its main purpose. The gross profit calculated in the trading account is transferred to the income & expenditure account.

Exhibit:
Torquin Drama Club has a bar. The following information for the year ended 31st July 20x1 is provided by the treasurer of the club:

	$
Inventory at 1st August 20x0	460
Inventory at 31st July 20x1	500
Sales	4,000
Purchases	1,340
Wages of bar tender	2,000

Required: Prepare a Bar trading account for the year ended 31st July 20x1.
Solution:

Torquin Drama Club Bar trading account for the year ended 31st July 20x1

	$	$
Sales		4,000
Less Cost of sales:		
Inventory at 1st August 20x0	460	
Add: Purchases	1,340	
	1,800	
Less: Inventory at 31st July 20x1	500	1,300
		2,700
Less: Wages of bar tender		2,000
Profit on Bar transferred to income & exp.A/c		700

√ Tip: It should be remembered that if either purchases or sales or both figures are missing, they should be calculated using the method outlined in the chapter on single entry and incomplete records.

Exercise 6.3

The Roadrunners Club is a non – profit organisation. They run a cafe and the following information is provided for the year ended 30th June 20x3:

	$
Inventory at 1st July 20x2	3,000
Inventory at 30th June 20x3	3,500
Sales	5,000
Purchases	1,500
Wages of part-time cafe staff	600

Required: Prepare a trading account for the year ended 30th June 20x3.

INCOME AND EXPENDITURE ACCOUNT

This account is similar to the profit & loss account of a trading firm.

√ Tip: The matching principle should be applied to both expenses as well as income (e.g. subscriptions).

THE STATEMENT OF FINANCIAL POSITION

Again, this is similar to that of a trading firm. The only difference is that there is no capital. The accumulated fund of the non – trading firm is shown in a similar way to the capital of a trading firm.

√ Tip: If the opening accumulated fund figure or the closing accumulated fund figure is missing, they are calculated by using the method outlined in the chapter on Single Entry. Also, if the subscriptions for the year is not evident, it is calculated using the method outlined in the chapter on Accruals and Prepayments. It should be remembered that subscriptions represents income to a non – profit organisation.

Exhibit:

The following trial balance was extracted from the books of Middletown Football Club as at 31st December 20x3:

	Dr	Cr
	$	$
Clubhouse	20,000	
Equipment	15,600	
Profits from competitions		5,000
Subscriptions received		22,000
Wages of bar staff	2,400	
Bar inventory 1st Jan. 20x3	1,600	
Bar purchases	10,000	
Bar sales		15,000
Groundsman's wages	3,000	
Sundry expenses	2,500	
Secretary's salary	1,000	
Cash at bank	1,460	
Accumulated fund 1st Jan. 20x3		15,560
	57,560	57,560

Notes:

i) Bar purchases and sales were on a cash basis. Bar inventory at 31st Dec. 20x3 were valued at $1,000.

ii) Subscriptions paid in advance at 31st December 20x3 amounted to $150

iii) Provide for depreciation of equipment $ 600.

Required:

a) Draw up a bar trading account for the year ended 31st December 20x3.

b) Draw up an income & expenditure account for the year ended 31st December 20x3 and a statement of financial position as at 31st December 20x3.

Solution: (The Bar Trading Account should be completed by you)

Middletown Football Club
Bar trading account for the year ended 31st Dec., 20x3

	$	$
Sales		....
Less Cost of Sales:		
Inventory at 1st Jan. 20x3	....	
Add Purchases	....	
	....	
Less: Inventory at 31st Dec.20x3	....	....
		....
Less: Bar staff wages		....
Profit from bar transferred to		
Income & expenditure A/c		....

Middletown football Club Income & expenditure account for the year ended
31st Dec. 20x3

	$	$
Income		
Profit from bar		2,000
Subscriptions (22,000 – 150)		21,850
Profit from competitions		5,000
		28,850
Expenditure		
Groundsman's wages	2,500	
Sundry expenses	3,000	
Secretary's salary	1,000	
Depreciation	600	7,100
Surplus of Income over Expenditure		21,750

Statement of financial position as at 31st Dec. 20x3

Non-current Assets:	Cost	Depr.	N.B.V.
	$	$	$
Clubhouse	20,000	-	20,000
Equipment	15,600	600	15,000
	35,600	600	35,000
Current Assets:			
Inventory		1,000	
Cash at bank		1,460	2,460
Total assets			37,460
Current Liabilities:			
Subscriptions paid in advance			150
Accumulated fund:			
Balance at 1st Jan. 20x3		15,560	
Add surplus of income over			
expenditure		21,750	37,310
Total liabilities and accumulated fund			37,460

√ Tip: The surplus is added to the accumulated fund, above. However, if there was an excess of expenditure over income, then the figure of the excess should be subtracted from the accumulated fund.

Exercise 6.4

The following trial balance was extracted from the books of Silas Social Club on 31st December 20x1:

	Dr	Cr
	$	$
Accumulated Fund, 1st January 20x1		40,000
Bar inventory 1st January 20x1	5,000	
Bar Purchases	35,000	
Land and buildings	40,000	
Cash at bank	4,000	
Cash in hand	2,000	
Bar Takings		60,000
Wages	20,000	
Equipment	10,500	
Secretary's salary	4,500	
Treasurer's salary	3,000	
Sundry expenses	2,200	
Subscriptions received		18,000
Profit from social events	_____	8,200
	126,200	126,200

The treasurer gives the following information:

a) All bar purchases and takings were for cash.

b) At 31st Dec. 20x1 :

   Subscriptions due but unpaid were $ 800.

   Bar inventory was $ 5000

c) Of the wages total, wages of bar staff were $ 10,000.

d) Depreciation to be written off equipment $ 500.

Required :

i)   Bar trading account for the year ended 31st December 20x1

ii)   Income & expenditure account for the year ended 31st December 20x1

iii)   The club statement of financial position as at 31st December 20x1

√ Tips: a) The figure for wages should be $ 20,000 – 10,000 in the Income & Expenditure A/c
*   b) Subscriptions due but unpaid should be entered as a current asset.*

Exerccise 6.5

On Jan 1st 20x3 Linden Golf club had $1,400 in the bank and equipment valued at $ 2,000. At that date, $20 was outstanding for travelling expenses and insurance was prepaid by $50. The treasurer provided the following information relating to the year ended 31st December 20x3:

	$
Subscriptions received	2,400
Payment of fees	40
Rent received	350
Traveling expenses	400
Sundry expenses	2,300
Insurance	320
Purchase of new equipment	1,500
Receipts from spectators	2,000

Net proceeds from annual ball   500

Additional notes:
  i)   All receipts were paid into the bank and all payments were made by cheque.
  ii)   At 31st December 20x3, insurance prepaid amounted to $30 and subscriptions owing amounted to $140.
  iii)   Equipment is to be depreciated by $ 500.

Required:
a) The Receipts & Payments Account for the year ended 31st December 20x3.
b) The Income & Expenditure Account for the year   ended 31st December 20x3.

Exercises 6.6
The following is a summary of the receipts & payments of the Happy Fishing Club during the year ended 31st July 20x2.

Happy Fishing Club Receipts and Payments Account for the year ended 31st July 20x2.

Receipts	$	Payments	$
Cash and bank bal b/f	300	Secretary's salary	150
Sales competition tickets	500	Rates	1,000
Subscriptions	2,000	Visiting speaker's expenses	900
Donations	100	Prizes for competitions	300
Refund of rates	300	Balance c/f	850
	3,200		3,200

The following valuations are also available:

As at 31st July	20x1	20x2
	$	$
Equipment (original cost $ 1,000)	950	900
Subscriptions in arrears	75	80
Subscriptions in advance	20	30
Stocks of competition prizes	40	50

Required:
a) Calculate the value of the accumulated fund as at 1st August 20x1
b) Reconstruct the subscriptions account.
c) Prepare the income & expenditure account for the year ended 31st July 20x2 and the statement of financial position as at that date.

√ *Tip: a) Accumulated fund at 1st August 20x1 = Assets – Liabilities (at 1st Aug.20x1)*
= (950+75+40+*300) – (20)
* *This is the balance at the Bank at that date.*

b)   *Subscriptions Account*

	$		$
Balance (owing) b/f	75	*Balance (Prepaid) b/f*	20
Balance (prepaid) c/f	30	*Cash and cheques*	....
Income & Expenditure A/c (Balancing figure)	......	*Balance (owing)c/f*	80
	2,100		2,100

Q. How should life subscriptions and entry fees be treated in the financial statements?
Ans. These are normally received as lump sums. The full amount should not be credited to the income and expenditure account but to a deferred income account. It should then be spread equally over a period of time, usually five years, as per the policy of the non-profit organization.

Q. How are donations treated in the financial statements?
Ans. Donations and funds left in a will (legacies) must be credited to an account opened for the purpose stipulated by the person/organization making the donation. A separate bank account is usually opened for the purpose and the money placed in it to ensure that it is not spent elsewhere.

EXHIBIT

The Hardunby Sports and Social Club had the following Assets and Liabilities as at 31 May 20x8:

Assets	$	Liabilities	$
Buildings at cost	40,000	Bar supplies	6,400
Pool tables	3,000	Subscriptions in advance	400
Lawn Mower	100		
10% Debentures	4,500		
Subscriptions due	500		
Bar Stock	7,200		
Bank	2,500		

The following are the receipts and payments for the year ended 31 May 20x9:

Receipts	$	Payments	$
Subscriptions	24,000	Dance expenses	2,500
Annual dance	3,000	Competition prizes	950
Competition entries	1,400	Bar inventory	26,500
Bar sales	58,700	Groundsman's wages	15,000
Takings from		Maintenance	2,200
Pool Tables	650	Deposit Account	6,000
Donation	6,000	Lawn Mower	500
		Bar wages	17,000

The following balances occur at 31 May 20x9:

	$
Bar inventory	5,400
Subscriptions in advance	650
Subscriptions in arrears	700
Bar stock unpaid	3,200
Wages due to groundsman	1,500

Pool Tables were depreciated at 25% at 31 May 20x9 on book value at 31 May 20x8. A trade-in was allowed when the new lawn mower was purchased. This transaction took place on 1 June 20x8 and a full year's depreciation at 25% was charged to the new mower in the final accounts in May 20x9. No depreciation was charged to the old mower. The new mower cost $700. The donation of $6,000, which was received at the end of May 20x9, was placed in a bank deposit account. The interest is to be used in future years to pay for an annual prize called the 'Hardunby People's Prize'.

Required:
(i)   Prepare the Club Bar Trading Account for the year ended 31 May 20x9
(ii)   Prepare the Club Income and Expenditure Account for the year ended 31 May 20x9
(iii)   Prepare the Club Statement of financial position as at 31 May 20x9.

NOTE: A debenture is a loan given to a company. It carries the right to a fixed rate of interest which is credited as income to the Income and Expenditure Account.

Solution:
(i) Bar Trading Account for the year ended 31 May 20x9

	$	$	$
Sales			58,700
Less Cost of Sales:			
Opening inventory		7,200	
Purchases	26,500		
Less unpaid at start	6,400		

```
                20,100
Add unpaid at end   3,200    23,300
                             30,500
Less Closing inventory        5,400
                             25,100
Add Bar wages                17,000    42,100
Bar Profit                             16,600
```

ii)   Income and Expenditure Account for the year ended 31 May 20x9

INCOME	$	$
Subscriptions		*23,950
Debenture Interest		450
Profit on Dinner Dance		500
Profit from competitions		450
Bar Profit		16,600
Takings from pool Tables		650
Profit on sale of Lawn Mower		100
		42,700
Less EXPENDITURE		
Groundsman's wages	16,500	
Maintenance	2,200	
Depreciation of Lawn Mower	175	
Depreciation of Pool Tables	750	19,625
Surplus of income over expenditure		23,075

Subscriptions Account

	$		$
Bal b/d	500	Bal B/d	400
Bal c/d	650	Bank/cash	24,000
Income and			
Expenditure	23,950	Bal c/d	700
	25,100		25,100

(iv)   Statement of financial position as at 31 May 20x9

	$	$	$
Non-current Assets:			
Buildings			40,000
Pool Tables			2,250
Lawn Mower			525
			42,775
Investments: 10% Debentures			4,500
Current Assets:			
Bar inventory		5,400	
Subscriptions in arrears		700	
Debenture Interest due		450	
Bank		25,600	
**Deposit Account		6,000	38,150
			85,425
Current Liabilities:			
Subscriptions in advance	650		
Other payables	4,700		5,350
Accumulated Fund		51,000	
Add Surplus		23,075	74,075
**Prize Fund			6,000
			85,425

** The donation can also be shown as follows:
Alternate Statement of financial position
Statement of financial position as at 31 May 20x9

	$	$	$
Non-current Assets:			
Buildings			40,000
Pool Tables			2,250
Lawn Mower			525
			42,775
Investments: 10% Debentures			4,500
Current Assets:			
Bar inventory		5,400	
Subscriptions in arrears		700	
Debenture Interest due		450	
Bank		25,600	32,150
			79,425
Current Liabilities:			
Subscriptions in advance	650		
Other payables	4,700		5,350
Accumulated Fund		51,000	
Add Surplus		23,075	74,075
			79425
**Prize Fund			6,000
Represented by: Deposit account			6,000

Exercise 6.7

During the year ended 31 December 20x2, Mel's hobby club received $6,700 for subscriptions. At 31 December 20x1 subscriptions owing were $ 490 and subscriptions received in advance were $350. At 31 December 20x2, subscriptions owing were $260 and subscriptions paid in advance were $4000.
Required:
Calculate the figure for subscriptions in the Income and Expenditure Account for the year ended 31 December 20x2.

Exercise 6.8

The Maestro Piano Club had the following assets and liabilities as at 31 May 20x5:

Assets	$	Liabilities	$
Buildings at cost	15,000	Bar supplies	2,300
Pianos	12,000	Subscriptions in advance	100
Lawn Mower	220		
10% Debentures	6,000		
Subscriptions due	250		
Bar Stock	3,400		
Bank	2,000		

The following are the Receipts and Payments for the year ended 31 May 20x6:

Receipts	$	Payments	$
Subscriptions	13,000	Dance expenses	2,500
Annual Dance	5,400	Competition prizes	950
Competition entries	2,500	Bar stock	26,500
Bar sales	43,600	Tuner's wages	15,000
Donations	4,000	Maintenance	2,200
Deposit Account	4,000	Lawn Mower	450

The following balances occur at 31 May 20x6:

	$
Bar stock	4,000
Subscriptions in advance	470
Subscriptions in arrears	580
Bar stock unpaid	2,450
Wages due to tuner	750

Pianos were depreciated at 25% at 31 May 20x6 on book value at 31 May 20x5. A trade-in was allowed when the new lawn mower was purchased. This transaction took place on 1 June 20x5 and a full year's depreciation at 25% was charged to the new mower in the final accounts in May 20x6. No depreciation was charged to the old mower. The new mower cost$600. The donation of $4,000, which was received at the end of May 20x6, was placed in a bank deposit account. The interest is to be used in future years to pay for an annual prize called the `Maestro's Prize'.

Required:

(i) Prepare the Club Bar Trading Account for the year ended 31 May 20x6
(ii) Prepare the Club Income and Expenditure Account for the year ended 31 May 20x6
(iii) Prepare the Club Statement of financial position as at 31 May 20x6.

TEST YOURSELF

6.1   Multiple-Choice Questions.

i) The Mannana Bowling Club has 100 members. The annual subscription is $ 25 a member. Subscriptions not paid in one year are written off if not paid by the end of the next year. During the year ended 31 December 20x4, the following amounts were received:

	$
Subscriptions for the year ended 31 December 20x4	2,000
Subscriptions for the year ended 31 December 20x3	500
Subscriptions for the year ended 31 December 20x5	750

At 31 December 20x3 subscriptions owing were $1,000. What was the amount of subscriptions owing showing in the Statement of financial position as at 31 December 20x4 as current assets?

A) $ 2,500   B) $500   C) $750   D) $2250

ii) The Mountaineering Club charges $40 as annual subscriptions per member. The following information is available:

	$
Subscriptions owing at 1 January 20x2	160
Subscriptions received during the year ended 31 December 20x2	2000
Subscriptions received in advance at 31 December 20x1	200

How many members did the Club have?

A) 50   B) 51   C) 55   D) 54

iii) Which of the following takes the place of the Income statement in a Non-profit Making company?

A) Accumulated fund
B) Receipts payments account
C) Income and expenditure account
D) Bar trading account

iv) From the following information, calculate the total income for the year:

	$
Subscriptions received	3,000
Proceeds of sale refreshments	6,000
Opening stock of refreshments	1,000
Closing stock of refreshments	600
Purchases of refreshments	3,600

A) $9,000   B) $6,400   C) $5,000   D) $2,400

v) Which of the following will not be found in the accounts of a Club?
A)   Accumulated fund
B)   Capital
C)   Non-current assets
D)   Accruals (other payables)

vi) Clubs should treat life membership subscriptions as:
A) Loans to the club
B) Deferred income
C) Additions to the accumulated fund
D) Income of the year in which they were received

vii) The following information is given to you by a club's treasurer.

	$
Closing stock of equipment	780
Purchases of equipment	4,500
Opening stock of equipment	1,200
Subscriptions received	12,000
Sale of equipment	5,000

What was the total income of the club for the year?
A) $12,080   B) $7,000   C) $2,500   D) $12,000

viii) A donation to a club to build tennis courts will be shown as
A)   a special fund in the statement of financial position
B)   income in the club's income and expenditure account
C)   an asset in the statement of financial position
D)   an addition to the accumulated fund

ix) The following information is given to you about a club's subscription for the year ended 31st July 20x6.

Number of members	10
Annual subscriptions	$30
Subscriptions owing at 1st August 20x5	$280
Subscription in advance at 31st July 20x6	$130

What is the amount that should be credited to the Income and Expenditure of the Club for the year ended 31st July 20x6?
A) $180   B) $300   C) $520   D) $450

x) You are given the following information about a club's records for the year ended 31st December 20x3.

	$
Life subscriptions received during the year	2,000
Balance of life subscriptions account at 1st January 20x3	800
Annual subscriptions received in the year	5,000
Annual subscriptions received for year ended 31st Dec, 20x4	40

The club has a policy of crediting the life subscriptions to the Income and Expenditure Account over five years. How much should be credited to the Income and Expenditure Account for subscriptions for the year ended 31st December 20x3?
A) $6960   B) $5,000   C) $5,200   D) $5160

6.2   The Bernard Shaw's Drama club hold three performances per year, and also attend several performances together in the city. The club is dependent upon grants and donations. The size of the grant each year depends upon the costs and revenues of the performances held in the previous year, being 80% of the difference. The programme, however has to be decided upon at least one season in advance, so that the venues and musicians can be booked.   For the 20x3 season, the club will give one performance requiring an orchestra and expensive props. The grant for 20x2 was $4,500.

The treasurer of the club resigned in December 20x1, and a club member, who has kept records ever since, provides the following information:

 i) The company purchased scripts which it sells to members at a mark-up of 10%, and also hires scripts for members. The hire charge to the club is 90% of the charge made to members. In the year ended 31st December 20x3 the club bought 150 scripts, which were sold to members for $6 each. It paid hire charges for scores of $400.

ii)   The club had 85 members in 20x2 and 100 in 20x3. Couple members are given a discount of 10% on their total subscription.   Over 60's obtain a reduction of 20%. In the year ended 31 December 20x3, the normal subscription was $40.   During the year ended 31December 20x3 there were 10 couple members and 5 over 60's, all of whom paid their subscriptions on time. However, subscriptions of 8 ordinary members was owing.

iii)   A discount of 5% was given on tickets sold a month or more before the show. The ticket prices were $4 and $5 each. For the 20x3 season, 750 tickets of $4 and 600 tickets of $5 were sold of which 250 and 120 respectively were at discounted rates for early payment.

iv.) The club transports its members to performances at the cost of $200 for a 50-seater coach.

It charges its members $5 each and in the year ended 31 December 20x3 it had 175 coach seats paid for.

Additional receipts and payments for the year ended 31st December 20x3 were:

Receipts	$	Payments	$
Sale of programmes	650	Printing charges	390
Donations	780	Hire of venues	4,500
		Musician's fees	5,680
		Hire of equipment	1,970

Required:

A)   Prepare the club's Income and Expenditure account for the year ended 31st December 20x3 and from those figures, calculate the grant the club should receive for the following season, not including i) in your calculations. State whether or not the club can budget effectively for the future on the basis of the grants it can expect to receive.

B)   What financial records do you suggest a club should keep?

C)   What differences would you expect to find between the records of a club or society and those of a small limited company?

Chapter 7
Manufacturing Accounts

Q. When is a Manufacturing account required to be drawn up?
Ans. A Manufacturing Account is prepared by manufacturers in addition to the Income statement and Statement of financial position.

Q. How are costs divided in a manufacturing firm?
Ans. The costs are:
1. Cost of raw materials consumed = opening inventory of raw materials + purchases of raw materials – closing inventory of raw materials + carriage inwards
2. Prime Cost = Direct materials (or cost of raw materials consumed) + Direct labour + Direct Expenses
3. Production Cost of goods completed = Prime cost + Factory overheads

Q. What is meant by the term: direct labour?
Ans. This is the cost of labour that can be directly traced to the manufacture of an item. Hence, wages of people working in the factory are included but wages and salaries of people working in the office, supervisors, cleaners, cranes drivers etc. are excluded.

Q. What is meant by the term: direct expenses?
Ans. These are expenses that can be directly traced to the manufacture of an item e.g. royalties, hire of a special machine for a job.

Q. What are 'Factory overhead costs'?
Ans. These include all those costs incurred in the factory where the production process is carried out, but which cannot be directly identified with each item produced. e.g. rent of factory, depreciation of plant machinery, factory lighting.

Q. What is meant by: work-in-progress?
Ans. Items that are not yet completed and only partly made are referred to as 'work-in-progress'.

Exhibit:
The following balances were taken from the books of Abraham, a manufacturer, on 31st December 20x6:

	$
Raw materials - Inventory at 1st January 20x6	3,000
Purchases	10,000
Inventory at 31st December 20x6	4,000
Carriage on raw material	400
Factory wages - Direct	1,000
Indirect	4,000
Factory rent	2,000
Factory machinery repairs	500
Depreciation of factory machinery	700
Factory lighting	1,200

Required:
Prepare the Manufacturing Account of Abraham for the year ended 31st December 20x6

Solution:

Abraham's Manufacturing Account for the year ended 31st December 20x6

	$	$
Opening Inventory of raw material		3,000
Add: Purchases of raw material		10,000
		13,000
Less Closing Inventory of raw material		4,000
		9,000
Add Carriage Inwards		400
Cost of raw materials consumed		9,400
Add Direct Costs:		
Direct wages		1,000
Prime Cost		10,400
Add Factory Overheads:		
Indirect factory wages	4,000	
Factory rent	2,000	
Factory machinery repairs	500	
Depreciation of factory machinery	700	
Factory lighting	1,200	8,400
Production cost of goods completed		18,800

Exercise 7.1

The balances of Y Company's books at 30th June 20x8 include the following:

	$
Raw materials: Inventory at 1st July 20x7	12,000
Purchases	55,000
Carriage inwards	3,700
Factory wages: Direct	16,000
Indirect	10,000
Factory fuel and power	15,000
Factory Rent	8,000

Additional information:

a) Inventory of Raw materials at 30th June 20x8 was $10,000.

b) There was no work in progress at the beginning or end of   the year.

c) Depreciation $4,000 is to be charged on factory machinery for the year ended 30th June 20x8

Required:

Prepare The Y Company's Manufacturing Account for the year ended 30th June 20x8. Show Prime Cost and Cost of Production.

Exercise 7.2

S. Rehman owns a manufacturing business. Her accounts are prepared annually to 31st December.

Balances in Rehman's books at 31st December 20x6 included the following:

	$
Raw materials:	
Inventory at 1st January 20x6	11,000
Purchases	37,000
Carriage inwards	3,000
Factory wages and salaries:	
Direct	20,000
Indirect	11,900
Factory overheads:	
Fuel and power	12,000
Rent and rates	6,000

Additional information:
a) Inventory of raw materials at 31st December 20x6 was valued at $ 13,000.
b) There was no work in progress at the beginning or at the end of the year.
c) Depreciation of plant and machinery is to be charged as $ 12,000 for the year ended 31st Dec., 20x6.
Required:
Prepare The Rehman's Manufacturing Account for the year ended 31st December 20x6. Show Prime Cost and Cost of Production.

WORK-IN-PROGRESS

Exhibit:
The following balances were taken from the books of Mully's Manufacturing Company on 31st August, 20x5:

	$
Inventory at 1st Sept., 20x4:	
Raw materials	16,500
Work in progress	11,650
Wages and salaries:	
Factory Direct	5,000
Factory indirect	12,000
Purchase of raw materials	20,000
Power and fuel (indirect)	4,000
Inventory at 31st August 20x5:	
Raw materials	13,700
Work in progress	12,000

Notes:
   a. Fuel and power $360 in arrears at 31st August 20x5.
   b. Factory machinery is to be depreciated by $600.

Required:
A Manufacturing Account for the year ended 31st August 20x5 showing clearly:
a) Cost of Raw materials consumed.
b) Prime Cost
c) Cost of production.

Solution: Manufacturing Account for the year ended 31st August 20x5.

	$	$
Opening Inventory of raw materials		16,500
Add Purchases		20,000
		36,500
Less Closing Inventory of raw materials		13,700
Cost of raw materials consumed		22,800
Add Direct costs:		
Wages and salaries		5,000
Prime cost		27,800
Add Factory overheads:		
Wages and salaries	12,000	
Power and fuel (4000 + 360)	4,360	
Depreciation	600	16,960
		44,760
Add Opening Inventory of work in progress		11,650
		56,410
Less Closing Inventory of work in progress		12,000
Production cost of goods completed		44,410

Exercise 7.3

The following balances were taken from the books of Molly's Manufacturing Company on 31st August, 20x5:

Inventory at 1st Sept., 20x4:	$
Raw materials	10,500
Work in progress	12,000
Wages and salaries:	
Factory Direct	3,000
Factory indirect	15,000
Purchase of raw materials	10,000
Power and fuel (indirect)	5,000
Inventory at 31st August 20x5:	
Raw materials	10,000
Work-in-progress	13,000

Notes:
 a. Fuel and power $200 in arrears at 31st August 20x5.
 b. Factory machinery is to be depreciated by $1000.

Required:
A Manufacturing Account for the year ended 31st August 20x5 showing clearly:
a) Cost of Raw materials consumed.
b) Prime Cost
c) Cost of production.

INCOME STATEMENT AND STATEMENT OF FINANCIAL POSITION

The Trading Account section of the income Statement is very similar to that of any other type of business. The only difference is that the Production Cost of Goods Completed is added to the opening inventory of finished goods in addition to purchases of finished goods (if any). If there are no purchases of finished goods then the production cost of goods completed takes the place of purchases in the Trading account.

The Profit & Loss Account section of the income statement is very similar to that of any other type of business too. It must be remembered that the expenses listed in the Profit & Loss Account will be Administrative, Financial and Selling and Distribution expenses that cannot be directly traced to the manufacturing process.

The Statement of financial position is similar to that of any other type of business. The only difference is that there may be more than one kind of closing inventory: that of finished goods, raw materials and work in progress.

Q. What is meant by the term: Factory Profit?
Ans. This is a percentage of the cost of production that is added onto the production cost of goods completed as profit. This percentage is decided on by management and is debited to the Manufacturing Account. It is then credited to the Income Statement.

Exercise 7.4

Kotze is a manufacturer. His trial balance at 31st August 20x8 is as follows:

	$	$
Motor Van repairs	3,600	
Electricity: Factory	1,980	
Office	1,500	
Manufacturing wages	12,000	
Sundry expenses: Factory	4,580	
Office	3,470	

Commission of sales team	4,600	
Purchase of raw materials	24,600	
Rent: Factory	1,300	
Office	2,500	
Machinery	12,000	
Office Equipment	6,000	
Office salaries	3,000	
Trade receivables & Payables	2,800	3,500
Bank	400	
Sales		28, 370
Premises	20,000	
Opening inventory:		
Raw materials	4,000	
Finished goods	16,000	
Work in progress	3,670	
Drawings	2,000	
Capital		98,130
	130,000	130,000

Additional information:
a) Inventory at 31 August 20x8: Raw materials $3,500, Finished goods $2,300, Work in Progress $1,200.
b) Depreciate machinery $2,000, Office Equipment $1,000, Premises $2,000.
c) Manufacturing wages due but unpaid at 31 August 20x8 $230.
d) Factory profit is to be calculated at 20% on cost of production.

Required:
Prepare the Manufacturing account and Income Statement for the year ended 31 August 20x8 and a Statement of financial position as at that date.

Notes
1.   Profit for the year on Trading does not include factory profit. It is profit made on trading activities and excludes manufacturing activities.
2.   Factory Profit is added to the profit for the year on trading to arrive at total profit. However, if there is closing inventory then unrealised profit included in the cost of such Inventory is to be treated as unrealised profit and subtracted (see point 3).
3.   Unrealised profit = $\frac{2300 \times 20}{120}$ = $ 383

Q. What is meant by the term: unrealised profit?
Ans. Unrealised profit is profit that has not been realised on inventory that has not yet been sold. The realisation concept states that unrealised profit is not to be included in the Net Profit for the year.

Q. How is unrealised profit on unsold inventory (closing inventory of finished goods) treated?
Ans. The double entry for unrealised profit is: debit the income statement and credit the Provision for Unrealised Profit. If such an account exists then it will be adjusted for only the increase or the decrease in the provision. If such an account does not exist, then a new Provision for Unrealised Profit Account should be opened.

Q. How is unrealised profit calculated?
Ans. The formula is:
Unrealised profit = $\frac{\text{Closing inventory x percentage of factory profit}}{100+ \text{percentage of factory profit}}$

Q. How is a decrease in the provision for unrealised profit calculated?
Ans. Decrease in unrealised profit = Balance in the provision for unrealised profit (old) – new provision for unrealised profit.

Q. How is a decrease in the provision for unrealised profit treated?
Ans. A decrease in the provision for unrealised profit is treated as follows: Debit the provision for unrealised profit account and credit the Income Statement with the amount of the decrease.

Q. How is an increase in the provision for unrealised profit calculated?
Ans. An increase in unrealised profit = New provision for unrealised profit – old balance in the provision for unrealised profit account.

Q. How is an increase in the provision for unrealised profit treated?
Ans. An increase in the provision for unrealised profit is treated as follows: Debit Income Statement and credit the provision for unrealised profit account with the amount of the increase.

√ *Tip: The treatment for Provision for Unrealised Profit is similar to that of a Provision for Doubtful Debts*

Exercise 7.5
M. Mosabi is a manufacturer. His trial balance at 31st December 20x6 is as follows:

	$	$
Capital		137,450
Drawings	8,560	
Motor Van repairs	2,000	
Electricity : Plant	2,059	
Office	1,110	
Manufacturing wages	45,470	
General expenses : Plant	5,640	
Office	3,810	
Commission to sales team	7,860	
Purchase of raw materials	30,054	
Rent: Plant	4,800	
Office	3,000	
Machinery	33,000	
Office equipment	11,000	
Office salaries	6,285	
Trade Receivables	13,337	
Trade Payables		19,500
Cash in bank	28,370	
Sales revenue		136,450
Premises	40,565	
Inventory at 1 January 20x6:		
Raw materials	8,000	
Work in progress	9,480	
Finished goods	29,000	
	293,400	293,400

Additional Information:
a) Inventory at 31 December 20x6 were: raw materials $3,600; work in progress $1,200; finished goods $ 3,700.
b) Depreciate Machinery $1,000; Office Equipment $1,300.

c) Factory rent prepaid at 31 December 20x6 was $400, office general expenses unpaid at 31 December 20x6 were $350.

d) Completed production is transferred to the warehouse at a mark-up on factory cost of 15%.

Required:

The Manufacturing account and Income Statement for the year ended 31 December 20x6 and a Statement of financial position as at that date.

Exercise 7.6

At the end of a financial year the following information is available:

	$
Sales revenue	150,000
Opening inventory	24,000
Closing inventory	11,000

If the business makes a standard mark-up of 20%, what were the purchases?

Exercise 7.7

An extract from the accounts of a manufacturing company shows:

	$
Direct factory labour	134,900
Indirect factory labour	47,000
Factory supervisor's salary	15,800
Opening inventory of raw materials	22,500
Heat, light and power	15,600
Purchases of raw materials	170,900
Depreciation of factory machinery	20,000
Factory cleaning costs	16,400
Closing inventory of raw materials	15,700

What is the prime cost of production?

Exercise 7.8

A manufacturer has paid $5,000 for electricity from his private bank account. The electricity charges are apportioned as follows:

Factory 40%

Sales office 20%

Private 40%

Required:

Pass the necessary journal entry to record this information.

Exercise 7.9

A manufacturing business calculates factory profit at 20% of cost of production. The following information is available:

	Statement of financial position as at31 December 20x1	Manufacturing account for the year ended 31 December 20x2	Trading account for the year ended 31 December 20x2
	$	$	$
Inventory of finished goods	35,000	-	-
Cost of goods produced	-	180,000	-
Closing inventory of finished Goods	-	-	48,000

Required:
Calculate the amount that will be credited in the Income Statement for the year ended 31 December 20x2 as factory profit.

Exercise 7.10
A company transfers its finished inventory from the factory to the warehouse at cost plus 20%. In 20x9, the transfer value was $80,000. At the end of 20x9, the closing inventory was 25% of the year's production.

Required:
How will inventory of finished goods be shown in:
a) The Trading Account
b) The Statement of financial position.

Exercise 7.11
The following balances were extracted from Aurora's accounts at 31 March 2007.

	$000
Sales revenue	3 200
Purchases of raw materials	450
Purchases returns	18
Carriage inwards	10
Direct labour	400
Direct overheads	60
Rent	40
Electricity	30
Insurance	55
Factory supervision salaries	65
Office salaries	70
Indirect factory wages	13
Factory cleaning	50
Office cleaning	50
Inventory at 1 April 2006:	
Raw materials	110
Work in progress	55
Finished goods	80
Factory machinery at cost	640
Provision for depreciation on factory machinery	280

Additional information at 31 March 2007:

	$000
Rent prepaid	5
Electricity accrued	15
Insurance prepaid	10
Inventory:	
Raw materials	140
Work in progress	75
Finished goods	170

Depreciation on factory machinery is to be provided at 25% per annum reducing balance.
Rent, electricity and insurance are apportioned on the basis of 80% to factory and 20% to office
Finished goods are transferred to the trading account section of the Income Statement at total factory cost plus one third.
Required: Prepare Aurora's manufacturing account for the year ended 31 March 2007.
(UCLES, 2007, AS/A Level Accounting, Syllabus 9706, May/June/02)

TEST YOURSELF

7.1 Multiple choice questions

i) In the first year of activity, Moosa's closing inventory was $5,600. It was decided that inventory would be transferred to the trading account at a mark-up of 12%. In the second year, the closing inventory was $3,600. What is the adjustment now required in the Provision for unrealised profit account that was opened in year 1?

A) The Provision for unrealised profit account will be credited with $432
B) The Provision for unrealised profit account will be debited with $432
C) The Provision for unrealised profit account will be credited with $240
D) The Provision for unrealised profit account will be debited with $240

ii) Which of the following is shown as inventory under current assets in the Statement of financial position of a Manufacturing company?

A) Closing inventory of finished goods at factory cost of production
B) Closing inventory of finished goods at factory cost less balance on Provision for Unrealised Profit Account.
C) Closing inventory of finished goods at factory cost plus the balance on the Provision for Unrealised Profit.
D) B & C

iii) The following information relates to a manufacturing company that adds a factory profit of 15% to its cost of production:

	$
Inventory of finished goods as per statement of financial position as at 1 July 20x2	35,000
Cost of goods produced as per manufacturing account for the year ended 30 June 20x3	100,000
Closing inventory of finished goods as per the Trading account for the year ended 30 June 20x3	24,000

How much will be credited as factory profit in the Income Statement for the year ended 30 June 20x3?

A) $ 2,120   B) $ 17120   C) $ 15,000   D) $ 5,250

7.2

Ali Ahmed started the Ahmed Manufacturing Company on 1 October 2000. He did not intend to take any part in the running of the business and appointed Tarek Alam as general manager. The following information is extracted from the books at the end of the first financial year.

	$
Sales revenue	70600
Purchases of raw materials	16781
Direct factory wages	13120
Indirect factory wages	8000
Carriage inwards	781
Factory rent	5600
Factory fuel and power	5850

Additional information:
1) Inventory was valued at: Raw materials $4100
                              Work-in-progress $250
                              Finished goods $2290
2) Factory rent prepaid amounted to $1400
3) Factory machinery was valued at $25,000. It had been purchased for $30000 on October 1 2000.
4) Completed production is transferred to the warehouse at a mark-up on factory cost of 20%.

Required:
a) Prepare the Manufacturing Account of the Ahmed Manufacturing Company for the year ended 30 September 2001.
b) Prepare the Trading Account section of the income statement of the Ahmed Manufacturing Company for the year ended 30 September 2001.

7.3 A manufacturing company transfers its products from factory to warehouse at cost of production plus 15%.   The following information is available:

	$
unrealised	
Provision for unrealised profit brought forward at 1 January 20x2	10,000
Closing inventory of finished goods at 31 December 20x2	30,000

Required:
Calculate the amount shown in the Income Statement for the year ended 31 December 20x2 for the provision of unrealised profit. State whether it is a debit or a credit.

7.4   The following information for a manufacturing company is available:

	$
Royalties paid	5,000
Closing inventory of finished goods	6,500
Office salaries	22,400
Factory wages	109,000
Depreciation on plant	4,100
Cost of raw materials	99,600
Depreciation on office equipment	2,500

What is the production cost of completed goods?

7.5 Kendall Manufacturing Ltd. adds 10% factory profit to the goods transferred to the warehouse from the factory. The opening inventory of finished goods in the Income Statement for the year ended 31st December 2014 was $137,500 and the closing inventory in the Income Statement for the year ended 31st December 2014 was $159,500.

Required:
How much should be debited in the Income Statement for the year ended 31st December 2014 for provision for unrealised profit on inventory?

CHAPTER 8
LIMITED COMPANIES

Q. What is a limited company?

Ans. A limited company, unlike other forms of legal business structures, is a separate legal entity. The shareholders (owners) of a limited company enjoy limited liability which means that they do not stand to lose more than the sum invested in the company, in the event of a bankruptcy or liquidation.

Q. What are the two main characteristics of a limited company as opposed to other forms of business organisations?

Ans. The two main characteristics are:

1) If the company is declared insolvent, it is the creditors who lose as they can only be paid to the extent of the issued capital of the business. If they are owed more than that sum, they risk not being paid.

2) Ownership and management are divorced, in that shareholders are not entitled to help manage the company. It is the directors that manage the company for them.

Q. What are the two documents that are required, by the Companies Act of 1985, to be filed with the Registrar of Companies?

Ans. The two documents are:

1. The Memorandum of Association: This document contains information regarding the relationship of the company with the rest of the world. It should contain the following information:
a) The name of the company which must be followed by the suffix plc, if it is a public limited company, or Ltd. if it is a private limited company.
b) A statement that the liability of the company is limited.
c) The amount of authorised capital.
2. The Articles of Association: This document defines the rights and duties of the company's shareholders and directors. Regulations for meetings, forfeiture of shares, voting rights, and directors' qualifications are also contained in this important document.

Q. What is the difference between a private and public limited company?

Ans. A private limited company cannot sell its shares to the general public. Therefore, its shares cannot be sold on the stock exchange. They may have authorised capitals of less than fifty thousand pounds. Their names should be followed by the suffix Ltd. which stands for 'Limited'. A public limited company may offer their shares to the general public and its shares can be traded on the stock exchange. Their authorised share capital should be at least fifty thousand pounds of which one quarter must have been paid by shareholders. The whole of any premium on shares must have also been paid.

Q. What is authorised share capital?

Ans. Authorised share capital is the maximum amount of capital that a company may raise. This capital may cover possible expansion of the company in the future. It must be remembered that the company has to pay duty on the amount of registered capital.

Q. Who are the directors of a company?

Ans. The directors of a company are shareholders who act as stewards of the shareholders' investments. They are elected by the body of shareholders and are in a position of trust.

Q. Name the documents that the shareholders are expected to receive annually.

Ans. The documents that are sent to the shareholders annually are:

1. Statement of Comprehensive Income
2. Statement of Financial Position
3. Statement of Cash Flows
4. Directors' report

5. Auditors' report.

These documents must be sent to shareholders in advance of every annual general meeting. They must also be sent to debenture holders. The directors must file an annual return, which includes the annual accounts, with the Registrar of Companies, and the returns may be inspected by any member of the public.

Q. Name five groups of stakeholders who would be interested in a company's accounts.

Ans. The following stakeholders would be interested in a company's accounts:
   a. Shareholders
   b. Debenture holders
   c. Financial analysts
   d. Stock exchanges
   e. Trade and other creditors

Q. What is meant by the term: directors' qualification?

Ans. This stands for the number of shares a director must hold in the company.

Q. How are partnerships different from limited companies with reference to the number of owners?

Ans. In a partnership, the minimum number of partners is two and the maximum is twenty (except in certain professional firms e.g. lawyers' and accountants'). In a limited company the minimum number of shareholders should be two and the maximum number is decided on by the number of shares permitted by the authorised share capital.

Q. How are partnerships different from limited companies with reference to the liability of the owners?

Ans. Partners have unlimited liability (except for limited partners in a limited partnership), whereas shareholders in a limited company have limited liability.

Q. How do partnerships differ from limited companies with reference to the management of the business?

Ans. All partners, except those with limited liability, may manage the affairs of a partnership. However, the management of a company is left entirely to the directors by the shareholders.

Q. What is the difference between partnerships and limited companies as far as taxation is concerned?

Ans. Partnerships are not required by law to pay tax on their profits. Partners pay individual tax on the income they make from the profits of the partnership. Companies are liable to pay tax on their profits. The tax paid is treated as an appropriation of profit.

Q. What is the difference between partnerships and limited companies as far as distribution of profit is concerned?

Ans. Partners share profits and losses as per their partnership deed or equally if there is no partnership deed. Companies distribute their profits to their shareholders in the form of dividend. They may not distribute all the profits made and any undistributed profit is retained in the company as a reserve.

Q. Name the act that governs limited companies.

Ans. The companies Act 1985 governs limited companies.

Q. What is the difference between liabilities, provisions and reserves?

Ans. Liabilities are defined as that which the company owes. They are determined with substantial accuracy. They are created by carrying down credit balances on personal or expense accounts.

Provisions are created by the company to provide for liabilities that are known to exist but cannot be determined with substantial accuracy. They are created by debiting the approximate amount of the known liability to the profit and loss account (or income statement) and crediting it to provision accounts. e.g. Provision for depreciation of non-current assets.

Reserves are amounts set aside apart from the ones mentioned above. They are an appropriation of profits and are created by debiting the Appropriation Account and crediting the Reserve accounts. They may also be created by premiums paid on ordinary or preference shares or by revaluing non-current assets.

Q. What are the different types of reserves?
Ans. There are two classes of reserves: revenue reserves or capital reserves.

Revenue reserves are created by transferring profit from the appropriation section of the profit and loss account (or the income statement) to the reserve. Hence the creation of such reserves (usually termed a general reserve) reduces the amount of profit available to pay dividends.

Capital reserves are not normally created by transferring profit from the profit and loss account (or income statement). They generally represent gains that have not been realised. Capital reserves may never be credited back to the income statement and can never be used to pay cash dividends.

Q. What are the different types of revenue reserves?
Ans. If revenue reserves are created for a specific purpose such as a replacement of a non-current asset or for the planned expansion of the business, then they are named accordingly. However, if they are just retained profits to strengthen the financial position of the company, then they are known as general reserves. Retained profit is also a revenue reserve.

Q. What are the different types of Capital reserves?
Ans. The following are the more common types of Capital reserves:
1) Share Premium Account.
2) Capital Redemption Reserve
3) Revaluation reserve

Q. Write a short note on 'Share Premium Account'.
Ans. When shares are issued at a price above their face (nominal) value they are said to be issued at a premium. The premium on each share is credited to a special account called the Share Premium Account. The Companies Act 1985 permits the Share Premium Account to be used only for the following purposes:
1) To write off preliminary expenses incurred by the company in its formation.
2) To provide for any premium payable on the redemption of debentures.
3) To provide any commission payable on the redemption of shares and debentures.
4) To write off expenses incurred in the issue of shares or debentures including any commission payable on the issue of shares.
5) To pay up bonus shares.

Exhibit
The directors of Ace & Co issued 100,000 Ordinary shares of $1 at $1.20 a share. All the shares were subscribed for and issued.
Required:
Prepare Journal Entries to record the issue of the shares.

Solution:

	DR $	CR $
Bank	120,000	
Ordinary Share capital		100,000
Share Premium Account		20,000
(Issue of 1,00,000 ordinary shares of $1 at $1.20 a share)		

Exercise 8.1

Belling and Co. issued 50,000 ordinary shares of a nominal value of $1 for $1.30 a share.
Required:
Pass Journal entries to record the issue of these shares.

Exercise 8.2

Vital and Co. issued 100,000 ordinary shares of a nominal value of $1 for $1.50 a share.
Required:
Pass Journal entries to record the issue of these shares.

Q. Write a short note on 'Revaluation Reserve'.

Ans. This reserve is created with the gain on revaluation of non-current assets that the company may undertake from time to time. This is unrealised profit and may not be credited to the income statement. However, this reserve may be used to issue bonus shares.

Exhibit

An extract from Malini Ltd's Statement of financial position is as follows:

	$
Premises at cost	50,000
Provision for depreciation	12,000
Net book value	38,000

The Premises have been professionally revalued at $80,000. A decision has been made to revalue the premises in the books of the company.
Required:
Prepare journal entries to revalue the premises in the company's books.

Solution	DR	CR
	$	$
Premises at cost	30,000	
Provision for depreciation	12,000	
Premises revaluation reserve		42,000

Exercise 8.3

An extract from Tosca and Company's Statement of financial position is as follows:

	$
Property at cost	100,000
Provision for depreciation	42,000
Net book value	58,000

The property has been professionally revalued at $180,000. A decision has been made to revalue the property in the books of the company.
Required:
Prepare journal entries to revalue the premises in the company's books.

Exercise 8.4

An extract from Massca and Company's Statement of financial position is as follows:

	$
Property at cost	150,000
Provision for depreciation	40,000
Net book value	110,000

The property has been professionally revalued at $200,000. A decision has been made to revalue the property in the books of the company.
Required:
Prepare journal entries to revalue the premises in the company's books.

Q. Write a short note on 'Issued Capital'.
Ans. This is made up of the total nominal value of shares issued to shareholders. It is always less than the authorised capital.

Q. Write a short note on 'Called-up capital'.
Ans. A company may require its shareholders to pay only part of the amount due on their shares until further sums are required. That part of the shares that the shareholders are required to pay immediately is called 'called up capital'. For instance if a share has a nominal value of $1, and the company's immediate requirement is for them to pay only 25 cents, then the called-up capital is 25 c. If there are 100,000 shareholders, then the called-up capital is $25,000.

Q. Write a short note on 'uncalled capital'.
Ans. That portion of the nominal value of the share that has not been called up is uncalled share capital.

Q. What are forfeited shares?
Ans. If shareholders do not pay their calls then their shares are forfeited and may be re-issued to other shareholders. These are forfeited shares.

Q. What is meant by the term 'paid-up capital'?
Ans. This is the total money received from shareholders on the called-up capital. It may not be equal to called-up capital as some shareholders may pay their calls late or not at all.

Q. What is meant by the term 'calls in advance'?
Ans. This is money received from shareholders who have paid their calls before they are due.

Q. What is meant by the term 'calls in arrears'?
Ans. This is money due from shareholders who are late in paying their calls.

Q. What are the different types of shares?
Ans. There are two types of shares: Ordinary shares and Preference shares.

Q. What are ordinary shares?
Ans. Ordinary shares form what is known as the equity of a company. Ordinary shareholders are entitled to vote at annual general meetings. They are, however, paid dividend out of the remaining profit left after the dividend of the preference shareholders has been paid. All the reserves also go up to make up the ordinary shareholders' fund and belong to ordinary shareholders. When a company is wound up the assets remaining after all the creditors, debenture holders and preference shareholders are paid, belong to the ordinary shareholders. Hence the ordinary shareholders may receive more or less than their original investment in the company.

Q. What are Preference shares?
Ans. Preference shares entitle their holders to certain rights which ordinary shareholders do not enjoy. Preference shareholders receive a dividend at a fixed rate which is expressed as a percentage of the nominal value of the share. This percentage is mentioned when the share is described. These dividends are paid before the ordinary shareholders get paid their dividend. In the event of a company being wound up, preference shareholders are entitled to have their capital repaid before ordinary shareholders receive their capital.

Q. What are the different types of Preference Shares?
Ans. The different types of Preference Shares are:
1) Cumulative Preference shares
2) Non-cumulative Preference Shares
3) Redeemable Preference Shares
4) Non-Redeemable Preference Shares
5) Secured Preference Shares

6) Non-secured preference shares.
7) Participating preference shares.

Q. What is the difference between cumulative and non-cumulative preference shares?

Ans. Cumulative preference shares are entitled to have arrears of their dividend carried forward in the event of there being insufficient profit in the current year. Non-cumulative preference shares, however, are not entitled to have any arrears of dividend carried forward to future years if the profit of the current year is insufficient to pay their dividend.

Exhibit

The Magic Company Ltd. have the following share capital break-up:

20,000 10% preference shares of $1 each

50,000 ordinary shares of $1 each.

The profits available for dividend were as follows: $

20x1	2,000
20x2	1,900
20x3	3,000
20x4	1,000
20x5	900
20x6	6,000

Required:

Calculate the dividends paid to the preference shareholders and the rate of dividend available to their Ordinary shareholders from the balance of profits if the preference shares were:

a) Non – Cumulative

b) Cumulative

a) Solution:

In the case of Non – Cumulative Preference Shares

	20X1	20X2	20X3	20X4	20X5	20X6
	$	$	$	$	$	$
Profit	2,000	1,900	3,000	1,000	900	6,000
Preference dividend pd	2,000	1,900	2,000	1,000	900	2,000
Profit left for ordinary shareholders	nil	nil	1,000	nil	nil	4,000
Maximum ordinary dividend paid	nil	nil	2%	nil	nil	8%

b. Solution:

In the case of Cumulative Preference Shares

	20X1	20X2	20X3	20X4	20X5	20X6
	$	$	$	$	$	$
Profit	2,000	1,900	3,000	1,000	900	6,000
Preference dividend pd	2,000	1,900	2,000	1,000	900	2,000
Arrears of dividend b/f			100		1,000	2,100
Profit left for ordinary shareholders	nil	nil	900	nil	nil	1,900
Maximum ordinary dividend paid	nil	nil	1.8%	nil	nil	3.8%

Exercise 8.5

Marlebee & Co.'s share capital consists of 100,000 ordinary shares of $1 each and 40,000 8% preference shares of $1 each. Profits for six years were as follows:

	$
20x1	3,200
20x2	3,000
20x3	2,000
20x4	8,000
20x5	2,900
20x6	7,000

Required:

Calculate the dividends paid to the preference shareholders and the rate of dividend available to their ordinary shareholders from the balance of profits if the preference shares were:
a) Non – Cumulative
b) Cumulative

Exercise 8.6

Lars & Co.'s share capital consists of 100,000 ordinary shares of $1 each and 50,000 5% preference shares of $1 each. Profits for six years were as follows:

20x1 $3,500

20x2	$3,000
20x3	$2,100
20x4	$8,000
20x5	$2,600
20x6	$7,000

Required:

Calculate the dividends paid to the preference shareholders and the rate of dividend available to their ordinary shareholders from the balance of profits if the preference shares were:
a) Non – Cumulative
b) Cumulative

Q. What is the difference between redeemable and non-redeemable preference shares?

Ans. Redeemable preference shares: should be shown as non-current liabilities in the Statement of Financial Position.

If they are redeemable within the next twelve months, then they should be shown as a current liability in the Statement of Financial Position. Dividends paid on these shares should be shown under financial costs in the Statement of Comprehensive Income.

Non-redeemable preference shares: form part of the capital of the company and should be shown under the equity section in the Statement of Financial Position.

Any dividend payable on non-redeemable preference shares should be accounted for under finance costs in the Statement of Comprehensive income.

Q. What is the treatment of unpaid dividends on preference shares?

Ans. Any dividends due on preference shares, whether they are redeemable or non-redeemable, should be accounted for in full in the year the financial statements are drawn up for. Hence, preference share dividend that has remained unpaid, should be shown as an accrual in current liabilities.

Q. How is distributable profit calculated?

Ans. Distributable profits of the company = accumulated realised profit unused –
accumulated realised losses not written off
= Profit after interest and tax + retained profit from previous years – accumulated realised losses not written off

Exercise 8.7

You are given the following information:

A company has profit after interest and tax of $56,000 and accumulated realised losses that have not been written of amounting to $3,000. The retained profit brought forward is $34,000.
Required:
Calculate the distributable profits of the company.

Q. Define:
a) Dividend
b) Interim dividend
c) Final dividend
d) Dividend policy

Ans. Dividend is defined as the share of profits that is distributed to each shareholder. Dividends are paid out of distributable profits. Dividends are expressed as cents per share or as a percentage of the nominal value of the shares.

Interim dividend may be paid to shareholders during a company's financial year if the directors feel that the profits and cash resources are sufficient for the purpose. These dividends are debited in the company's income statement for the year to which they relate.

Final dividends are proposed by the directors of the company but must be approved by shareholders at the Annual General Meeting before they can be paid. They are paid after the end of the financial year.

Dividend Policy-Before a decision is made by the directors of a company to pay or recommend a dividend, the following factors must be considered:
1. That the company has sufficient distributable realised profits available.
2. That the company has sufficient liquid funds to pay the dividend.
3. Whether some of the profits should be ploughed back into the business as reserves to strengthen it.
4. It must be remembered that the company is not obligated to declare dividend. Having said that, a generous dividend policy may increase the value of shares on the stock exchange and a mean policy may have the opposite effect.
5. That there is a balance between dividend growth and capital growth. Share values should increase along with dividends for this to happen.

Q. What is a debenture?
Ans. A debenture represents a loan taken by the company from many debenture holders. A document called a debenture states the amount of the loan and the interest payable. It also includes the dates on which the loan is to be repaid by the company. Repayment is spread over a period and the dates of the start and end of the period are also included in the document. Debenture holders are not members of the company and cannot vote at annual general meetings. A Debenture is listed as a long term liability in the statement of financial position and not under share capital and reserves. If the debenture is due for redemption within one year, then it is shown as a current liability. Debenture holders are repaid before the shareholders of a company in the event of the company being wound up. Interest on debentures must be paid even if the company has not made a profit and this interest is debited as an expense in the income statement.
Note: Debentures are included as a deduction when calculating net assets.

Q. What is a secured debenture?
Ans. A secured debenture is one which is secured on all or some of the company's assets. If the company gets into financial difficulties, these assets are sold and the proceeds are used to repay the loans to the debenture holders.

Exercise 8.8
A newly formed company issues 100,000 shares of $1 at $3.00 each. It also issues $400,000 5% debentures. The operating profit was $340,000. The directors recommend an ordinary dividend of 6% for the year (disregard tax).
Required:
What is the retained profit for the year?

Note: Operating profit is also known as PBIT – Profit before interest and tax.

Q. What is a private limited company?
Ans. A private limited company is not traded on the stock exchange.

Q. How is the income statement of a private limited company different from that of a sole trader?
Ans. The income statement follows the same format as for a sole trader. However, interest on debentures and remuneration of directors may also be included as expenses in the profit and loss section.

Q. What does IAS 1 say about the financial statements of public limited companies?
Ans. IAS 1 changes the titles of financial statements as they will be used in IFRSs:
1. The statement of financial position will now be known as the **statement of financial position.**
2. The income statement will become the **statement of comprehensive income**
3. The cash flow statement will become the **statement of cash flows.**

Q. What does IAS 1 say about the purpose of financial statements?
Ans. IAS 1 states that the purpose of financial statements is: 'To provide information about the financial position, financial performance and cash flows of an entity that is useful to a wide range of users in making economic decisions.'

Q. What does IAS 1 say about the components of financial statements?
Ans. IAS 1 says that a complete set of financial statements comprises of:
1. A Statement of financial position or **a statement of financial Position**
2. An income statement or **a statement of comprehensive income**
3. A statement of changes in equity
4. A statement of cash flow
5. Accounting policies and explanatory notes

Q. How is revenue defined?
Ans. Revenue is defined as sales revenue less sales returns.

Q. What data is to be contained in the statement of comprehensive income?
Ans. The details included in the statement can be summarised, rather than detailing every single item as follows:
1. Revenue
2. Finance costs
3. Charge for taxation
4. The after-tax profit or loss for the period from discontinued operations.
The statement ends by showing the profit or loss for the period attributable to the equity shareholders.

Q. How are expenses analysed?
Ans. Expenses can be analysed:
1. by nature – for example depreciation, raw materials etc. This may be more applicable for a manufacturing company
2. by function – for example cost of sales, administration expenses etc.
Which method is used will depend on which provides the more reliable and relevant information.

Q. For expenses analysed by function, how are the following decided
1. administrative costs
2. distribution costs?

Ans. 1. Administrative costs will include office costs, heat and light etc.
2. Distribution costs will include such things as delivery vehicle costs, driver's wages, warehouse costs etc.

Exhibit:
EXAMPLE – by function

XYZ Limited
Statement of comprehensive income for the year ended ....

	*This year $000	*Last year $000
Revenue	100,000	80,000
Cost of Sales	(60,000)	(45,000)
Gross Profit	40,000	35,000
Distribution Costs	(8,000)	(7,000)
Administration Expenses	(11,000)	(10,000)
Profit/(Loss) from Operations	21,000	18,000
Finance Costs	(3,000)	(2,000)
Profit/(Loss) Before Tax	19,000	16,000
Tax	(4,500)	(4,000)
Profit/(Loss) for the year attributable to equity holders	14,500	12,000

Other comprehensive income and revaluation gains can be shown after the profit or loss attributable to equity holders.

NOTE: Finance costs will include:
- **Interest paid**
- **Dividends on redeemable preference shares paid.**

EXAMPLE - Statement of Changes in Equity
Retained Earnings

	*This year $000	*Last year $000
Balance at start of year	43,000	35,000
Profit for the year	14,500	12,000
Transfers from other reserves**	-	-
	57,500	47,000
Dividends Paid	(5,000)	(4,000)
Transfers to other reserves**	-	-
Balance at end of year	52,500	43,000

#Dividends (Note for the published accounts)

	*This year $000	*Last year $000
Amounts recognised as distributions to equity holders during the year:		
Final dividend for last year of $0.075per share	3,000	2,200
Interim dividend for this year of $0.050 per share	2,000	1,800
	5,000	4,000
Proposed final dividend for this year of $0.095 per share	3,800	3,000

#NOTE: These included dividends on ordinary shares as well as dividends on non-redeemable preference shares.

NOTE: Unpaid dividends on redeemable preference shares will be treated as an accrued expense (current liability) in the Statement of financial position.

EXAMPLE

XYZ Limited

Statement of financial position at ....

	*This year $000	*Last year $000
Non – current Assets		
Intangible		
Goodwill	7,700	8,000
Tangible		
Property, Plant & Equipment	90,000	80,100
Investments	10,000	12,000
	107,700	100,100
Current Assets		
Inventories	1,000	800
Trade and other receivables	5,000	4,000
Cash and cash equivalents	500	300
Total assets	**114,200**	**105,200**
Current liabilities		
***Trade and other payables	1,200	1,000
Tax liabilities	3,500	4,000
	4,700	5,000
Non-current liabilities:		
Bank Loan	3,000	
10% Debentures 2005/2008	2,000	5,200
Total liabilities	9,700	10,200
Share capital and reserves:		
Share Capital	20,000	20,000
8% preference shares of $1 each	20,000	20,000
Share Premium	2,000	2,000
General Reserve	10,000	10,000
Retained Earnings	52,500	43,000
	114,200	**105,200**

Note that no dates are included. This would not be the case in practice where the actual date of the year end and previous year e.g. 31 December, would be stated.

** *The transfer to and from reserves would include movements to revaluation reserves, share premium, revenue reserves etc.*

*** *These would include accrued preference share dividend (both redeemable as well as non-redeemable preference share dividends)*

Q. What does the IAS say about ordinary dividends: paid and proposed?
Ans. For dividends paid: Only dividends paid during the year should be included in the financial statements. They are to be shown as deductions in the Statement of Changes in Equity.

For proposed dividends: As this is subject to the approval of the shareholders at the AGM, it is to be included only by way of a note to the financial statements. It is not included in the financial statements as a liability.

Q. What does IAS 1 say about the figure for retained earnings?

Ans. The figure for retained earnings should be the closing figure from the statement of changes in equity.

Exercise 8.9

Magnum Plc has an authorised capital of 1.5 million $1 ordinary shares of which 1 million have been issued as fully paid.

The following information was extracted from the accounts for the year ended 30 September 20x6:

	20x6 $000	20x5 $000
Revenue	150	80
Cost of sales	65	43
Distribution costs	5	4
Administration expenses	10	13
Finance costs	6	6
Tax	2	3

Required:

Draw up a statement of comprehensive income for the year ended 30 September 20x6 in the format laid out by IAS 1

Exercise 8.10

The retained earnings at the start of the year ended 31March 20x9 for Maxmillan plc was $3m

Additional information for the year ended 31 March 20x9:

	$000
Profit	4,500
Transfer to general reserve	1,000
Dividends paid	2,000

Required:

Prepare a statement of changes in equity for the year ended 31 March 20x9.

Exercise 8.11

Patni plc has an authorised capital of $ 3.5m $1 ordinary shares, of which 2m have been issued.

The following information is extracted from the records of Patni plc for the year ended 30 June 20x6:

Final dividend for the year ended 31 March 20x5 was proposed and approved at the AGM @2.5c a share.

Interim dividend paid during the year ended 31 March 20x6 was $0.050 a share.

Final dividend for the year ended 31 March 20x6 @ 0.090 a share was proposed.

Required:

Note to published accounts regarding dividends prepared in the format prescribed by IAS1.

Exercise 8.12

So Young plc. has an authorised capital of 4.9m ordinary shares of $1 each of which 70,000 have been issued at a premium of $1.5 a share.   Additional information as at 31 December 20x4 and 20x5:

	20x4 $000	20x5 $000
Goodwill	8.5	8.5
Property, Plant & Equipment	60	75
Motor vehicles	6	10
Inventories	78.5	45
Trade receivables	4	3
Other receivables	1	2.3
Trade payables	1	1.5
Other payables	2	2.4

	Dr	Cr
Tax liabilities	4	5
Bank loan	6	6
Retained profits	40	23.9

Required:
Prepare a statement of financial position in good form and style from the information given above, for the year ended 31 December 20x5

Exhibit
The Trial Balance of Molly and Company private limited at 31 December 20x6 is as follows:

	Dr $	Cr $
Sales revenue		450,000
Purchases of ordinary goods	157,000	
Carriage outwards	12,000	
Land and Buildings	158,750	
Motor Vehicles	80,000	
Machinery	76,000	
Provision for depreciation:		
Property		41,000
Motor Vehicles		20,000
Machinery		30,000
Inventory at 1 January 20x6	37,000	
Directors' remuneration	20,000	
Salaries	58,000	
General expenses	34,000	
Interest on debentures	5,000	
Goodwill at cost	150,000	
Trade receivables	75,000	
Trade payables		40,000
Bank	41,000	
1,00,000 ordinary shares of $1		100,000
10% debentures 20x8/2010		100,000
50,000 5% Non- Redeemable preference shares of $1		50,000
Share premium account		45,000
General reserve		20,000
Retained profit b/f		12,000
Interim dividends paid: preference	1,250	
ordinary	3,000	
	908,000	908,000

Additional information:
1) Inventory at 31 December 20x6 was $46,000
2) Depreciation for the year is to be provided as follows:
   Property $ 5,000
   Motor vehicles $2,000
   Machinery $ 3,000
3) Provision is to be made for taxation on the year's profits in the sum of $40,000.
4) A transfer of $52,000 is to be made to general reserve.
5) Debenture interest is payable on 1 June and 1 December.
6) The directors have recommended a final dividend of 10% per share on ordinary shares.
7) Of the salaries, $50,000 was paid to sales staff.
8) The Motor Vehicles were used for delivery purposes.

Required:
a. Prepare Molly and Co's Income statement (Statement of financial position) for the year ended 31 December 20x6 in as much detail as possible.
b. Prepare Molly and Co's Satement of Financial position (Statement of financial position) as at 31 December 20x6 in as much detail as possible.

Solution:

a)   Molly and company
Income statement for the year ended 31 December 20x6

	$	$
Sales revenue		450,000
Less Cost of sales:		
Inventory at 1 January	37,000	
Purchases of ordinary goods	157,000	
	194,000	
Less inventory at 31 December 20x6	46,000	148,000
Gross Profit		302,000
Selling and distribution expenses:		
Sales staff salaries	50,000	
Carriage outwards	12,000	
Motor vehicles- depreciation	2,000 64,000	
Administration expenses:		
Administrative salaries	8,000	
Directors' remuneration	20,000	
General expenses	34,000	
Depreciation: Property	5,000	
Machinery	3,000 70,000	134,000
Operating Profit		168,000
Debenture interest		10,000
Preference dividend: Paid	1,250	
Proposed	1,250	2,500
Profit before taxation		155,500
Taxation		40,000
Profit/(Loss) for the year attributable to Equity Holders		115,500

b) Statement of Changes in Equity

	31st Dec 20x6
Retained profit:	$000
Balance at start of year	12,000
Profit for the year	115,500
Transfers from other reserves	-
	127,500
Dividends Paid	(3,000)
Transfers to general reserves	(52,000)
Balance at end of year	72,500

c) Dividends (Note for the published accounts)

	31st Dec 20x6
	$000
Amounts recognised as distributions to equity holders during the year:	
Interim dividend for this year of	3,000
	3,000

Proposed final dividend for this year of $10,000

d) Statement of Financial position as at 31 December 20x6

	$	$	$
Non-current Assets	Cost	Depreciation	NBV
Intangible: Goodwill	150,000	-	150,000
Tangible:			
Property	158,750	46,000	112,750
Machinery	76,000	33,000	43,000
Motor vehicles	80,000	22,000	58,000
	314,750	101,000	213,750
Total non-current Assets			363,750
Current Assets:			
Inventory		46,000	
Trade receivables		75,000	
Bank		41,000	162,000
Total assets			525,750
Current liabilities:			
Trade payables		40,000	
Debenture interest		5,000	
Taxation		40,000	
Dividends: Preference		1,250	86,250
Non-current liabilities:			
10% debentures 20x8/2010			100,000
			186,250
Share capital and reserves:			
100,000 ordinary shares of $1 each			100,000
50,000 5% NR preference shares of $1 each			50,000
Share premium account			45,000
General reserve (20,000 + 52,000)			72,000
Retained profit (12,000 +60500)			72,500
Liabilities and equity			**525,750**

NOTE: Under IAS proposed ordinary dividends are not to be mentioned either in the Statement of Comprehensive Income or in the Statement of Financial position.

Exercise 8.13
The Trial Balance of Billy Merchants plc. at 31 December 20x2 is as follows:

	Dr	Cr
	$	$
Sales revenue		370,000
Purchases of ordinary goods	149,000	
Carriage outwards	5,250	
Property	158,750	
Motor Vehicles	77,000	
Machinery	79,000	
Provision for depreciation:		
Property		38,000
Motor Vehicles		40,000
Machinery		30,000
Inventory of finished		
goods at1January 20x2	47,000	
Salaries	65,000	
General expenses	47,000	
Interest on debentures	5,000	
Goodwill at cost	70,000	
Trade receivables	85,000	

Trade payables		50,000
Bank	35,000	
1,00,000 ordinary shares of $1		100,000
10% debentures 20x4/20x6		100,000
50,000 8% Non-redeemable		
preference shares of $1		50,000
Share premium account		36,000
General reserve		10,000
Retained profit b/f		6,000
Interim dividends paid:		
preference	4,000	
ordinary	3,000	
	830,000	830,000

Additional information:
1) Inventory of finished goods at 31 December 20x2 was $44,000
2) Depreciation for the year is to be provided as follows:
   Property $ 6,000
   Motor vehicles $4,000
   Machinery $ 5,000
3) Provision is to be made for taxation on the year's profits in the sum of $10,000.
4) A transfer of $35,000 is to be made to general reserve.
5) Debenture interest is payable on 1 June and 1 December.
6) The directors have recommended a final dividend of 5% per share on ordinary shares.
7) Of the salaries, $50,000 was paid to sales staff.
8) The Motor Vehicles were used for delivery purposes.
9) Accrued general expenses at 31 December 20x2 were $1,000

Required:
a) Prepare Billy Merchant plc.'s Statement of Comprehensive Income for the year ended 31 December 20x2 in as much detail as possible.
b) Prepare Billy Merchant plc.'s Statement of financial position as at 31 December 20x2 in as much detail as possible.

Q. What are bonus shares?
Ans. When a company capitalises its reserves by using them to issue shares to ordinary shareholders as fully paid up shares, these shares are called bonus shares. These shares are so called as the shareholders do not have to pay for them.

Q. Why are bonus shares issued?
Ans. A company issues bonus shares for the following reasons:
1) In the event of the issued share capital not adequately supporting the long-term assets of the company.
2) If the company distributed the reserves to their shareholders as dividend, then the shareholders would receive a very hefty rate of dividend that could cause problems with the workforce and the company's customers. The workforce would feel cheated if the shareholders were rewarded when they themselves received no increase in their wages. The customers would want the company to reduce their prices rather than shore up profits to pay excessive dividends to shareholders.

Exhibit
Kingston and company's summarised statement of financial position is as follows:

	$
Non-current assets	300,000
Net current assets	120,000
	420,000
Ordinary shares of $1	150,000
Share premium	50,000

Revaluation reserve	150,000
General reserve	50,000
Retained profit	20,000
	420,000

The directors have decided to make a bonus issue of three shares for every five shares already held. They also wish to leave the reserves in the most flexible form.

Required:

Kingston and company's statement of financial position immediately after the bonus issue.

Tip √ *As any of the reserves could be used to issue bonus shares, directors prefer to use capital reserves and leave the revenue reserves intact.*

Solution

Kingston and Company statement of financial position immediately after the issue of bonus shares

	$
Non-current assets	300,000
Net current assets	120,000
	420,000

Ordinary shares of $1	240,000
Revaluation reserve	110,000
General reserve	50,000
Retained profit	20,000
	420,000

Exercise 8.14

Barrington and company's summarised statement of financial position is as follows:

	$
Non-current assets	400,000
Net current assets	130,000
	530,000

Ordinary shares of $1	200,000
Share premium	280,000
General reserve	30,000
Retained profit	20,000
	530,000

The directors have decided to make a bonus issue of four shares for every five shares already held. They also wish to leave the reserves in the most flexible form.

Required:

Barrington and company's statement of financial position immediately after the bonus issue.

Q. What is a rights issue?

Ans. This is an issue of shares made to the existing shareholders of the company. The offer price is generally below market price.

Q. What are the advantages of a rights issue?

Ans. The advantages are:

1) The company can raise more capital.

2) A rights issue is a shorter and cheaper procedure than a fresh issue of shares.

3) Shareholders are rewarded for their loyalty as rights issues are generally made at a price that is cheaper than market price. If shareholders do not wish to subscribe to a rights issue, they may sell their rights.

Exhibit

What follows is a summary of the statement of financial position of Ling and company as at 1 June 20x3:

	$
Net non-current and current assets	1,200,000
Share capital and reserves:	
Ordinary shares of $1	900,000
Share premium	100,000
Retained profit	200,000
	1,200,000

On 1 June 20x3, the directors made a bonus issue of one share for every five held, leaving the reserves in the most flexible form. Following the issue of bonus shares, Ling and company made a rights issue on 10 June 20x3 of 108,000 ordinary shares of $1 at a price of $1.50 a share. All the shares were subscribed for by the shareholders.

Required:

a) Ling and company's statement of financial position immediately after the bonus issue

b) Ling and company's statement of financial position immediately after the rights issue had been completed.

Solution

a.	$
Net Non-current and current assets	1,200,000
Share capital and reserves:	
Ordinary shares of $1	1,080,000
Retained profit	120,000
	1,200,000

b.	$
Net non-current and current assets	1,362,000
Share capital and reserves:	
Ordinary shares of $1	1,188,000
Share premium	54,000
Retained profit	120,000
	1,362,000

Exercise 8.15

The capital structure of a company was as follows:

	$
100,000 Ordinary shares at $1 each	100,000
Share premium account	25,000

The financial year ends on 31 December. On 1 May 20x4 the company made an issue of 30,000 shares for $ 54,000. Subsequent to that, on 1 July 20x4 a bonus issue of one share for every five in issue was made. The share premium account was used for the purpose.

Required:

Calculate the balance on the share premium account at 31 December 20x4.

Exercise 8.16

A company has issued 100,000 ordinary shares of $0.50 each. These are quoted on the stock exchange at $1.50 each. The company makes a rights issue on a 1 for 5 basis at a price of $1.10 each. The rights issue was fully subscribed.

Required:

a. Calculate the balance on the share capital account after the rights issue.
b. Calculate the balance on the share premium account.

Exercise 8.17

The following is an extract of a company's statement of financial position:

	$
500,000 ordinary shares of $1 each	500,000
Retained profit	300,000
10% debentures	200,000
	1,000,000

Net assets	1,000,000

A rights issue of 1 for 5 shares is made at $2 per share and 50% of the debentures are repaid at par. The rights issue was fully subscribed.

Required:

A statement of financial position extract reflecting the above mentioned changes.

Exercise 8.18

The table below shows extracts from a company's statement of financial position at 31 December 20x2 and at 31 December 20x3:

	31 December 20x3 $m	31 December 20x2 $m
Ordinary shares of $1 each	200	40
Share premium account	231	73

On 1 April 20x3 there was a bonus issue of 1 ordinary share for every 10 held.
On 1 June 20x3 there was a rights issue.

There were no other reserves.

Required:

Calculate the amount of cash received from the issue of shares in the year ended 31 December 20x3.

Q. What is convertible loan stock?

Ans. Convertible loan stock is stock that starts out as straightforward debt, but can be converted by the lender into equity. The loan is usually unsecured, which means that it is not tied to specific assets of the borrowing company. To this extent it is not as safe as debenture stock. However, like debentures, interest is paid on convertible loan stock at a fixed rate. The holders of convertible loan stock can convert their loan into shares in the company at a predetermined price. If, when the time arrives for the loan stock holders to exercise their option, the market value of the company shares is higher than the predetermined price, the holders could find the exchange attractive. They will be unlikely to exercise their option if the market value of the company's shares is below the predetermined price.

Q. List three advantages to loan stock holders of exercising their option when the time arrives to convert their loan into shares.

Ans. The advantages are:
a. Dividends in the shares may likely exceed the interest on the loan stock.
b. The loan stockholders will be entitled to attend and vote at company AGMs.
c. A possibility exists where loan stockholders may see the value of their shares increase over time to counteract inflation.

Q. What are the disadvantages of holding convertible loan stock?
Ans. Convertible loan stock is 'deferred equity' but it is not equity until it is converted. Hence, its holders are not owners of the company and so do not have voting right. This stock is usually an unsecured loan and is therefore not as secure as debentures.

Q. Where are redeemable preference shares shown in the Statement of financial position of a Public Limited company?
Ans. If the shares are redeemable *more than twelve months after the date* of the Statement of financial position, then the shares are shown under Non-current liabilities.
If the company has the option to redeem the shares *immediately*, then the shares are not identified as redeemable and are shown in the equity section of the Statement of financial position as simply 'Preference Shares'.
In both cases, creditors must still be protected.

Q. What does IAS 32 say about irredeemable Preference shares?
Ans. Irredeemable preferences shares are a part of equity and should be shown in the equity section of the Statement of financial position.

Q. How are dividends payable on non-redeemable preference shares shown?
Ans. Dividend of such shares should be treated as a financial cost in the Income Statement if presenting under IAS.

Q. How are dividends on redeemable preference shares shown?
Ans. Dividends payable on redeemable preference shares are shown as a financial cost in the Income Statement if presenting under IAS.

Q. How are unpaid dividends on Accumulative Preference shares shown?
Ans. Dividends due on Accumulative Preference Shares, redeemable or otherwise, should be accounted for in full in the year. Thus, any dividend unpaid at the end of the year should be shown as an accrual in current liabilities.

Q. What is a capital instrument?
Ans. A capital instrument is a document which is evidence of the provision of long term capital to a company. E.g. Ordinary shares, debentures.

Exercise 8.19	$ 000
Non-current assets	1 500
Net current assets	800
	2 300
SHARE CAPITAL AND RESERVES	
Ordinary shares of $1each	1 000
10% redeemable preference shares $ 0.50	600
Share premium	300
Retained earnings	400
	2 300

The following transactions took place during January 2010.
1. The non-current assets are revalued at $ 2000 000.
2. The company made a bonus issue on the basis of 2 new ordinary shares for every 5 already held.
3. Following the bonus issue, the company made a rights issue of 2 new ordinary shares for every 7 already held at $ 1.50 per share.
Required: Redraft the statement of financial position at 31 January 2010 of Eastern Ltd immediately after the above transactions took place.

Exercise 8.20
The draft statement of financial position at 30 April 2007 for O'Really Ltd, an electrical goods retailer, is shown

below. Unfortunately it did not balance, and a suspense account was created.

Statement of financial position at 30 April 2007

	$	$
Non-current assets		
Premises		500 000
Other tangible fixed assets		710 000
		1 210 000
Current assets		
Inventory	60 000	
Trade receivables	8 000	
Bank	14 000	82 000
Suspense account		180 000
Total Assets		1 472 000
Current liabilities		42 000
Share capital and reserves:		
Ordinary shares of $1 each fully paid		750 000
7% redeemable preference shares		250 000
Share premium		62 500
Income Statement		367 500
Total liabilities and equity		1 472 000

After the preparation of the draft final accounts for O'Really Ltd for the year ended 30 April 2007 the following items were revealed, all of which need to be included in the final accounts.

1. On 1 May 2006 O'Really Ltd purchased the business of a rival retailer. As part of the purchase price O'Really paid $180 000 for goodwill. The directors were unsure how to treat the goodwill. It had been entered in a suspense account. It is estimated that the economic life of the goodwill will be 4 years.

2. O'Really's sales have doubled over the past few years and the directors believe that they have a very good business reputation. As a result they propose to introduce a further $120 000 as additional goodwill.

3. The directors of O'Really Ltd valued inventory at cost. The closing inventory at 30 April 2007 has been valued at $60 000. Included in the closing inventory were 6 air conditioning units that had been damaged in a recent flood. The units cost $220 each and normally sell for $350 each. The 6 damaged units could be sold for $250 each after undertaking total repair costs of $400. The 6 units could be replaced for $200 each.

4. On 1 May 2006 the business premises were re-valued from a net book value of $500 000 to $750 000. Premises are depreciated at 2 % per annum. The revaluation had not been included in the books of account.

5. No provision has been made for irrecoverable debts. The directors feel that 5 % would be appropriate.

Required

(a) Identify the appropriate accounting standard for each of the items 1-5.

(b) Calculate the profit and loss account balance at 30 April 2007 showing clearly the effect of each of the items 1-5.

(c) Prepare a statement of financial position at 30 April 2007 taking into account items 1-5.

(Adapted from: UCLES, 2007, AS/A Level Accounting, Syllabus 9706/4, Oct/Nov)

TEST YOURSELF

8.1 Multiple choice questions

i) A company has an authorised share capital of $300,000 and an issued 100,000 ordinary share capital of $1 each.   Their operating profit is $40,000. The company has issued $200,000 10% debentures. The directors have proposed a transfer of $10,000 to the general reserve.
What is the maximum dividend that can be paid on ordinary shares?
A) 3%   B) 10%   C) 30%   D) 5%

ii) Out of an authorised share capital of 200,000 ordinary shares of $0.50 each, the directors have issued 80,000 shares. If the proposed dividend is 60 cents in the dollar, what is the amount of the dividend?
A) $24,000   B) $6,000   C) $48,000   D) $12,000
B; iv-

iii) What follows is relevant information extracted from a company's Statement of financial position:

	$000
Freehold premises at cost	500
Provision for depreciation of freehold premises	240
Ordinary shares of $1 each	600
5% preference shares of $1 each	100
Share premium a/c	80
Retained profit	60

It has been decided to revalue freehold premises to $800,000. What will be the statement of financial position value of the ordinary shares after revaluation?
A) $2.3   B) $1.3   C) $2.13   D) $1.5

iv) Adventure Ltd has an authorised share capital of 400,000 shares of $0.50 each and has issued 100,000 shares. They decide to make a bonus issue of 1 share of every 5 shares held.
Which of the following shows the position of the company after the bonus shares issue?

	Authorised share capital	Ordinary share capital
A	Increases by 80,000 shares	No effect
B	No effect	Increases by 20,000 shares
C	No effect	Increases by 80,000 shares
D	Increases by 20,000 shares	Increases by 20,000 shares

v) A company has an ordinary share capital of 200,000 shares of $1 each. It makes a bonus issue of three shares for every two shares held. It follows that with a rights issue of one share for every five held at $1.50 a share. The rights issue was fully subscribed.
What was the increase in the Share Premium account as a result of the bonus and rights issue?
A) $300,000 B) $100,000 C) $150,000 D) $50,000

8.2   A newly formed company issues the following:
a) 1,000,000 ordinary shares of $1 at $2 each
b) $200,000 5% debentures.

Operating profit for the year was $390,000. The directors recommend a 6% ordinary dividend for the year.
Required: Calculate the retained profit for the year.

8.3   A company's share capital consists of 100,000 ordinary shares of $1 each. It makes a rights issue of 1 ordinary share for every 4 held at $1.10 a share.   It then makes a bonus issue of 1 share for every 5 held.
Required: Calculate the amount shown in the Statement of financial position for share capital.

8.4   A company is financed by:
20,000 ordinary shares of $0.50 each.
$4,000 10% loan.
Its profit for the year before interest and taxation is $3,000.
Tax payable is $300
 Required: Calculate the maximum dividend payable per share from this year's profits.

8.5 An extract from the statement of financial position of a company is as follows:

	$
40,000 ordinary shares of $1	40,000
Convertible loan stock	20,000
Share premium account	10,000

It has been decided to convert the loan stock on the basis of 1 new ordinary share for every $4 of Convertible stock held.
Required: The capital structure after the conversion.

8.6   A company decides to convert $600,000 of its convertible loan stock into ordinary shares so that every $1 loan stock receives a $1 ordinary share.
Additional information:

	$
Assets	2,700,000
Liabilities (excluding loan)	810,000
1,500,000 ordinary shares of $1	1,500,000
Profit & loss account	(210,000) dr

Required:
 Calculate the value of each ordinary share after conversion, on a net assets basis.

8.7   A company has an 8% debenture loan of $ 100,000 at 1 January 20x5. Its policy is:
a. To redeem $20,000 of the debenture each 31 December
b. To pay the interest every 31 December.
Required:
What are the amounts that should be disclosed in the statement of financial position at 31 December 20x5 regarding:
i. accrued interest
ii. current liabilities
iii. long term loan

8.8   A company issues a debentures of $1000,000 in 20x0, payable in 5 years' time. The interest for 20x0 and 20x1 is 10% p.a. The interest for 20x2, 20x3 and 20x4 is 12% p.a.
Required:
Calculate the amount of interest shown in the company's profit & loss account for:
a. 20x0
b. 20x1

c. 20x2

d. 20x3

e. 20x4

8.9 Birdlington plc prepares accounts annually to 30 September. The directors provide the following information.

Trial Balance at 30 September 2013

	Debit $	Credit $
Revenue		936,011
Purchases	479,352	
Distribution costs	108,376	
Administrative expenses	236,758	
Ordinary share capital		400,000
Share premium		40,000
Retained earnings		57,386
Land and buildings		
Cost	380,000	
Accumulated depreciation		66,500
Motor vehicles		
Cost	65,000	
Accumulated depreciation		37,578
Loss on disposal of motor vehicle	850	
Inventory at 1 October 2012	177,838	
Provision for doubtful receivables		6,834
Trade receivables	138,450	
Trade payables		51,243
Cash and cash equivalents		17,672
	1,691,624	1,691,624

Additional information

1. Land, which cost $100,000 is not to be depreciated.
2. Depreciation is to be provided as follows:
    | Buildings | 4% on cost, |
    | Plant and machinery | 10% on cost, |
    | Motor vehicles | 25% reducing balance |

    A full year's depreciation is charged in the year of acquisition and none in the year of disposal.

    The charge is split in the ratio 3:1 between administrative expenses and distribution costs.

    Plant and machinery costing $10,000 was acquired on 1 April 2013.

    A motor vehicle which had been purchased on 1 February 2011 for $16,000 was sold on 1 June 2013 for $8,150.
3. The inventory at 30 September 2013 was valued as follows:

    Net realisable value $212,653

    Cost $172,927
4. The provision for doubtful receivables is to be provided at 4% of the trade receivables and the movement is to be treated as an administrative expense.

5. An invoice for an administrative expense of $4,525 remained unpaid at 30 September 2013.
6. There was a prepayment for a distribution cost at 30 September 2013 of $2,760
7. The tax charge for the year is estimated to be $16,730.

Required

a. Prepare an income statement for the year ended 30 September 2013.
b. Prepare a schedule of property, plant and equipment at 30 September 2013 suitable to be used as a note to the accounts.
c. Prepare a statement of financial position at 30 September 2013.

Additional information

During October 2013 the following transactions took place:

6ᵗʰ October: A rights issue of 1 share for each 8 held was made at $1.50 a share. The rights were fully taken up. Nominal value of each share is $1.

15 October: A bonus issue of 1 share for every 10 held was made. The company maintains its reserves in the most flexible form.

31 October: Land was revalued at 200,000.

Profit for the month of October was $2,615

Required

Prepare the equity section of the statement of financial position at 31 October 2013

(UCLES, 2014, AS/A Level Accounting, Syllabus 9706/41, May/June)

8.10 The financial statements of Manik plc showed the following in respect of non-current assets:

	$000
Cost at 1 January 2012	2,000
Less: accumulated depreciation	200
Net book value at 1 January 2012	1,800

During the year ended 31 December 2012 the following took place.

New machinery costing $100,000 was purchased. This had been entered in the ledger. Machinery which had cost 200,000 and had been depreciated by $50,000 was sold. The proceeds of the sale were $145,000 and this had been credited to the suspense account. No depreciation has been charged on the plant and machinery for the year. Depreciation is charged at 10% on the net book value of plant and machinery at 31 December 2012. The charge is to be included in the Administrative expenses for the year.

Required

a.   Prepare a statement suitable for inclusion in the published accounts to show the cost, accumulated depreciation and net book value of plant and machinery at 31 December 2012.

The trainee accountant at Manik plc has provided the following financial information at 31 December 2012

	$000
Revenue	4,000
Cost of sales	1,000
Administrative expenses	1,700
Distribution costs	450
Suspense account	145
Dividends paid and proposed	135

Inventory	400
Trade receivables	385
Trade payables	120
Cash and cash equivalents	170
Long term loan	300
Ordinary shares of $1 each	1,250
Retained earnings at 1 January 2012	265

Additional information

1. No adjustments have been made in respect of distribution costs owing of $20,000 and administrative expenses prepaid of $15,000.

2. Interest on the long-term loan is chargeable at 10% per annum. Only the interest paid during the year of $20,000 has been included in administrative expenses.

3. The estimated tax charge for the year is $365,000.

4. The figure for dividends paid and proposed is made up as follows:

Final dividend for the year ended 31 December 2011 paid in 2012	$50,000
Interim dividend paid 30 September 2012	$25,000
Proposed final dividend to be paid in March 2013	$60,000

5. On 1 December 2012 the company issued a further 500,000 shares of $1 each at $1.50. These shares would qualify for the proposed final dividend to be paid in March 2013.

Required

b. Prepare the company's income statement for the year ended 31 December 2012.

c. Prepare a statement of changes in equity for the year ended 31 December 2012.

d. Prepare the company's statement of financial position at 31 December 2012.

e. Explain how proposed dividends are treated in the published account

(UCLES, 2013, AS/A Level Accounting, Syllabus 9706/41, May/June)

CHAPTER 9
BUSINESS PURCHASE AND MERGERS

Q. What is a business purchase?
Ans. The methods that can be used are:
   a.   The company making the purchase may purchase the net assets of the company it wishes to acquire.
   b.   The company making the purchase may purchase shares in the company it wishes to acquire.
   c.   A third company may be formed to purchase the share capitals and/or assets and liabilities of the two companies that are merging. This is called a merger or an amalgamation.

Q. Give examples of mergers.
Ans. The following methods of mergers can be considered:
   a.   A sole trader merges with an existing partnership to form an enlarged partnership.
   b.   Existing businesses of sole traders merge to form a partnership.
   c.   A sole trader's business or a partnership is acquired by a limited company.

Q. Why would businesses merge?
Ans. Businesses may merge for the following reasons:
1. **Synergy**: this is the idea that by combining business activities, performance will increase and costs will decrease. Essentially, a business will attempt to merge with another business that has complementary strengths and weaknesses. One of the reasons why costs would decrease would be due to economies of scale.
2. **Diversification / Sharpening Business Focus**: These two conflicting goals have been used to describe thousands of merger and acquisition transactions. A company that merges to diversify may acquire another company in a seemingly unrelated industry in order to reduce the impact of a particular industry's performance on its profitability. Companies seeking to sharpen focus often merge with companies that have deeper market penetration in a key area of operations.
3. **Growth**: Mergers can give the acquiring company an opportunity to grow market share without having to really earn it by doing the work themselves - instead, they buy a competitor's business for a price. Usually, these are called horizontal mergers. For example, a beer company may choose to buy out a smaller competing brewery, enabling the smaller company to make more beer and sell more to its brand-loyal customers.
4. **Increase Supply-Chain Pricing Power**: By buying out one of its suppliers or one of the distributors, a business can eliminate a level of costs. If a company buys out one of its suppliers, it is able to save on the margins that the supplier was previously adding to its costs; this is known as a vertical merger. If a company buys out a distributor, it may be able to ship its products at a lower cost.
5. **Eliminate Competition**: Many merger deals allow the acquirer to eliminate future competition and gain a larger market share in its product's market.
6. **To avoid entry barriers**: Entry barriers are the existence of high start-up costs or other obstacles that prevent new competitors from easily entering an industry or area of business. New businesses will therefore chose to merge with existing businesses to avoid these barriers.
7. **Capital:** To increase the amount of capital for business expansion.
8. **Skills & expertise:** To make use of the skills and expertise available in one of the business merging.
9. **Geographical areas**: To cover different geographical areas.
10. **Contracts:** To attract more profitable contracts.

Q. What is goodwill?

Ans. Goodwill is an intangible non-current asset that is recognised at the time of a business purchase. Some of the reasons that goodwill arises are:

a. Good business reputation
b. Strong brand
c. Well – trained employees
d. Favourable location
e. Good customer and employee relations
f. Any other circumstances that enhances the intangible value of the business.

Goodwill is calculated by using the following formula:

Goodwill = Purchase consideration – fair value of separately identifiable net assets purchased.

When the result is a negative figure, it is termed 'Negative goodwill'.

Goodwill is usually amortised using the straight-line method.

Q. How is negative goodwill treated?

Ans. IAS 22 (not in CIE syllabus) states: 'Negative goodwill is presented as a deduction from the assets of the enterprise, in the same statement of financial position classification as (positive) goodwill'.

Hence negative goodwill must be subtracted from the non-tangible assets in the statement of financial position in the non-current assets section.

Q. What is the difference between purchased goodwill and inherent goodwill?

Ans. Purchased goodwill has been paid for whereas inherent goodwill has not been paid for. Inherent goodwill arises when a business decides to show the value of its intangible assets e.g. a trained workforce, in its statement of financial position. IAS states that only purchased goodwill should be shown in the statement of financial position as an intangible non-current asset.

Q. When will goodwill not arise in a business sale?

Ans. If the business is sold as a going concern, then goodwill will arise as the purchasing business will have acquired an established trade with all its assets, customers, rights and obligations. However, if the assets of a business are sold independently to another business then this may not give rise to goodwill as the business selling the assets may continue to operate as, and thus enjoy the advantages of, a going concern.

Q. How is purchase consideration calculated?

Ans. Purchase consideration = assets taken over – liabilities taken over.

Assets should be professionally valued. Liabilities are normally taken over as agreed upon by the sellers and the buyers. Outstanding loans in the books of the sellers are normally discharged by the purchasing company issuing its own debentures.

Exhibit:

The statement of financial positions of Ami Ltd. and Tal Ltd. at 31 March 20x0 are given below:

	Ami Ltd.		Tal Ltd.	
	$	$	$	$
Non-current assets:				
Property, plant and equipment		39,000		12,000
Delivery vans		11,000		8,000
Fixtures and fittings		-		3,000
		50,000		23,000

Current assets:				
Inventory	4,000		1,200	
Trade receivables	5,400		900	
Bank	31,700	41,100	1,000	3,100
Total assets		91,100		26,100
Less current liabilities:				
Trade payables		3,600		475
Capital and reserves:				
Ordinary shares of $1		75,000		25,000
Profit & loss account		12,500		625
		91,100		26,100

Ami Ltd. takes over all the assets and liabilities of Tal Ltd. at book value with the exception of the bank account for a purchase consideration of $20,000 in the form of ordinary shares in Ami Ltd at par and the balance in cash.

Required:
The statement of financial position of Ami Ltd. immediately after the acquisition of Tal Ltd.

Solution:

Ami Ltd
Statement of financial position as at 1 April 20x0

	$	$
Non-current assets:		
Property, plant and equipment		51,000
Delivery vans		19,000
Fixtures and fittings		3,000
		73,000
Current assets:		
Inventory	5,200	
Trade receivables	6,300	
*Bank	27,075	38,575
		111,575
Less current liabilities:		
Trade payables		4,075
Share capital and reserves:		
Ordinary shares of $1(75,000+20,000)		95,000
Profit and loss account		12,500
		111,575

Working:
Value of net assets acquired = 25,625 – 1000 (bank account) = $24,625
Purchase consideration = 20,000 (shares) + 4,625(cash)
*Bank = 31,700 - 4,625 = $ 27,075

Exercise 9.1
The statement of financial positions of Sharon Ltd. and Stone Ltd. at 31 December 20x1 are given below:

	Sharon Ltd.		Stone Ltd.	
	$	$	$	$
Non-current assets:				
Property, plant and equipment		52,000		10,000
Delivery vans		15,000		5,000
Fixtures and fittings		7,000		9,000
		74,000		24,000

Current assets:				
Inventory	3,000		2,700	
Trade receivables	1,400		1,900	
Bank	20,500	24,900	1,500	6,100
Total assets		98,900		30,100
Current liabilities:				
Trade payables		3,900		3,100
Capital and reserves:				
Ordinary shares of $1		55,000		20,000
Retained earnings		40,000		7,000
		98,900		30,100

Sharon Ltd. takes over all the assets of Stone Ltd. at the following valuations with the exception of the bank account:

	$
Property, plant and equipment	12,000
Delivery vans	4,000
Fixtures & fittings	6,000
Inventory	2,000
Trade receivables	1,500

Sharon Ltd. also assumes responsibility of Stone Ltd's creditors.

The purchase price was fixed at $25,000, which was to be settled by the issued to Stone Ltd's shareholders of 15,000 ordinary shares of $1 each in Sharon Ltd. at a premium of 50c each and the balance in cash.

Required:
The statement of financial position of Sharon Ltd. immediately after the acquisition of Stone Ltd.

Exhibit:
Malika Ltd. was formed to acquire the net assets of two sole trader businesses: Kailash Socks owned by Kailash Sheth and Madhuben knitwear owned by Madhuben Shirodkar. Kailash and Madhuben subscribed for a total of 100,000 ordinary shares of $1 each in Malika Ltd and paid the cash for the shares into the newly formed company's bank account.

At 31 March 20x1, the statement of financial positions of Malika Ltd., Kailash Socks and Madhuben Knitwear were as follows:

	Malika Ltd	Kailash Socks		Madhuben Knitwear	
	$	$	$	$	$
Non-current assets:					
Freehold property			40,000		15,000
Motor vans			8,000		6,000
Fixtures & fittings			10,000		12,000
			58,000		33,000
Current assets:					
Inventory		40,000		66,000	
Trade receivables		5,000		17,000	
Bank	100,000	-	45,000	-	83,000
Total assets	100,000		103,000		116,000
Current liabilities:					
Trade payables			32,000		76,000
Bank overdraft			16,000		22,000
			48,000		98,000

Capital:

100,000 ordinary shares of $1	100,000		
Kailash& Madhuben – capital	___-___	55,000	18,000
Capital and liabilities	<u>100,000</u>	<u>103,000</u>	<u>116,000</u>

Malika Ltd. would take over the assets of the two businesses at their net book value except for the following assets which would be taken over at the values shown below:

	Kailash socks	Madhuben Knitwear
Freehold property	$75,000	$25,000
Motor vans	N.B.V	$5,000
Fixtures & fittings	$7,000	N.B.V.
Inventory	$38,000	$55,000
Trade receivables	$4,000	$60,000

Malika Ltd. would pay $100,000 for Kailash socks to be settled by the allotment of 60,000 ordinary shares of $1 each in Malika Ltd and $28,000 in cash.

Malika Ltd. would pay $60,000 for Madhuben Knitwear, to be settled by the allotment of 40,000 ordinary shares of $1 each in Malika Ltd. and $12,000 in cash.

Required:

Prepare the statement of financial position of Malika Ltd. as it would have appeared immediately after the above scheme has been implemented.

Solution:

Malika Ltd.

Statement of financial position as at 1 July 20x1

	$	$
Non-current assets:		
Intangible: Goodwill		17,000
Tangible:		
Freehold property	100,000	
Motor vans	13,000	
Fixtures & fittings	<u>19,000</u>	<u>132,000</u>
		149,000
Current assets:		
Inventory	93,000	
Trade receivables	64,000	
*Bank	<u>22,000</u>	<u>179,000</u>
		328,000
Current liabilities:		
**Trade payables		108,000
Capital and reserves:		
200,000 ordinary shares of $1		200,000
Share premium		<u>20,000</u>
		<u>328,000</u>

Working:

* Bank = 100,000 – 16,000 -22,000 – 40,000 = $22,000

** Trade payables = 32,000 + 76,000 = $ 108,000

    1. Calculation of goodwill:

Kailash socks:

Goodwill = 100,000 – {(75,000 + 8,000+7,000+38,000+4,000) – (48,000)} =$16,000

Madhuben knitwear:

Goodwill = 60,000 – {(25,000+5,000+12,000+55,000+60,000) – (98,000)} = $1,000

Total goodwill = $ 17,000

2. Calculation of share premium:

	$
Total consideration	160,000
Cash payments	(40,000)
Consideration in shares	120,000
Number of shares	100,000

Each share = $\dfrac{120,000}{100,000}$

= $1.20

Premium = $0.20

Exercise 9.2
Leo, a sole trader sold his business to Lamington Ltd. on 31 December 20x1. The net assets of his business at that date had a net book value of $160,000 and a fair value of $200,000.

The consideration for the sale was satisfied by the issue of 200,000 $1 ordinary shares and a cash payment of $20,000.

Required:
Calculate the amount of goodwill arising on the transfer.

Exercise 9.3
A sole trader's business is acquired by a limited company. The sole trader gives you the following information:

	$
Net assets at valuation	167,000
Purchase consideration	137,000
Cash paid in part settlement	50,000
Ordinary shares of $1 each	60,000

Required:
Calculate the premium on each ordinary share.

Exercise 9.4
A business has assets with a fair value of $150,000 and agreed negative goodwill of $30,000. 16,000 ordinary shares of $2 each were issued at a premium of $3 each to acquire the net assets.

Required:
Calculate the value of the liabilities acquired.

Exercise 9.5
The statement of financial position (extract) of Kensignton & sons is given to you:

	$
Intangible non-current assets: goodwill	20,000
Tangible non-current assets	162,000
Net current assets	58,000

A company wants to acquire the tangible non-current and net current assets of Kensington & sons for an agreed price of $200,000. It brings the assets into its books at the original book values.

Required:
Calculate the goodwill (positive or negative) that will appear in the company's statement of financial position after the acquisition.

Exercise 9.6

Negative goodwill amounted to $20,000.

The purchase consideration was settled by the issue of 200,000 ordinary shares of $1 each.

Required

Give the entry in Malcolm's share premium account.

Q. Why would two sole traders or two partnerships want to convert into a limited company?

Ans. A limited company enjoys the following advantages that a sole trader or a partnership does not enjoy:

    a. Limited liability

    b. Separate legal identity

    c. Continuity

Q. What accounting procedures should be followed when two partnerships decide to convert into a limited company?

Ans. As the partnerships dissolve, the same accounting procedure that is followed for the dissolution of a partnership should be used. However, the purchase consideration may not be cash, but shares (ordinary & preference), debentures or cash; or a combination of all three. Moreover, the shares may be valued at a premium. The distribution of the purchase consideration between the partners could be agreed upon. In the absence of such an agreement the following will apply:

1. Ordinary shares received from the purchasing company will be distributed in the existing profit and loss sharing ratio.
2. Partnership loans are converted into debentures. The face value of the debentures is dictated by the amount of interest the loan attracted and the amount of interest the debentures command. Sufficient debentures are issued so that the partner continues to receive the same amount of interest as he was receiving on the partnership loan.
3. The remaining amount due to the partners is normally settled by cash or preference shares. Sometimes a partner may have capital that does not reflect his high profit-sharing ratio. If such is the case, then the partner may have to be content with a sufficient number of shares to clear his account. If is want his equity in the newly-formed company to reflect his profit-sharing ratio, then he will be required to contribute a sufficient amount of cash to make up the difference.

Q. Give the journal entries to record the purchase of a business.

Ans. The journal entries are:

                       Dr   Cr

1. *Assets   xxx

    Business purchase a/c   xxx

    (Assets purchased from partnership at agreed values)

* The assets should be named individually at agreed values, normally given in the examination question.

                       Dr   Cr

2. Business purchase a/c xxx

    Liabilities   xxx

    (Liabilities acquired by the purchasing business at agreed values)

		Dr	Cr
3.	Business purchase a/c	xxx	
	Selling business a/c		xxx

(Liability for purchase consideration to selling business recognised)

		Dr	Cr
4.	Goodwill a/c	xxx	
	Business purchase a/c		xxx

(Being the excess of purchase consideration over agree value of net assets purchased)

		Dr	Cr
5.	Business purchase a/c	xxx	
	Goodwill a/c		xxx

(Being the excess of the agreed value of net assets acquired over the purchase consideration)

		Dr	Cr
6.	Selling business	xxx	
	Bank		xx
	Ordinary/preference shares		xx
	Share premium a/c		x
	Debentures		xx

(Being the full settlement of the purchase consideration to the selling business)

Exhibit:

A partner receives 8% interest on a partnership loan of $100,000.
A company takes over all the assets and liabilities of the partnership. The consideration of $1m is partly satisfied by the issue of 10% debentures in place of the partnership loan, but the total interest payable is to remain the same.
The balance will be settled by the issue of 800,000 $1 ordinary shares to the partners.
Required:
An extract of the company's opening statement of financial position showing the amount of debentures, ordinary shares and reserves.

Solution:

The company's opening statement of financial position will contain the following:

	$
*10% Debentures	80,000
Ordinary shares of $1	800,000
**Reserves	120,000

Working:
*Debentures = $\frac{8 \text{ (old rate of interest)}}{10 \text{ (new rate of interest}} \times 100000$
= $80,000
** Reserves = 1m – (800,000 +80,000)
= $120,000

Exercise 9.7

A partner receives 6% interest on a partnership loan of $60,000.
A company takes over all the assets and liabilities of the partnership. The consideration of $1m is partly satisfied by the issue of 10% debentures in place of the partnership loan, but the total interest payable is to remain the same.
The balance will be settled by the issue of 600,000 $1 ordinary shares to the partners.
Required:
An extract of the company's opening statement of financial position showing the amount of debentures, ordinary shares and reserves.

Exercise 9.8

Akram, Bhupesh and Chuck were in partnership. Their partnership agreement provided that:
1. Akram received a partnership salary of $80,000 per annum.
2. Partners be credited with interest on capital at 6% per annum.
3. Residual profits be shared in the ratio of 3:2:1 respectively
4. Chuck be guaranteed a minimum share of residual profits of $7,200.

The partnership trial balance at 31st March 2010, after the preparation of the partnership trading account, was a follows:

	Dr $	Cr $
Gross Profit		383,000
Trade receivables	24,000	
Trade payables		18,000
Inventories at 31 March 2010	37,000	
Non-current assets at cost:		
Buildings	310,000	
Machinery	170,000	
Vehicles	120,000	
Provision for depreciation:		
Buildings		105,000
Machinery		68,000
Vehicles		77,000
General expenses	327,000	
Bank		14,000
Capital accounts:		
Akram		160,000
Bhupesh		110,000
Chuck		80,000
Current accounts:		
Akram		14,000
Bhupesh		27,000
Chuck		37,000
Drawings:		
Akram	40,000	
Bhupesh	30,000	
Chuck	35,000	
	1,093,000	1,093,000

ADDITIONAL INFORMATION:
1. A family holiday taken by Bhupesh, costing $3,400 had been entered in general expenses.
2. A irrecoverable debt of $500 was written off during the year. It had not been entered in the books of account.
3. A irrecoverable debt of $400 written off in the year ended 31 March 2009 was partially recovered. The debtor paid, by cheque, $0.50 for each $1 owed. No entries had been made in the books of account.
4. A machine purchased in January 2010 for $17,000 had been included in general expenses.
5. Depreciation is to be provided at the following rates:
a. Buildings at 2% per annum on cost
b. Machinery at 10% per annum on cost
c. Vehicles at 40% per annum reducing balance.
A full year's depreciation is provided on non-current assets acquired during the year.

Required:
   a. **Prepare an income statement and an appropriation account for the year ended 31 March 2010.**
   b. **Prepare the partners' current accounts at 31 March 2010.**

At the close of business on March 2010 the partnership was taken over by EDC Ltd. The company took over all the assets and liabilities, with the exception of the bank balance, for a purchase consideration of $60,000.

The purchase consideration comprised:
$30,000 in cash;
150,000 $1 debentures at par shared equally between the partners;
300,000 ordinary shares of $1 in EDC Ltd. These were shared among the partners in their profit sharing ratios.

The partnership expenses incurred in the takeover amounted to $20,200.

Required:
   c. **Prepare the partners' capital accounts to close the books of accounts of the partnership.**
   d. **Prepare the partnership bank account to close the books of account.**
(UCLES, 2010, AS/A Level Accounting, Syllabus 9706/41, Oct/Nov)

Q. How is return on investment calculated?
Ans. Return on investment or capital employed (ROCE) = $\frac{profit}{Investment}$ x 100

Q. When can an investment in a new company be considered worthwhile?
Ans. In order to discern whether an investment in a new company was worthwhile, it is necessary to calculate the incremental profitability.

Exhibit
S Ltd had a capital of $200,000 with an annual average profit of $76,000. S Ltd purchases T Ltd for $100,000 settled by the issue of shares in S Ltd. S Ltd.'s profit for the year following the purchase was $90,000.

Profitability before the purchase = $\frac{76000 \times 100}{200000}$ = 38%

Profitability after the purchase = $\frac{90000 \times 100}{300000}$ = 30%
The profitability has **fallen** by 8%

However, to get a more reliable picture, incremental profit is calculated:
Incremental profitability = $\frac{(90000 - 76000) \times 100}{100000}$ = 14%
Hence, S Ltd has profited by the acquisition.

Exercise 9.9
Tonigton Ltd had a capital of $100,000 with an annual average profit of $38,000. Tonnington Ltd purchases T Ltd for $100,000 settled by the issue of shares in Tonnington Ltd. Tonnington Ltd.'s profit for the year following the purchase was $40,000.
Required:
   a. **Calculate the profitability of Tonnington Ltd before the purchase.**

b. Calculate the profitability of Tonnington Ltd after the purchase.
c. Comment on the acquisition.

Exercise 9.10   A & U Ltd is a company formed to take over the partnership business of Amal and Ushi on 1 November 2009. Profits and losses are shared equally. The partnership statement of financial position at that date was as follows:

Amal and Ushi
Statement of Financial Position at 31 October 2009

	$	$
Non-current assets (net book value)		60 000
Current assets		
Inventory	34 000	
Trade receivables	41 000	
Cash equivalents	9 650	
	84 650	
Less Current liabilities		
Trade payables	21 300	
Net current assets (working capital)		63 350
		123 350
Less Non-current liabilities		
Loan from Ushi at 10% per annum		20 000
		103 350

	$	$
Financed by:		
Capital accounts: Amal	60 000	
Ushi	40 000	100 000
Current accounts: Amal	2 000	
Ushi	1 350	3 350
		103 350

The terms of the sale of the partnership business to A & U Ltd are:
1.   All the assets and liabilities of the partnership are to be taken over by A & U Ltd. The assets
are to be valued as shown below.

	$
Non-current assets	85,000
Inventory	31,000
Trade receivables	37,650

2. The consideration for the partnership business is to be $170 000 satisfied as follows:

Amal will be issued with 8% debenture stock sufficient to ensure that she receives the same amount of interest annually as she had received on her own loan to the partnership. 100 000 ordinary shares of $1 issued as fully paid to Amal and Ushi in proportion to the balances on their capital accounts in the partnership at 31 October 2009.

Any balances remaining on the partners' capital accounts to be settled in cash through the company's bank accounts.

After purchasing the partnership business, the company will issue 20 000 ordinary shares of $1 each to their friend Djamel on the same terms as those issued to Amal and Ushi.

Required
(a) Calculate the value of the goodwill and the shares issued to Djamel and show the relevant entries in the partners' capital accounts to dissolve the partnership.
(b) Calculate the balance on the bank account and prepare the statement of financial position of A & U Ltd, as it will appear immediately after the above transactions have

been completed.

(c) (i) Explain what is meant by the term 'capital instrument'. Name the capital instruments in A & U Ltd's statement of affairs (statement of financial position).

(UCLES, 2010, AS/A Level Accounting, Syllabus 9706/4, SP)

TEST YOURSELF

9.1 Multiple choice questions:

i. Melingue Ltd has the following statement of financial position extract:

	$	$
Non-current assets at cost		200,000
Depreciation to date		80,000
		120,000
Current assets:		
Inventory	20,000	
Trade receivables	15,000	
	35,000	
Less current liabilities:		
Trade receivables	5,000	30,000
		150,000
Capital and reserves		150,000

The net current assets were valued at $20,000 and the non-current assets were valued at $180,000. Melingue Ltd was acquired by Basil Ltd for a purchase consideration of $225,000.

The goodwill paid by Basil Ltd was:

A. 85,000
B. 115,000
C. 25,000
D. 55,000

ii. Alice runs a successful sole trader business. Wonderland Ltd wants to purchase her business. Her net assets have a book value of $90,000. The market value of her net assets is $100,000. She has valued her goodwill at $30,000. The purchase price has thus been agreed upon and will be settled by an issue of $1 ordinary shares at a premium of $0.25. How many shares did Alice receive in Wonderland Ltd?

A. 104,000
B. 105,000
C. 120,000
D. 80,000

iii. Donny is in partnership with Jenny. Donny has made a loan to the partnership of $200,000 @8% p.a. The partnershp is now being sold to a limited company, Jade Ltd. Donny is to receive sufficient 10% debentures to ensure that he continues to receive the same amount of interest.

What is the nominal amount of debentures that Donny will receive?

A. 200,000
B. 250,000
C. 160,000
D. 128,000

9.2 A company acquires the assets of another company for $200,000. The purchase price comprises of:

a. An issue of $50,000 debentures at a discount of 5%

b. Cash of $60,000

c. 18,500 ordinary shares of $0.50 each.

Required:

Calculate the market value of each ordinary share.

9.3 A company has the following statement of financial position(extract):

	$
Non-current assets	400,000
Net current assets	120,000
Long term loan	200,000

The business was purchased for $600,000

Required:

Calculate the goodwill paid.

9.4 Stanley & sons is a sole trader business with net assets of $500,000. Warrington Ltd. buys Stanley & sons for $800,000 by issuing new share capital. The market value of the net assets taken over by Warrington Ltd. is $700,000.

Required:

Calculate the increase in the net assets of Warrington Ltd.

9.5 Argy and Bargy were in partnership sharing profit and losses in the ratio of 2:1. The partnership's statement of financial position at 30 April 2004 was:

	$	$
Non current assets: Freehold land		5,000
Freehold buildings		20,000
Equipment		8,000
		33,000
Current assets: Inventory	11,000	
Trade receivables	6,000	
Bank	2,000	
	19,000	
Less current liabilities:		
Trade payables	3,000	16,000
		49,000
Less long term liability:		
Loan from Argy at 10%		4,000
		45,000
Capital accounts: Argy	50,000	
Bargy	25,000	75,000
Less Drawing accounts: Argy	(18,000)	
Bargy	(12,000)	(30,000)
		45,000

Shindig Ltd offered to purchase the partnership business. The offer was based on the following re-valuation of assets.

	$
Freehold land	10,000
Freehold buildings	16,000
Equipment	5,000
Inventory	9,000
Trade receivables	5,000

Shindig Ltd would not take over the partnership bank account.

The purchase consideration was $62,000, settled as follows:

1. Argy received sufficient 8% debentures in Shindig Ltd to ensure that he continued to receive the same amount of interest as he ahd been entitled to on his loan to the partnership.
2. Shindig Ltd paid $12,000 into the partnership bank account.
3. The balance of the purchase price was settled in ordinary shares of $1 each in Shindig Ltd at a prices of $1.50.

The shares were distributed among the partners in their profit/loss sharing ratios and any remaining balances on their capital accounts were settled in cash.

Required:

a. Prepare the partners' capital accounts in columnar form to show the closing entries.

The statement of financial position of Shindig Ltd at the 30 April 2004 before the purchase of the partnership business was:

		$	$
Fixed assets:	Leasehold buildings		10,000
	Office furniture		2,000
			12,000
Current assets:	Inventory	20,000	
	Trade receivables	12,000	
	Bank	24,000	
		56,000	
Current liabilities:	Trade payables	14,000	42,000
			54,000
Share capital and reserves:			
Ordinary shares of $1			50,000
Profit and loss account			4,000
			54,000

Required:

b. (i) Prepare the statement of financial position of Shindig Ltd as it will appear after the purchase of the partnership business.

(ii) Describe how your answers to (a) and (b)(i) would have been different if Shindig Ltd had purchased the partnerhsip assets only, instead of the partnership business.

(UCLES, 2004, AS/A Level Accounting, Syllabus 9706/4, May/June)

CHAPTER 10
JOINT VENTURE AND CONSIGNMENT ACCOUNTS

Q1. What is a joint venture?

Ans. A joint venture is a business arrangement in which two or more parties agree to pool their resources for the purpose of accomplishing a specific task, sharing risks, profits and liabilities. This task can be a new project or any other business activity. It is a contractual business undertaking and is similar to a business partnership, with one key difference: a partnership generally involves an ongoing, long-term business relationship, whereas a joint venture is based on a single business transaction. A

Joint Venture is a temporary undertaking without the use of the firm name. Example of such a business is joint construction of a building, joint underwriting of a particular issue of shares or debentures, transport and travel industries that operate in different countries etc.

Q1. What is a consignment?

Ans. When a trader sends goods to an agent to sell them for him, the goods are said to be on consignment.

Q2. What are the main features of goods on consignment?

Ans. The main features of goods on consignment are:

1. The goods are sent to an agent.
2. The goods do not legally belong to the agent. They belong to the trader till they are sold. Hence they are included as part of the consignor's closing inventory till they are sold.
3. The agent is called the **consignee** whereas the sender/trader or the principal is the **consignor**.
4. The agent stores the goods till they are sold. All the expenses he incurs is refunded by the consignor.
5. The consignee receives a commission for his work.
6. The consignee collects money from the customers to whom the goods are sold. This money is paid to the consignor after expenses and commission are deducted.
7. The statement from the consignee to the consignor showing this is known as the **account sales**.
8. The consignor opens a **consignment account** for each consignment. It is similar to an Income Statement for each consignment and is used to calculate the profit or loss on each consignment.
9. Any irrecoverable debt arising as a result of credit sales of consigned sales are borne by the consignor. However, the consignee would have to bear this loss if he has agreed to this against del-credere commission.

Q3. What is ordinary commission that the consignee receives?

Ans. Ordinary commission is an agreed – upon commission calculated using a fixed percentage on the gross sales of the goods on consignment.

Q4. What is del-credere commission?

Ans. It is a fee received by the consignee from the consignor for guaranteeing the payment of goods sold. It is usually calculated on total gross sales (cash and credit).

Q. What is a consignment account?

Ans. A consignment occurs when the owner of goods leaves them with another party to be sold. When the goods are eventually sold, the consignee retains a commission and pays the consignor the residual amount. Consignment deals are made on a variety of products - from artwork, to clothing, to books. In recent years, consignment shops have become rather trendy, especially those offering specialty products, infant wear and high-end fashion items. Selling on consignment is a great option for individuals or businesses that do not have a brick-and-mortar presence, although consignment arrangements can also exist in cyberspace. To a certain degree, online companies like eBay are consignment shops, because, for a percentage of the sale, they offer people a marketplace to exhibit and sell their wares.

Q. Outline the major differences between consignments and joint ventures.

Ans. The following table pinpoints the differences between the two:

Basis of distinction	Joint Venture	Consignment
Nature	It is a temporary partnership business without a firm name.	It is an extension of a business owned by the principal through the agent.
Parties involved	The parties involved in a joint venture are known as co-ventures.	The parties involved are: the consignor and consignee.
Relation	Each co-venture is a partner as well as the agent of other co-ventures.	The relation between the consignor and consignee is that of 'principal and agent'. The consignee is the agent of his principle i.e., consignor.
Profit sharing	The profits and losses of joint venture are shared among the co-ventures in their agreed proportion.	The profits and losses are not shared between the consignor and consignee. The consignee only gets a commission.
Rights	The co-ventures have equal rights and powers e.g. to buy and sell goods, to collect dues etc.	The consignor enjoys a principal's rights whereas consignee enjoys the rights of an agent.
Exchange of information	The co-ventures exchange information on a regular basis.	The consignee prepares an account sale which contains the details of business activities carried on. This is sent to the consignor
Ownership	All the co-ventures are the owners of the joint venture.	The consignor is the owner of the business.
Capital	Capital in cash or in kind is contributed by the co-ventures.	Capital in cash or in kind is contributed as dictated by the principal.

Purpose	The object of the business could be buying or selling, contract work or any other activity.	Consignments are meant for the sale of goods alone.
Termination	A joint venture comes to an end when venture is completed.	The relationship between the consignor and the consignee continues until terminated by the parties concerned.
Scope	Any movable or immovable property.	Only movable property.
Number of persons	Two or more persons.	Just two people- the consignor and the consignee.
Laws	As it is like a temporary partnership, it is governed by the Partnership Act.	As it is a principal/agent relationship, it is governed by the Law of Agency.

JOINT VENTURES

Q. Why are joint ventures undertaken?

Ans. A joint venture can:

- help a business grow faster resulting in increased productivity and greater profits.
- offer access to new markets and distribution networks
- result in increased capacity
- result in sharing of risks and costs with a partner
- offer access to greater resources, including specialised staff, technology and finance. You may be able to use your joint venture partner's customer database to market your product, or offer your partner's services and products to your existing customers.
- result in economies of scale
- enable each co-venture to gain from the synergistic effect of the pooling of diversified skills. Joint venture partners benefit from being able to join forces in purchasing, research and development.
- offer increased capital. Joint ventures often enable growth without having to borrow funds or look for outside investors.
- be very flexible e.g. a joint venture can have a limited life span and only cover part of what you do, thus limiting the commitment for both parties and the business' exposure.

Q. What are the risks of joint ventures?

Ans. Partnering with another business can be complex. It takes time and effort to build the right relationship. Problems are likely to arise if:

- the objectives of the venture are not totally clear and communicated to everyone involved
- the partners have different objectives for the joint venture
- there is an imbalance in levels of expertise, investment or assets brought into the venture by the different partners
- different cultures and management styles result in poor integration and co-operation
- the partners don't provide sufficient leadership and support in the early stages

Success in a joint venture depends on thorough research and analysis of aims and objectives. This should be followed up with effective communication of the business plan to everyone involved.

Q. What is the difference between accounting for large joint ventures and smaller joint ventures?

Ans. For large-scale joint ventures, a separate bank account and a separate set of books are maintained. The calculation of profit is not difficult as the financial statements are similar to that of an ordinary business. For smaller joint ventures, no separate bank accounts or books need be maintained. Each party will record transactions that concern them in their own books.

Exhibit

Somena and Jules enter into a joint venture. Somena is to provide the capital, the transport to markets and the selling skills. Jules is to grow the produce. The profits are shared equally. The following transactions took place:

Jules supplied produce costing $1,500
Jules paid wages 300
Jules paid for storage expenses $230
Somena paid transport expenses $450
Somena paid selling expenses $280
Somena received cash from sales of all the produce $3,000.

Stage 1

Somena and Jules will each enter their part of the transactions. Somena will open an account named 'Joint venture with Jules' and Jules will open an account names 'Joint venture with Somena'. The entries are:

In Jules books:	**dr**	**cr**
Payments by Jules:	Joint venture with Somena	Cash book
Produce supplied	Joint venture with Somena	Purchases

In Somena's books:	**dr**	**cr**
Payments by Somena	Joint venture with Jules	Cash book
Cash received by Somena	Cash book	Joint venture with Jules

The joint venture accounts in each of the co-venture's books will appear as follows:

Jules books:

Joint venture with Somena a/c

	$		$
Purchases	1,500		
Cash wages	300		
Cash: storage expenses	230		

Somena's books:

Joint venture with Jules a/c

	$		$
Cash: transport expenses	450	Cash: sales	3,000
Cash: selling expenses	280		

Stage 2

As Jules and Somena do not know the details in each other's books, they cannot calculate profit or find out how much cash has to be paid or received to close the venture. Hence, they must send each other a copy of their joint venture accounts. On receipt of these accounts, Jules and Somena will each draw up a memorandum joint venture account to include all the details as follows:

Jules and Somena
Memorandum Joint Venture Account

	$	$		$	$
Purchases		1,500	Sales		3,000
Wages		300			
Storage expenses		230			
Transport expenses		450			
Selling expenses		280			
Net profit:					
Jules (1/2)	120				
Somena (1/2)	120	240			
		3,000			3,000

This account is NOT a double entry account. It is merely drawn up to calculate the each person's share of profit or loss as well as to calculate the amounts payable or receivable to close the venture.

Stage 3

The net profit shares for Jules and Somena will now be brought into their books as follows:
Jules' books:
Debit share of profit to Joint Venture with Somena's a/c
Credit Jules's Income Statement

Somena's books:
Debit share of profit to Joint Venture with Jules's a/c
Credit Somena's Income Statement

The Joint Venture accounts are now balanced down showing:
1. If the balance c/d is a credit balance, the person has received more from the joint venture than they should keep. They will then have to pay that amount to the other person to close the venture.
2. If the balance c/d is a debit balance, the person has received less from the joint venture than they should get. They will therefore need to receive cash from the other person to close the venture.

The complete Joint Venture accounts are:
Jules books:

Joint venture with Somena

	$		$
Purchases	1,500	Balance c/d	2,150
Cash wages	300		
Cash: storage expenses	230		
Share of profit transferred			
to Income Statement	120		
	2,150		2,150
Balance b/d	2,150	Cash in settlement from Jules	2,150

Somena's books:

Joint Venture with Jules

	$		$
Cash: transport expenses	450	Cash: sales	3,000
Cash: selling expenses	280		
Share of profit transferred			
to Income Statement	120		
Balance c/d	2,150		
	3,000		3,000
Cash settlement to Jules	2,150	Balance b/d	2,150

Exercise 10.1

A, B and C entered into a joint venture. A shop was rented by A at $50 per month. Profit and loss is to be split in the ratio of 3:2:1The following transactions took place:

20x3

June 1   A paid three months' rent for the shop.
June 3   B bought a motor vehicle for $2,700.
June 4   B purchased$650 of goods.
June 15   C sold some products for cash $3,790.
June 28   A purchased $1,200 worth of goods for the business.
July 11   C started using his personal motor vehicle for the venture, at an agree charge of
          $400 as the business' motor vehicle broke down.
Jule 13   The motor vehicle bought on June 3 was sold for $2,100, cash, by A.
July 15   Cash sales by B $780.
July 18   Electricity charges paid by C $120.
July 30   C purchased $440 worth of products for the business.
Aug 4   General expenses of $800 were shared equally by A and C.
Aug 19   Cash sales made by C $990.
Aug 31   The joint venture ended. Inventory left over was taken over by B at a value of $2,100.
Any outstanding balances between the co-ventures were settled.

Required:
1. **Joint venture accounts in the books of A, B and C.**
2. **Detailed workings to calculate the profit or loss incurred by the venture.**

Exercise 10.2

Henry and John entered into a joint venture for the purchase and sale of antiques. They agreed to share profits and losses equally. The following transactions took place in the month of July:

July 1   Henry purchased antiques for $88,900 and paid carriage of $273.
July 5   John purchases antiques for $7,560 and paid carriage of $51.
July 14   John paid Henry $40,000.
July 20   Henry sold some antiques for $73,400 and sent a cheque of $30,000 to John.
July 24   Unsold inventory was taken over by Henry at a valuation of $26,000.
July 31   The amounts due to each party was paid and the joint venture was dissolved.

Required:
1. **A statement to show the profit or loss of the joint venture.**
2. **The accounts for the joint venture in the books of Henry and John.**

Exercise 10.3

Viola and Innis and Helen entered into a joint venture to share profits and losses in the ration of 7:3:2. They have no joint banking account or a separate set of books. All parties agreed to take an active part in the business, each recording their own transactions. The transactions connected with the venture were:

20x9

Jun 8   Viola rented land at a cost of $156.
Jun 10   Innis supplied seeds at a valuation of $48.
Jun 17   Viola employed labour for planting paying cash wages of $105.
Jun 19   Innis charged motor expenses $17.
Jun 30   Viola employed labour for fertilising $36.
Jul 21 Viola paid the following expenses: Sundries $10, Labour $18, Fertiliser $29.
Aug 17   Helen employed labour for lifting carrots $73.
Aug 30   Helen paid selling expenses $39.
Aug 31   Helen received cash from sales $987.
Aug 31   Outstanding balances between the parties were settled by cheque.

Required:
a **Show the joint venture accounts in the books of Viola, Innis and Helen.**
b **Show how profit on the venture was calculated.**

Exercise 10.4

Greaves and Hurst participated in a joint venture sharing profits and losses in the ratio 2:1.
Greaves provided goods valued at $15 000 and incurred costs of $900.   Hurst provided goods
valued at $10 000 and incurred costs of $800.
Greaves sold all of the goods for $35 000.
It was agreed that a commission of 10% of the sales value would be paid to the person making
the sale.
The joint venture was then dissolved.

REQUIRED

(a) Explain two benefits to Greaves and Hurst of forming a joint venture.

(b) Calculate the share of profit made by Greaves and Hurst from the joint venture.

Additional information

A separate set of books of account are maintained to record the transactions of the joint venture.
Greaves and Hurst kept their own transactions with the joint venture in their own books.

REQUIRED

(c) Prepare the following ledger accounts:

(i) Greaves account with the joint venture

(ii) Hurst account with the joint venture

Additional information

Following the closure of the joint venture, Greaves and Hurst have received more orders and are
considering forming a partnership.

REQUIRED

**(d) Advise Greaves and Hurst whether or not they should form a partnership. Justify your
answer by discussing advantages and disadvantages of forming the partnership
(UCLES, 2017, AS/A Level Accounting, Syllabus 9706/33, May/June)**

ACCOUNTING FOR CONSIGNMENT ACCOUNTS

Q. What is a consignment account?

Ans. A consignment account is an Income Statement for one consignment.

Q. What does the consignee's account show?

Ans. The consignee's account is used to show the double entry for items concerning him/her.
All of these details are contained in the Account Sales that was sent by the consignee to the
consignor after selling the goods.

Q. Where do the transactions take place?

The transactions relating to the consignment in total take place both at the place of the consignor
as well as that of the consignee. Transactions relating to sending goods and the related aspects
happen at the place of the consignor and the transactions relating to the sale of the goods happen
at the place of the consignee.

Q. Who needs to have all the information regarding transactions taking place?

Ans. The consignor is the risk bearer of the business. Therefore, the consignor is the person who
has to make decisions about the different aspects of the business. She needs to know everything
about the transactions that take place at the consignor's and consignee's place.
The consignee being just an agent, would only be interested in the information relating to those
transactions concerning what she has to receive or give the consignor. Most of these transactions
will take place at the consignee's place.

Q. How does the consignor know about the transactions at the consignee's place?

Ans. Information is passed by the consignee to the consignor in the form of a statement called
the 'Account Sales Statement'.

Q. What is meant by the term: Account Sales?

Ans. An 'account sales' is a statement of affairs relating to the consignment. This is a statement prepared and sent by the consignee to the consignor to keep him informed of the transactions of the business. It is a periodic statement i.e. it is made for a certain period with a starting date and an ending date. The details in the account sales form a basis for accounting for the transactions at the consignees end.

√*Tip: If the account sales is not given in an examination question, prepare one.*

Q. How is a consignment different from a sale?
Ans. The table below outlines the difference between a consignment and a sale:

BASIS OF DIFFERENCE	CONSIGNMENT	SALE
Expenses	All expenses are ultimately borne by the consignor.	Expenses after the sale are borne by the buyer unless otherwise agreed upon.
Ownership	The ownership remains with the principal (the consignor).	The ownership passes to the buyer.
Relationship	The relationship between the consignor and consignee is that of principal and agent which will continue until terminated.	The relationship between buyer and seller terminates as soon the goods are delivered and payment made.
Returns	Goods may be returned at any time.	The buyer cannot return the goods unless otherwise agreed upon.
Payment	Payment is only due when goods are sold.	Payment is due immediately, unless otherwise agreed upon.
Account sale	An account sale is prepared	An account sale is not needed.

Exhibit: Account Sales for sales made on consignment for the period ...... to ...

Gross Sale proceeds:	$	$	$
Cash sales			
1.	XX		
2.	XX	XXX	
Credit Sales:			
1.	XX		
2.	XX	XXX	
Total sales proceeds			XXXX
Other receipts (Note 1)			
1.	XX		
2.	XX	XXX	
Total Receipts			XXXX
Less: Amounts to be deducted:			
Advances sent (Note 2)			
1.	XX		
2.	XX		XXX
Expenses paid to be reimbursed (Note 3):			
1.	XX		
2.	XX		XXX
Commissions receivable (Note 3):			
1.	XX		

2.	<u>xx</u>	<u>xxx</u>
Total Deductions		(xxx)
Gross Amount Due		xxx
Less: Irrecoverable debts		
(Consignor's responsibility (Note 4)		(xx)
Net amount due		xxx
Less: Amounts still to be collected (Note 5)		(xx)
<u>Cash due</u>		xxx
Less: Amounts sent (along with a/c sales)		(xx)
Net cash due		(xxx)

NOTES:

1. **<u>Other receipts:</u>** The amount to be paid by the consignee may include the amounts received on account of sale of abnormal loss stocks, insurance realisations and sale of salvaged stock.
2. **<u>Advances sent:</u>** The consignee may have sent advances to the consignee at the time when goods were consigned. These advances could have been in the form of cash, cheques, bills (Bills receivable to the consignor or bills payable to the consignee), etc.
3. **<u>Expenses paid to be reimbursed:</u>** Unless there is an agreement to the contrary, the consignor has to bear all the expenses of the consignment. Therefore if, during the course of conducting the business, the consignee incurs expenses, they will be reimbursed subsequently by the consignor.
4. **<u>Commissions Receivable:</u>** The consignee may be entitled to one or more types of commissions. All these are collected from the proceeds of sales.
5. **<u>Irrecoverable Debts:</u>** Where the irrecoverable debts are to be borne by the consignor, the sale proceeds representing the sales made to the consignment debtors who did not pay up would become unrealisable. Therefore they are deducted. If the consignee has agreed to bear the irrecoverable debt (in case where he is being given del-credere commission) such a deduction cannot be made.
6. **<u>Amounts still to be collected:</u>** The amount due to be received by the consignor would be the amount left over after setting off the advances, commissions and expenses to be reimbursed from the total receipts. The total receipts includes both cash receipts as well as collections in relation to credit sales. The net amount due to be sent to the consignor may not be available with the consignee in cash due to credit sales and this can be assessed from the balance in the consignment debtors account. The consignee will be able to send cash to the consignor only after he receives it. Therefore, the cash due can be arrived at by deducting the amount of cash that has not yet been collected. The consignee is obliged to pay up this amount to the consignor and if at all he sends only a part of it, the remaining can be identified as cash due.

Exhibit

$5,600 worth of goods were consigned by X Traders Ltd to Jisu Retailers. X traders paid carriage of $60. Jisu Retailers, the consignee, sends an account sales when all the goods were sold. It showed:

Sales of $ 7,000

Import duty $45

Distribution expenses $25

Jisu Retailers paid the balance owing to X Traders Ltd.

Required:

A. In X Traders' books:

1. **Consignment to Jisu Retailers' account**

2. Goods sent on consignment account
3. Excerpt of the cash book that reflect the transactions above
4. Jisu Retailers' account.

B. In Jisu Retailers' books:

1. Account sales
2. X Traders' Accounts
3. Excerpt of the cash book that reflect the transactions
4. Excerpt of Jisu Retailers' Income Statement to reflect the transactions.

Solution:

A1.

Consignment to Jisu Retailers' A/c

	$		$
Goods sent on consignment	5,600	Sales	7,000
Carriage	60		
Jisu Retailers: Import duty	45		
Distribution expenses	25		
Commission	350		
Profit on consignment	920		
	7,000		7,000

A2.

Goods sent on consignment

	$		$
		Consignment to Jisu Retailers	5,600

A3.

Cash book

	$		$
Jisu Retailers (consignee)	7,000	Consignment to Jisu Retailers: carriage	60

A4.

Jisu Retailers' Account

	$		$
Consignment sales	7,000	Consignment:	
		Import duty	45
		Distribution expenses	25
		Commission	350
		Bank	6,580
	7,000		7,000

B1. **Account Sales for sales made on consignment for the period.......**

Jisu Retailers

Date

To: X Traders

	$	$
Sale of goods received on consignment		7,000
Less Charges:		
Import duty	45	
Distribution expenses	25	
Commission	350	420
Cheque payment		6,580

In Jisu Retailers' books: **X Traders a/c**

	$		$
Bank:		Bank: Sales	7,000
Import duty	45		
Distribution expenses	25		
Commission transferred to			
income statement	350		
Bank	6,580		
	7,000		7,000

Cash book (extract)

	$		$
X Traders: Sales	7,000	X Traders: Import duty	45
		Distribution expenses	25
		To settle account	6,580

Income Statement (extract)

	$
Gross profit	xxx
Add income: Commission received on consignment from X Traders	350

Exercise 10.4

$10,000 worth of goods were consigned by Abigail & Daughters Ltd to Dong Yu Retailers.
Expenses of $400 were incurred on the consignment.
Required:
Pass journal entries to record the transactions in the Consignor's books

Exercise 10.5

$10,700 worth of goods were consigned by Penny Pinchers Ltd to Magnanimous Retailers.
Penny Pinchers paid carriage of $70. The consignee sent an account sales when all the goods
were sold. It showed:
Sales of $ 17,000
Import duty $105
Distribution expenses $92
Magnanimous Retailers paid the balance owing to Penny Pinchers Ltd.
 Required:
A. In Penny Pinchers' books:
> 1. **Consignment to Magnanimous Retailers' account**
> 2. **Goods sent on consignment account**
> 3. **Excerpt of the cash book that reflect the transactions above**
> 4. **Magnanimous Retailers' account.**
B. In Magnanimous Retailers' books:
> 1. **Account sales**
> 2. **Penny Pinchers' Accounts**
> 3. **Excerpt of the cash book that reflect the transactions**

Q. How is an irrecoverable debt treated?
Ans. In the absence of a del-credere commission agreement, the burden of the irrecoverable
debt is borne by the consignor, not the consignee. Hence, the amount is not to be paid by the

consignee. However, if there is a del-credere commission agreement, the money for the debt will be paid by the consignee, even though he has not collected it.

Q. What is meant by the term: incomplete consignments?
Ans. If the goods are consigned in the middle of the financial year and the final sales are not made by the end of that financial year, then an incomplete consignment is generated at the date of the balance sheet.

Q. What is the accounting treatment for incomplete consignments?
Ans. In the case of an incomplete consignment at the balance sheet date, the unsold inventory should be valued and carried down to the following period. This inventory will appear in the balance sheet of the consignor as a current asset.

Exhibit
Gaby consigns 12 cases of wine costing $300 per case to Naby on 1 June 20x7 and pays $10 per case for carriage.
Gaby receives an interim account sales statement with a cheque payment from Naby on 29th December, 20x7. It contains the following information:
   1. Naby has sold 8 cases of goods for $400 each.
   2. Naby has paid $140 for landing charges and import duties.
   3. Naby has paid selling and distribution costs of $50 in respect of the 8 cases sold.
   4. Naby deducted a commission of $400 for the 8 cases sold.
   5. Naby encloses a cheque for the remaining amount due to Gaby.
Gaby's financial year ends on 31 December and Gaby wishes to balance off his consignment account at 31 December 20x7. He wishes to transfer the profit to date to his income statement.
Required:
In Gaby's books:
   1. **The consignment to Naby's a/c**
   2. **Naby's a/c**
   3. **Profit on consignment transferred to the Income statement**
   4. **Value of inventory shown in the balance sheet.**
Solution:

1.   Consignment to Naby's a/c

20x7		$	20x7		$
June 1	Goods on consignment	3,600	Dec 29	Naby: sale of part consignment	3,200
June 1	Bank: carriage	120	Dec 31	Value of unsold inventory c/d	*1,080
Dec 29	Naby:				
	Landing charges &				
	import duty	140			
	Selling expenses	50			
	Commission	200			
Dec 31	Profit on consignment				
	to income statement	160			
		4,280			4,280

20x8
Jan 1   Value of unsold inventory b/d 1,080

Note1:* Value of unsold inventory at 31 Dec 20x7:

	$	$
Goods: 4 cases x $300 each		1,200
Add: Proportion of expenses for the 4 unsold cases:		
Carriage $10 x4	40	
Landing charges and import duties 4/12x240	80	120
		1080

Note 2: There are no selling expenses or commission added for the 4 unsold cases as these expenses were incurred for the cases sold.

2.   **Naby's a/c**

20x7		$	20x7		$
Dec 29	Consignment: sales	3,200	Dec 29	Consignment expenses:	
				Landing charges	140
				Selling expenses	50
				Commission	200
				Bank	2,810
		3,200			3,200

3. The profit on consignment transferred to the Income Statement is $160.
4. The value of inventory shown in the balance sheet is $1080.

Exercise 10.6

ABC Ltd. consigns 10 cases of wine costing $450 per case to XYZ Ltd. on 1 July 20x0 and pays $15 per case for carriage.

ABC Ltd. receives an interim account sales statement with a cheque payment from XYZ Ltd on 28th December, 20x0. It contains the following information:

6. XYZ Ltd. has sold 6 cases of goods for $560 each.
7. XYZ Ltd. has paid $100 for landing charges and import duties.
8. XYZ Ltd. has paid selling and distribution costs of $100 in respect of the 6 cases sold.
9. XYZ Ltd. deducted a commission of $300 for the 6 cases sold.
10. XYZ Ltd. encloses a cheque for the remaining amount due to ABC Ltd.

ABC Ltd.'s financial year ends on 31 December and the consignment account is balanced off at 31 December 20x0. The profit is transferred to the income statement.

Required:

In ABC Ltd.'s books:

a. The consignment to XYZ Ltd.s a/c
b. XYZ Ltd.'s a/c
c. Profit on consignment transferred to the Income statement
d. Value of inventory shown in the balance sheet.

Q. When is the consignment account closed?
Ans. When all the goods on consignment are sold, the consignment account can be closed. This is done by transferring the final profit or loss, found in the final account sales from the consignee, to the consignor's income statement.

Exhibit:
Taking the previous exhibit into account, the following details were obtained from the final account sales sent by Naby dated 31 May 20x7:
a. The final 4 cases were sold for $410 each.
b. Selling costs for these 4 cases amounted to $50.
c. Commission was deducted @5%.
d. A cheque payment was made by Naby to Gaby for the amount due.

Required:
In Gaby's books draw up:
1. A consignment to Naby's account.
Solution:

Consignment to Naby;s a/c

20x7		$	20x7		$
Jan 1	Value of unsold inventory b/d	1080	May 31	Naby: Sale of remaining cases	1,640
May 31	Naby:				
	Selling costs	50			
	Commission	82			
May 31	Profit to income statement	428			
		1,640			1,640

TEST YOURSELF

10.1. Multiple choice questions:

i. Clark Corporation invested $100,000 in a real estate corporate joint venture on January 2, 2002. During 2002, Clark received $9,500 from the joint venture, and its share of joint venture net income (after depreciation) was $12,000. The depreciation expense applicable to Clark's share of net income was $4,000. Clark values its joint-venture investment in its December 31, 2002, statement of financial position (under the equity method of accounting) at:
  A. $116,000   B. $112,000   C. $102,500   D. $100,000

ii. A temporary arrangement where two or more businesses pooled their economic resources together to attain a specific task is called
A. Partnership
B. Economic entity
C. Merger
D. Joint Venture

iii.The accounting entries to be made in the consignor's books upon despatch of the consignment to the consignee are:
A. Dr. Consignment to Consignee's account; Cr. Consignee's personal account with the selling price of the Consignment.
B. Dr. Consignment to Consignee's account; Cr. Sales account with the selling price of the Consignment
C. Dr. Consignment to Consignee's account; Cr. Consignment outwards account with the cost price of the Consignment
D. Dr. Debtors account and Cr. Sales account with the cost price of the Consignment

iv. The consignee becomes a debtor of the consignor when
   A. the goods are dispatched
   B. the goods are received
   C. the goods are sold
   D. None of these

v. An account sales is a statement which shows the details about the
   A. goods received   B. goods sold   C. goods lying unsold D. None of these

10.2. Y Limited is based in Mauritius and has recently sent a consignment of goods to Mahood who lives in Egypt. They agreed the following terms:
1. Mahood has to make an advance payment before the goods are delivered to him.
2. Mahood is entitled to a commission of 5% on all sales made by him. The commission is calculated on the sales value after the deductions of the commission.
The following transactions took place during the year ended 31 December 2017.

Y Limited:

- sent 1000 units to Mahood and invoiced him at $175 each
- paid freight of $15 400 and insurance of $3200.

Mahood:

- made an advance payment of $55 000 to Y Limited
- made cash sales of 480 units at $257.50 each
- made credit sales of 320 units at $270 each
- paid the following:

	$
import duty	1600
advertising	9700
carriage inwards	2800
carriage outwards	3300

All customers who bought on credit from Mahood settled their accounts in full at 31 December 2017 except a customer who bought 16 units. It was confirmed that nothing will be recovered from this customer.

At the year-end 60 units with minor faults were discovered by Mahood. Their net realisable value was $150 each.

Mahood paid the balance owing to Y Limited by cheque.

Answer the following questions in the Question Paper. Questions are printed here for reference only.

(a) **Calculate the cost per unit to be used when valuing inventory.**

(b) **Prepare the consignment account in the books of Y Limited for the year ended   31 December 2017.**

(c) **Prepare Mahood's account in the books of Y Limited for the year ended 31 December 2017.**

Additional information:

The directors of Y Limited are thinking of opening a branch overseas to sell its goods rather than having a consignment agreement with Mahood.

(d) **Suggest whether Y Limited should continue consigning goods to Mahood or open a branch overseas. Justify your answer.**

(UCLES, 2018, AS/A Level Accounting, Syllabus 9706/32, May/June)

CHAPTER 11
AUDITING AND STEWARDSHIP OF LIMITED COMPANIES

Q1. What is meant by the term: auditing?

Ans. Auditing refers to a systematic and independent examination of books, accounts, documents and vouchers of an organization to ascertain how far the financial statements present a true and fair view of the concern. It also attempts to ensure that the books of accounts are properly maintained by the concern as required by law and accounting standards applicable. The auditor then gives a professional opinion about how much reliance users can place on the audit topic at hand.

Q. Who is an external auditor?

Ans. External auditors are independent accounting or auditing firms hired by companies that are subject to an audit. External auditors express their own opinions on whether the financial statements of the company in question are free of material misstatements (these could be due to fraud, error or otherwise). They will have to make an attempt to comprehend the business's environment, both internal and external. A business's internal environmental factors could include management's leadership styles, their ethical values, risk management, governance process, control systems, organisational policies and objectives. The external factors could include industry practices, corporate rules, IAS guidelines etc.

Q. Who is an internal auditor?

Ans. The Institute of Internal Auditors has defined internal auditing as follows: "Internal auditing is an independent, objective assurance and consulting activity designed to add value and improve an organization's operations. It helps an organization accomplish its objectives by bringing a systematic, disciplined approach to evaluate and improve the effectiveness of risk management, control, and governance processes". It is a function that, although operating independently from other departments and reporting directly to the audit committee, resides within an organisation (i.e. the auditors are company employees). It is responsible for performing audits (both financial and non-financial) within a wide range of areas in a business, as directed by the annual audit plan. Internal audit looks at key risks facing the business and what is being done to manage those risks effectively in order to help the organisation achieve its objectives.

Q. What does an auditor do?

Ans. The auditor gathers appropriate and sufficient evidence through observation, testing, comparing and finally, confirming. The auditor then forms an opinion of whether the financial statements are free of material misstatement, due to fraud or error. Some of the more important auditing procedures include:

- Inquiring of management and others to gain an understanding of the organization itself, its operations, financial reporting, and known fraud or error.
- Evaluating and understanding the internal control system.
- Performing analytical procedures on expected or unexpected variances in account balances or classes of transactions.
- Testing documentation supporting account balances or classes of transactions.

- Observing the physical inventory count.
- Confirming accounts receivable and other accounts with a third party.
- Making sure that there is sufficient and competent evidential matter. Good evidence will be relevant and reliable. For the evidence to be relevant, it should directly relate to the facts that are being substantiated. Reliable evidence is that which can be depended upon to steer one in the right direction.
- Test management assertions regarding occurrence of transaction, completeness (transactions are recorded in their entirety), transactions are recorded in the correct account and for the correct period. The auditor also confirms that the business owns or holds the rights to assets and is indeed responsible for the liabilities shown in the statement of financial position.
- At the completion of the audit, the auditor may also offer objective advice for improving financial reporting and internal controls to maximize a company's performance and efficiency.
- The results of the audit will typically be documented within an audit report, with a 'close out' meeting held with all of the relevant stakeholders to discuss the findings and agree on the details and timing of any required remediation activities.

Q. What do auditors not do?
Ans. Auditors do not:
- Take responsibility for the financial statements on which they form an opinion. The responsibility for financial statement presentation lies squarely in the hands of the company being audited.
- Authorize or execute transactions on behalf of a business.
- Prepare or make changes to source documents.
- Close books of accounts.
- Prepare financial statements.
- Assume custody of business assets, including maintenance of bank accounts.
- Establish or maintain internal controls.
- Determine the value of a business's assets and liabilities.
- Supervise business employees performing normal day-to-day activities.
- Report to the board of directors on behalf of management.
- Serve as a business's stock agent.
- Serve as a business's general counsel.
- Sign payroll tax returns on behalf of a business.
- Approve of a vendor's invoices for payment.
- Design a Business's financial management system.
- Make modifications to the code underlying a business's management system.
- Hire or terminate employees

In short, the auditor may not assume the role and duties of management.

Q. What are the responsibilities of management that are fundamental to the conducting of an audit?
Ans. 1. Management is required to prepare and present the financial statements in accordance with an applicable financial reporting framework. They should:
- Design financial statements
- Implement and maintain internal controls to ensure that that preparation and presentation of financial statements are free from material error or fraud

2. Management is required to provide the auditor with the following information:

- All records, documentation and other matters relevant to the preparation and presentation of the financial statements
- Any additional information the auditor may request from management.
- Unrestricted access to those within the organization if the auditor determines it necessary to obtain audit evidence objectively.

Q. Who manages the running of a limited company?
Ans. A limited company is owned by its shareholders, but is managed by its board of directors.

Q. How are the board of directors appointed?
Ans. The board of directors are usually appointed by the shareholders at the AGM. However, they may also be appointed by other directors if permitted to do so by the Company's articles of association.

Q. What are the board of directors primarily responsible for?
Ans. The board of directors are primarily responsible for:
- determining the company's strategic objectives and policies;
- monitoring progress towards achieving the objectives and policies;
- appointing senior management;
- accounting for the company's activities to the shareholders.

Q. What role do the board of directors play in a limited company?
Ans. The role of the board of directors include the following:
ESTABLISH VISION, MISSION AND VALUES
- Determine the company's vision and mission to guide and set the pace for its current operations and future development.
- Determine the values to be promoted throughout the company.
- Determine and review company goals.
- Determine company policies

SET STRATEGY AND STRUCTURE
- Review and evaluate present and future opportunities, threats and risks in the external environment and current and future strengths, weaknesses and risks relating to the company.
- Determine strategic options, select those to be pursued, and decide the means to implement and support them.
- Determine the business strategies and plans that underpin the corporate strategy.
- Ensure that the company's organisational structure and capability are appropriate for implementing the chosen strategies.

DELEGATE TO MANAGEMENT
- Delegate authority to management, and monitor and evaluate the implementation of policies, strategies and business plans.
- Determine monitoring criteria to be used by the board.
- Ensure that internal controls are effective.
- Communicate with senior management

EXERCISE ACCOUNTABILITY TO SHAREHOLDERS AND BE RESPONSIBLE TO RELEVANT STAKEHOLDERS
- Ensure that communications both to and from shareholders and relevant stakeholders are effective.
- Understand and take into account the interests of shareholders and relevant stakeholders.
- Monitor relations with shareholders and relevant stakeholders by gathering and evaluation of appropriate information.

- Promote the goodwill and support of shareholders and relevant stakeholders.

Q. What are the duties of the board of directors as outlined by the Companies Act of 2006?

Ans. The duties as outlined by the Companies Act 2006 are:

1. The directors have a duty to act in accordance with the company's constitution and only exercise their powers for the purpose for which they are conferred.
2. They should promote the success of the company by:
   a. Thinking about the likely long term consequences of any decisions they make;
   b. Keeping the company's employees in mind;
   c. Fostering relationships with suppliers, customers and others;
   d. Maintaining a reputation for high standards of business conduct;
   e. Acting fairly and in good faith and
   f. Keeping the interests of creditors in mind.
3. The directors have a duty to exercise independent judgment in a way that is authorised by the company's constitution.
4. A director must exercise reasonable care, skill and diligence that would be expected of a director of a company.
5. The director of a company should avoid a situation in which he or she has, or can have, a direct or indirect interest that conflicts with the interests of the company. This applies in particular to the exploitation of any property, information or opportunity.
6. A director must not accept a benefit from a third party conferred by reason his being a director or his doing (or not doing) anything as a director.
7. If a director of a company is in any way, directly or indirectly, interested in a proposed transaction or arrangement with the company, he must declare the nature and extent of that interest to the other directors.

Q. List three duties that directors have to carry out as stewards of the company.

Ans. The directors should:
- Prepare a director's report for each financial year.
- Recommend and propose ordinary dividend for the purpose of approval by shareholders at the Annual General Meeting (AGM). They have to ensure that these dividends are paid out of distributable profits.
- Call an AGM.

Q. What is meant by the term 'true and fair view of financial statements'?

Ans. A true and fair view means that the financial statements should be free from material misstatements and faithfully represent the financial performance and position of the business.

True suggests that the financial statements are factually correct and have been prepared according to applicable reporting framework such as the IAS and they do not contain any material misstatements that may mislead the users. Misstatements may result from material errors or omissions of transactions & balances in the financial statements.

Fair implies that the financial statements present the information faithfully without any element of bias and they reflect the economic substance of transactions rather than just their legal form.

Section 393 of the Companies Act 2006 requires that the directors of a company must not approve accounts unless they are satisfied they give a true and fair view. The true and fair requirement has been fundamental to accounting in the UK for many years. It is a requirement of both UK and EU law.

Q. What precautions should be taken to ensure that the financial statements present a true and fair view?

Ans. Preparers of financial statements, directors and auditors should

- stand back and ensure that the accounts as a whole do give a true and fair view;
- use the true and fair override where compliance with the standards does not result in the presentation of a true and fair view;
- provide additional disclosures when compliance with an accounting standard is insufficient to present a true and fair view; and
- ensure that the consideration they give to these matters is evident in their deliberations and documentation.

Q. Discuss the importance of professional judgement with respect to ensuring that the financial statements present a true and fair view of the financial position and performance of a business entity.

Ans. The preparation of financial statements cannot be reduced to a mechanistic following of the relevant accounting standards. The use of excessive prudence, for example, resulting in the deliberate understatement of assets or overstatement of liabilities, does not lead to useful information. For example, hidden reserves or excessive provisions, which may be released later to boost profit, are not allowed. Objective professional judgement must be applied to ensure that financial statements give a true and fair view. This professional judgement is all important. It applies at all stages of preparation of the accounts, for example:

- Where there is a choice of accounting policies allowed under accounting standards, ensuring that those selected are appropriate, taking into account the circumstances of the company;
- When establishing accounting policies for items not specifically covered by accounting standards or where they are ambiguous. In such circumstances the approach in IAS 8 to consider standards dealing with similar items may be appropriate;
- Making judgements, for example about valuation, aimed at giving a true and fair view;
- Not using detailed accounting rules as an excuse for poor accounting;
- Considering what is and what is not material;
- Giving appropriate disclosures even where not specifically required by accounting standards; and
- Ensuring that significant information is not obscured by immaterial or irrelevant disclosures.

Q. How relevant is IAS 8 in ensuring that financial statements present a true and fair view?

Ans. IAS 8 states that for information to be reliable, it must be reported in accordance with economic substance, rather than strictly in adherence to its legal form. Indeed if material transactions are not accounted for in accordance with their substance it is doubtful whether the accounts present a true and fair view.

Q. What is the essence of accounting standards with respect to a true and fair view?

Ans. A true and fair is not something that is merely a separate add-on to accounting standards. Rather the whole essence of standards is to provide for recognition, measurement, presentation and disclosure for specific aspects of financial reporting in a way that reflects economic reality and hence that provides a true and fair view.

Q. What does IAS 1 have to say about a true and fair view of financial statements?

Ans. The statement in IAS 1 that departures from the standards should only be necessary in "extremely rare circumstances does not release directors from their legal obligation to only approve particular accounts if they are satisfied that they give a true and fair view and directors should not rely on it to avoid making appropriate judgements. Disagreement with a particular standard does not, on its own, provide grounds for departing from it.

Q. When is additional disclosure required?

Ans. Where the accounting standards clearly address an issue, but the requirements are insufficient to fully explain the issue, the solution is normally additional disclosure. For example, some companies have disclosed alternative measures, such as adjusted Earnings per Share measures, where such disclosures were considered necessary to provide a more complete picture of their performance. However, where directors and auditors do not believe that following a particular accounting policy will give a true and fair view they are legally required to adopt a more appropriate policy, even if this requires a departure from a particular standard. As IAS 1 states, an entity cannot rectify inappropriate accounting policies by disclosure.

Q. State some drawbacks of the true and fair view principle.

Ans. As the principle takes into consideration the fact that a business's or organization's management will declare financial statements based on management's own "judgements and estimates", hence, a true and fair view is a relative truth in relation to the business's larger picture and also depends on whether or not the business or organization is also complying with other accounting principles.

Moreover, businesses tend to interpret the concept according to specific historical, social, cultural, political and economic roots and environments. Thus the concept has been described by some as a formula for international disharmony and as "an exercise in deharmonization".

Q. State an important advantage of the true and fair view principle.

Ans. This principle helps ensure that accounts continue to demonstrate the high quality that users of financial statements have come to expect. Hence, stakeholders such as shareholders, employees, creditors, potential investors and the public, to name a few, can be assured that the financial statements are free from material misstatements and faithfully represent the financial performance and position of the business.

Q. How does New Zealand use the true and fair view practice?

Ans. The 'true and fair view' principle is one of two competing but not mutually exclusive legal standards for financial reporting quality that have been subject to debate on their meaning, use and importance. The other is 'present fairly in conformity with generally accepted accounting principles'. While the former is closely identified with judgement and is used in New Zealand, the latter is the standard for United States (US) financial reporting and tends to be more rule based.

Following a diverging path from UK influences, the Institute of Chartered Accountants in New Zealand (ICANZ) also uses the terms 'fairly reflect' and 'fair presentation' and states that the terms are equivalent. This may signal a move away from 'true and fair view' towards the US requirement for 'fair presentation'.

CHAPTER 12
STATEMENTS OF CASH FLOW

Q. What is meant by the term 'cash flow'?
Ans. It is the net amount of cash and cash equivalents moving into and out of the business. It is used to assess how liquid a business is and its ability to remain solvent.

Q. Define:
a. Cash inflow
b. Cash outflow
c. Positive cash flow
d. Negative cash flow
e. A cash flow statement
f. Cash and cash equivalents

Ans. a. Cash inflow refers to a business' income or sources of money. These could include payment in cash by debtors, the sale of an asset tec.
b. Cash outflow refers to a business' expenses paid in cash. Examples are: cash payments to creditors, rent paid in cash etc.
c. When a business generates a larger cash inflow than a cash outflow, they have a positive cash flow. Such a net positive cash flow indicate that a business' liquid assets are increasing thus enabling it to settle debts, pay dividends to shareholders, pay expenses such as rent, plough money back into the business etc.
d. When a business' cash outflows are greater than its inflows, the result is a negative cash flow. This is an indication that the liquid assets of a business are decreasing and the business could be heading into insolvency.
e. A cash flow statement in financial accounting shows how changes in income and the balance sheet accounts affect cash and cash equivalents. The statement breaks the analysis down to operating activities, investing activities and financing activities. The statement shows changes in cash and cash equivalents rather than working capital. The aim of a statement of cash flow is therefore to assist its users to:

- To assess the reasons for the differences between reported and related cash flows.
- To gauge the business' ability to generate future positive cash flows
- To assess the quality of a business' income and how liquid it is. This an indicate whether the business is positioned to remain solvent.
- To assess the effect of major transactions during the year on its finances.
- To assess the ability of the business to meet its obligations to pay dividends, service loans etc.

f. Cash and cash equivalents comprise cash on hand, demand deposits, together with short-term, highly liquid investments that are readily convertible to a known amount of cash, and that are subject to an insignificant risk of changes in value. Investments normally meet the definition of a cash equivalent when it has a maturity of three months or less from the date of acquisition. Bank overdrafts, repayable on demand are also included as a component of cash and cash equivalents.

Q. Why is 'profit' as stated in a balance sheet not enough for a shareholder to ascertain the health of a company?

Ans. 'Profit' does not always give a useful or meaningful picture of a company's operations. Shareholders reading a company's financial statements might even be misled by the profit figure reported therein. For instance, a shareholder might be led to believe that if the company makes a profit after tax of say $400,000, then this is the amount it can afford to pay out as dividend. However, the company should have sufficient cash available not only to pay a dividend, but also to stay in business. Its survival does not solely depend on profits, but on its ability to pay its debts when they fall due. These could include items listed in the Income statement such as purchases, wages etc. However, it could also include payments for capital items bought or the repayment of loan capital such as redemption of debentures.

Q. What does IAS 7 stipulate?

Ans. The objective of IAS 7 is to require the presentation of information about the historical changes in cash and cash equivalents of an entity by means of a statement of cash flows, which classifies cash flows during the period according to operating, investing and financing activities.

Q. Define:
a. Operating activities
b. Investing activities
c. Financing activities

Ans. a. Operating activities are the main revenue-producing activities. They would therefore include cash received from customers, cash paid to suppliers etc.
b. Investing activities are the acquisition and disposal of long-term assets and other investments that are not considered to be cash equivalents.
c. Financing activities are those that alter the equity capital and borrowing structure of the entity.

Q. How are 'interest and dividends received' classified?

Ans. Interest and dividends received and paid may be classified as operating, investing or financing cash flows provided that they are classified consistently from period to period.

Q. What is the difference between the direct and indirect method of calculating cash from operating activities?

Ans. The direct method shows each major class of gross cash receipts and payments. This is how it would appear:

	$'000
Cash receipts from customers	xxx
Cash paid to suppliers	(xx)
Cash paid to employees	(xx)
Cash paid for other operating expenses	(xx)
Interest paid	(x)
Income taxes paid	(xx)
Net cash from operating activities	**xxx**

The indirect method adjusts accrual basis profit or loss for the year, for the effects of non-cash transactions. This is how it would appear:

	$'000
Profit before interest and tax	xxxx
Add back depreciation	xxx
Add back impairment of assets	xx
Decrease in trade receivables	xx
Decrease in inventories	xx
Increase in trade payables	xx
Net cash from operating activities	**xxx**

Q. What are the cash inflows related to 'Returns on investments and servicing of finance'

Ans. Examples of cash inflows related to 'returns on investments and servicing of finance' would be: interest received, tax refunds, dividends received.

Q. Give examples of cash outflows from 'returns on investments and servicing of finance'.

Ans. Examples are: interest paid, dividends paid, the interest element of finance lease payments.

Q. Explain the term: Financing activities.

Ans. Financing activities result in changes in the size and composition of the equity capital and borrowings of the enterprise.

Financing cash outflows include: repayments of amounts borrowed, the capital element of finance lease rental payments, payments to re-acquire or redeem the entity's shares.

Financing cash inflows include: receipts from issuing shares or other equity instruments, receipts from issuing debentures, loans, notes and bonds.

Exercise 12.1

You are given the following extracts from the financial statements of Holby Ltd for the two years ended:

	30 June 20x1	30 June 20x2
	$	$
Operating profit	47 200	42 460
(after depreciation of	9 600	8 900)
Net current assets:		
Inventory	32 990	30 000
Trade receivables	16 200	14 000
Trade and other payables	10 340	10 000

Calculate:
The operating cash flow for the year ended 30 June 2002

Exercise 12.2

You are given the following information about Abbot Ltd:
Profit for the year $15,000
Depreciation $15,000
Loss on sale of assets $1000

During the year there was a decrease in working capital of $500.
Required:

Calculate the net cash flow generated from operations?

Exhibit:

Draw up a statement of cash flows for the year ended 31 December 20x5 given the following information:

	$'000
Profit for the year	332
Decrease in trade receivables	8
Increase in inventory	5
Increase in trade payables	6
Purchase of non-current assets	200
Issue of ordinary shares	45
Payment of dividends	15
Bank balance at 1 Jan, 20x5	8

Solution:

Statement of cash flows for the year ended 30 June 2016

	$000	$000
Cash from operating activities		
Profit for the year	332	
Decrease in trade receivable	8	
Increase in inventory	(5)	
Increase in trade payable	6	341
Investing activities		
Purchase of non-current assets		(200)
Financing activities		
Issue of ordinary shares	45	
Payment of dividends	(15)	30
Net cash inflow for the year		**171**
Bank balance at the start of the year		8
Bank balance at the end of the year		179

Exercise12.3

The following information has been extracted from a company's statement of cash flows.

	$000
Total cash from operating activities	200
Net cash used by investing activities	(300)
Net cash used by financing activities	(150)
Closing cash and cash equivalents	(50)

Required:

Calculate the opening figure for cash and cash equivalents.

Exercise12.4

Swamp Circus plc provides the following information:

Statements of financial position at

	31 March 2012			31 March 2011		
	$000	$000	$000	$000	$000	$000
Non-current assets						
Intangible:						
Patents			220			180
Tangible:						
Property			2 400			1 700
Equipment			920			610
			3 540			2 490
Current assets						
Inventory		480			509	
Trade receivables		611			569	
Cash and cash equivalents		79			000	
		1 170			1 078	
Current liabilities						
Trade payables	512			501		
Other payables	76			54		
Taxation	220			195		
Cash and cash Equivalents	000	808		71	821	
			362			257
			3 902			2 747
Non-current liabilities						
Debentures			500			400
			3 402			2 347
Equity						
Ordinary share capital			1 500			1 200
Revaluation reserve			700			
General reserve			400			200
Retained earnings			802			947
			3 402			2 347

Income statement for the year ended 31 March 2012

	$000
Profit from operations	636
Finance charges	61
	575
Taxation	220
Profit for the year attributable to equity holders	355

Additional information:
1. During the year the directors transferred $200 000 to the general reserve and paid dividends of $300 000.
2. At 31 March 2011 equipment had cost $905 000 and was shown after the provision of $295 000 depreciation. At 31 March 2012 equipment had cost $1 240 000 and depreciation of $320 000 had been provided.
3. During the year equipment which had cost $172 000 was sold for $90 000. Depreciation of $101 000 had been provided on it.
4. Other payables include $21 000 unpaid interest at 31 March 2012 and $11 000 unpaid interest at 31 March 2011.

5. During the year an issue of both ordinary shares and debentures had taken place, and the property had been re-valued.

REQUIRED
(a) Prepare a statement of changes in equity for the year ended 31 March 2012.
(b) Prepare a statement of cash flows in accordance with the provisions of IAS 7 for the year ended 31 March 2012.
(UCLES, 2012, AS/A Level Accounting, Syllabus 9706/41, May/June)

Exercise 12.5

Harrowgate & Co. issued 10 000 ordinary shares of $10 at a price of $20 each on 1 June 20x7. On 1 July 20x7, the company used $156 000 of the proceeds to repay an 8 % Loan Stock including six months' accrued interest due. The company prepared a cash flow statement just after repayment of the Loan Stock.
Required:
Calculate the amount of net cash inflow that will appear under the heading 'Financing' in the cash flow statement.

Exercise 12.6

Loco Ltd sold plant and machinery during the year ended 31 March 20x7, for $8000. This plant had cost $60 000 and had a book value of $10 000.
An additional $140 000 was spent on new plant and machinery, which was depreciated at the end of the year by 20 %.
Required: In preparing the cash flow statement at the end of the year, how are the above transactions shown under the capital expenditure heading?

Exercise 12.7

Manchi plc are preparing their budgets for the forthcoming year ending 30 September 2014. They provide the following information.

Statements of Financial Position at 30 September

	2013 (actual) $000	2014 (budgeted) $000
Assets		
Non-current assets		
Property plant and equipment	3050	3190
Goodwill	400	450
Investments	300	240
	3750	3880
Current assets		
Inventories	750	790
Trade and other receivables	460	425
Cash and cash equivalents	210	574
	1420	1789
Total assets	5170	5669
Equity		
Ordinary shares	1200	1400
Non-redeemable preference shares	500	500
Revaluation reserve	300	400
Retained earnings	930	834
Total equity	2930	3134

Liabilities

Non-current liabilities		
7% debentures	1000	1300
Current liabilities		
Trade and other payables	960	1075
Current tax liabilities	280	160
	1240	1235
Total liabilities	2240	2535
Total equity and liabilities	5170	5669

Budgeted Statement of Changes in Equity for year ending 30 September 2014

	$000
Retained earnings at 1 October 2013	930
Budgeted profit for year	214
	1144
Dividends payable	(110)
Transfer to share capital (bonus issue)	(200)
Retained earnings at 30 September 2014	834

Additional information

1. The tax charge for the year ending 30 September 2014 has been budgeted as $160 000.
2. Income from investments is budgeted at $40 000.
3. Manchi plc issued additional 7% debentures on 1 October 2013. Interest for the year will be paid on all the issued debentures on 30 September 2014.
4. A bonus issue of 1 new ordinary share for every 6 held is budgeted for 1 April 2014.
5. The following note was extracted from the financial statements at 30 September 2013.

Non-current assets

	Cost	Depreciation	Net book value
	$000	$000	$000
Property plant and equipment:			
Land	1500	–	1500
Buildings	800	250	550
Plant and equipment	1500	600	900
Motor vehicles	150	50	100
Total	3950	900	3050

6. The land is expected to increase in value by $100 000 during the year.
7. Budgeted capital expenditure for the year on buildings is $80 000; plant and equipment $280 000; motor vehicles $30 000 and goodwill $50 000.
8. Budgeted depreciation for the year on buildings is $50 000; plant and equipment $255 000 and motor vehicles $25 000.
9. Plant and equipment with an original cost of $35 000 and depreciation of $15 000 is budgeted to be disposed of for proceeds of $10 000.
10. An impairment review has shown that the carrying value of the investments should be $240 000 at 30 September 2014.

REQUIRED

(a) Calculate the company's budgeted profit from operations for the year ending 30 September 2014.

(b) Prepare a budgeted statement of cash flows for the year ending 30 September 2014 in accordance with IAS 7.

(c) Prepare the property, plant and equipment section of the non-current assets note to the budgeted statement of financial position at 30 September 2014.

(UCLES, 2013, AS/A Level Accounting, Syllabus 9706/41, Oct/Nov)

CHAPTER 13
ANALYSIS AND INTERPRETATION OF FINANCIAL STATEMENTS

Q. Why is it necessary to analyse and interpret accounting statements?
Ans. Analysis and interpretation of Financial Statements help stakeholders to assess the performance of the business. The liquidity, profitability and efficiency of a business can be ascertained by suitable analysis and subsequent interpretation.

Q. Who are the 'stakeholders' of a business and why would they be interested in a firm's performance?
Ans. The stakeholders are the parties who are interested in the firm's performance for one reason or another. They could be:
The owner. The owner of the business would like to know how his/her business is performing in comparison to another similar business or in comparison with targets set or in comparison with previous years.
Prospective investors. They would like to know how well the business is doing now, and its prospects for future profitability, in order to make good investment decisions.
A Bank manager. He/she will have to analyse and interpret accounting statements supplied by a business that has applied for a loan. The future liquidity position of the business will be the guiding factor in the manager granting loans and overdrafts to the business.
Creditors. Creditors, such as suppliers are also interested in a business's liquidity and its credit rating.
Members of a non-profit organisation. The members of a club, for example, will be interested its financial position. They would like to know whether the club has a deficit or a surplus since this will affect the future of the club and consequently the members.

Q. What is the need for ratios?
Ans. Accounting ratios form a basis of common measure so that comparisons become meaningful. It is impossible to compare absolute figures e.g. profits. What is needed is profitability, e.g. profit margins that are expressed in percentages and offer a platform for easy comparison.

Q. How can ratios be used?
Ans. Ratios can be used in the following ways:
- Ratios of a business for the current year can be compared with those of a previous year to ascertain whether there has been an improvement.
- Ratios of a business can be compared with those of another similar business
- Ratios of a business for the current year can be compared with ratios derived from budgets and forecasts made to ascertain whether the targets were in fact achieved and if not, the reason why they were not achieved so that corrective action can be taken.
- A company can also compare its ratios to the industry's average ratios. (Industry ratios might be available from an industry association, library reference desks, and from bankers. Many banks have memberships in Risk Management Association (RMA), an organization that collects and distributes statistics by industry.) A common-size statement of financial position also allows two businesspersons to compare the magnitude of a statement of financial position item without either one revealing the actual dollar amounts.

Q. What are the precautions to be borne in mind when making comparisons between two businesses using ratios?
Ans. The following points should be borne in mind when comparing ratios of two

businesses:

- The accounts may not be those of a typical year.
- The financial years of the two businesses may end on different dates and hence this may affect the ratios, making interpretation difficult.
- The two businesses may be different from each other. It is useless to compare the liquidity of a business selling electrical appliances with one that sells vegetables and fruits.
- The two businesses may be of a different size. There is no point in comparing a large business with a small one.
- The businesses may operate using different accounting policies, for example, one business may be using the straight-line method of depreciation and the other business may be using the reducing balance method.
- There may be differences that affect the items on the Statement of financial position and the profitability of the businesses. For example, one business may own a certain non-current asset and the other business may rent it.

Hence ratios should be used with caution.

Q. What are the limitations of accounting statements?

Ans. Accounting statements have the following limitations:

a. Due to the desire to keep to the money measurement concept, a lot of desirable information is excluded. For example, the following information is not revealed:
   o Whether the firm has good or bad managers.
   o Whether problems with the workforce that would affect the future of the business.
   o An impending law that would cause the firm additional expenditure.
   o Competitors waiting to take over some of the firm's most valuable customers.
   o Whether the firm is able to adapt to changing market conditions.
   o If the location of the business is fast becoming undesirable.

In addition, financial statements have the following limitations:

b. Financial statements contain information about the past and may not be relevant for the future since change is an integral part of any business.
c. Since the historic cost concept is used, inflation is not factored in. This makes the value of non-current assets, for example, useless.
d. Financial statements do not reveal pertinent information such as whether the firm is situated in a good location. If the location is fast becoming undesirable, for example, this would affect the profitability of the firm in the future.

When computing financial ratios and when doing other financial statement analysis always keep in mind that the financial statements reflect the accounting principles. This means assets are generally not reported at their current value. It is also likely that many brand names and unique product lines will not be included among the assets reported on the statement of financial position, even though they may be the most valuable of all the items owned by a company.

Q. Briefly discuss the limitations of a Statement of Financial Position.

Ans. The statement of financial position reports a company's assets, liabilities, and stockholders' equity as of a specific date, such as December 31, 2014, March 31, 2014, etc.

The historic cost principle and the monetary measurement assumption will limit the assets reported on the statement of financial position. Assets will be reported

(1) only if they were acquired in a transaction, and
(2) generally at an amount that is not greater than the asset's cost at the time of the transaction.

This means that a company's creative and effective management team will not be listed as an asset. Similarly, a company's outstanding reputation, its unique product lines, and brand names developed within the company will not be reported on the statement of financial position. Oftentimes, these items are the most valuable of all the things owned by the company. (Brand names purchased from another company will be recorded in the company's accounting records at their cost.)

The matching principle will result in assets such as buildings, equipment, furnishings, fixtures, vehicles, etc. being reported at amounts less than cost. The reason is these assets are depreciated. Depreciation reduces an asset's book value each year and the amount of the reduction is reported as Depreciation Expense on the income statement.

While depreciation is reducing the book value of certain assets over their useful lives, the current value (or fair market value) of these assets may actually be increasing. (It is also possible that the current value of some assets—such as computers—may be decreasing faster than the book value.)

Current assets such as Cash, Accounts Receivable, Inventory, Supplies, Prepaid Insurance, etc. usually have current values that are close to the amounts reported on the statement of financial position.

Current liabilities such as trade Payables (due within one year), Accounts Payable, Wages Payable, Interest Payable, Unearned Revenues, etc. are also likely to have current values that are close to the amounts reported on the statement of financial position.

Long-term liabilities such as other Payables (not due within one year) or Bonds Payable (not maturing within one year) will often have current values that *differ* from the amounts reported on the statement of financial position.

Stockholders' equity is the book value of the company. It is the difference between the reported amount of assets and the reported amount of liabilities. For the reasons mentioned above, the reported amount of stockholders' equity will therefore be different from the current or market value of the company.

By definition the current assets and current liabilities are "turning over" at least once per year. As a result, the reported amounts are likely to be similar to their current value. The long-term assets and long-term liabilities are *not* "turning over" often.

Therefore, the amounts reported for long-term assets and long-term liabilities will likely be different from the current value of those items.

Q. Discuss the limitations of Income Statements.

Ans. Although analysis of financial statement is essential to obtain relevant information for making several decisions and formulating corporate plans and policies, it should be carefully performed as it suffers from a number of the following limitations.

- **It could mislead the user:** The accuracy of financial information largely depends on how accurately financial statements are prepared. If their preparation is wrong, the information obtained from their analysis will also be wrong. This may mislead the user when making decisions.

- **Not useful for planning:** Since financial statements are prepared by using historical financial date, therefore, the information derived from such statements may not be effective in corporate planning, if the previous situation does not prevail.
- **Qualitative aspects:** Financial statement analysis provides only quantitative information about the company's financial affairs. However, it fails to provide qualitative information such as management – labour relations, customers' satisfaction, management skills etc. which are also equally important for decision making.
- **Comparisons not possible:** The financial statements are based on historical data. Therefore comparative analysis of financial statements of different years cannot be performed as inflation distorts the view presented by the statements of different years.
- **Wrong judgement:** Adequate skills and knowledge of the subject matter is necessary to for accurate judgements to be made on the basis of ratio analysis. Similarly, a biased analyst cannot be relied upon to make sound judgements.
- **Relevance and reliability:** Income statements include judgments and estimates, which means that items that might be relevant but cannot be reliably measured are not reported and that some reported figures have a subjective component.
- **Realism:** With respect to accounting methods, one of the limitations of the income statement is that income is reported based on accounting rules and often does not reflect cash changing hands.
- **Fraud:** Income statements can also be limited by fraud, such as earnings management, which occurs when managers use judgment in financial reporting to intentionally alter financial reports to show an artificial increase (or decrease) of revenues, profits, or earnings per share figures

The limitations mentioned above about financial statement analysis make it clear that the analysis is a means to an end and not an end in itself. The users and analysts must understand the limitations before analysing the financial statements of the company

Q. Define the following terms:
a) Capital invested (or capital owned)
b) Capital employed
c) Working capital
Ans. a) Capital Invested is the amount owed by the business to the owner at that date. It is the amount of money or money's worth brought into the business by the owner from his outside interests.
b) **Capital Employed** is the amount of money effectively being used in the business. It is sometimes referred to as Net Assets.
   Capital employed = non-current assets + current assets – current liabilities
   (Or)
   Capital employed = opening balance of owner's capital + profit for the year– drawings + long term liabilities.
c) **Working capital** is the amount available for the day - to - day running of the business.
   Working Capital = Current assets – Current liabilities

Q. Name the different types of ratios used.
Ans. The different types of ratios used are:
a) Profitability ratios
b) Liquidity ratios

Q. Name the profitability ratios.
Ans. The profitability ratios are:

1. Return on capital employed (ROCE)
It shows the net profit earned for every $100 of capital employed. The higher the ROCE, the better since the capital is being more effectively employed.

Return on capital employed = $\frac{\text{Net profit (profit for the year) x 100}}{\text{Capital employed}}$

[Capital Employed = Issued Shares + Reserves + Non-Current Liabilities]

2. Gross profit as a percentage of sales
This is also known as the Gross profit as a percentage of turnover. It shows the Gross profit for every $100 of sales. A higher rate indicates higher profitability.

Gross profit as a percentage of sales (or Gross profit ratio) = $\frac{\text{Gross profit x 100}}{\text{Net sales/Sales revenue}}$

Where Gross profit = Net sales – cost of sales and sales revenue is the income earned from the principle activities of the business.

NOTE: Mark-up = $\frac{\text{Gross profit x 100}}{\text{Cost of sales}}$

3. Profit margin (Net profit as a percentage of sales)
This measures the net profit for every $100 of sales. The higher the rate, the more profitable the business will be. It is an indication of the firm's efficiency, since it reveals how well the firm is able to control its expenses.

Net profit as a percentage of sales (or Net profit margin) = $\frac{\text{Net profit (NPBI) x100}}{\text{Net Sales/Sales revenue}}$

NOTE: NPBI = Net profit before interest (i.e. add back interest)

4. Return on Equity = $\frac{\text{Net Profit after Preference Dividends x100}}{\text{Equity}}$

[Equity = Issued Ordinary Shares + Reserves]

5. Return on Total Assets = $\frac{\text{NPBI x100}}{\text{Total Assets}}$

Total Assets = Non-current assets + current assets

6. Operating expenses to Revenue Ratio = $\frac{\text{Operating expenses x100}}{\text{Revenue}}$

7. Non-Current Asset Turnover = $\frac{\text{Net sales revenue}}{\text{Total Net Book Value of Non-Current Assets}}$

Q. What is the difference between 'profit' and 'profitability'?
Ans. 'Profit' is an absolute figure and as such does not lend itself to comparisons. 'Profitability' is a ratio and can be easily used for comparison purposes. 'Profitability ratios' are more accurate measures of a firm's profitability. For example: a price – cutting policy may reduce the profitability of a firm even though the profit of the firm has increased.

Q. List the factors that can influence the GP Margin.
Ans. The GP Margin can be influenced by internal as well as external factors. The factors that can impact the CP Margin include:
- Level of industry
- Level of competition in the industry
- Extent of product differentiation
- Cost structure of the organisation
- Economies of scale
- Efficiency of operations
- Cost of factors of production
- Market demand
- Product life cycle phases
- Accounting policies

Q. Outline the reasons why the GP Margin could change.

Ans. The GP Margin should be analysed over several periods in the context of the norms of the industry it operates in. A change in the ratio could be attributed to several factors:

1. **Increase in GP Margin & decrease in total gross profit:** This could be due to
   a. an increase in the selling price that does not result in greater sales revenue due to the demand being very price elastic.
   b. a decrease in production costs achieved in the later stages of the product life cycle (e.g. through better manufacturing efficiency) offset by a lower demand.
   c. an increase in competition forcing a decrease in selling price and reduction in market share.
   d. the burden of increasing production costs not being transferred to customers
   e. inefficient production
2. **Increase in GP margin & increase in total gross profit:** This could be due to an increase in the selling price of products whose demand is price inelastic or an increase in sales volume resulting in the decrease of production costs due to economies of scale.

Generally, a higher gross profit margin is desirable as it suggests a greater potential for earning larger profits. Businesses with higher gross profit margins are better equipped against unanticipated increase in the cost of production or competition. Businesses sometimes deliberately lower their GP margin to improve their overall profitability by lowering selling prices with the aim of increasing their market share in industries and market segments that are highly sensitive to price. It is important for such businesses however to operate highly efficiently in order to minimize their costs.

Exhibit:

ABC Plc gives you the following information:

	$ Million
Income	
Sales revenue from selling stationery	100
Gain on disposal of investments	10
Interest income on bank deposits	20
	130
Expenses	
Production expenditure	60
General and administrative expenses	20
Taxation	15
	95
Profit for the year (*Income Less Expenses*)	35

Gross profit margin = $\frac{100 - 60}{100} \times 100$

= 40%

Note:

- *A gain on disposal of investment and interest income are not considered revenue because they are not earned from the principal business activity of ABC, i.e. selling stationery*
- *Cost of sale includes only expenses that are directly associated with producing goods or rendering services and therefore does not include expenses such as general and administrative costs and tax expenses.*

Q. How can the Gross Profit as a percentage of sales ratio be improved?

Ans. The following measures could be used:

a) Increasing sales by increasing advertising and sales promotions.

b) Increasing selling prices. This may improve the gross profit, if the demand is price inelastic.

c) Using cheaper suppliers.

d) Increasing or changing product range.

e) Reduce deliver costs by streamlining the delivery procedure.

f) Find alternate ways to get the product to the customer. E.g joint ventures, web selling.

Q. Name and explain the 'Liquidity ratios'.

Ans. The Liquidity ratios are:

a) **Current ratio.** This ratio is also known as the 'Working Capital Ratio'. It measures the business's ability to meet its current liabilities. The ideal current ratio is 2:1. However, anything between 2:1 and 1.5:1 is considered desirable. A ratio of 1: 1 indicated the absence of working capital.

Current ratio = $\dfrac{\text{current assets}}{\text{current liabilities}}$

b) **Quick ratio.**

This ratio is also known as the 'Acid test ratio'. This ratio shows a comparison between assets in money or near money form with liabilities due for payment in the near future. The ideal current ratio is 1:1.

Quick ratio = $\dfrac{\text{current assets – inventory}}{\text{current liabilities}}$

c) **Rate of turnover.**

It is the amount of times a business sells and replaces its inventory in a given period of time. The rate of inventory turnover can be calculated in two ways:

1. Rate of inventory turnover = $\dfrac{\text{Cost of sales}}{(\text{opening inventory + closing inventory }) / 2}$

= $\dfrac{\text{Cost of sales}}{\text{average inventory}}$

This gives the number of **times** inventory is sold and replaced and is the more commonly used formula. The higher the rate, the greater the **efficiency** and gross profit (provided the profit margin is constant).

Inventory turnover can also be calculated in days using this formula:

2. Inventory turnover (days) = $\dfrac{\text{Average inventory}}{\text{Cost of sales}} \times 365$

This gives the number of **days,** on an average, the inventory is being held before being sold. The lower the number, the greater the **efficiency** and gross profit (provided the profit margin is constant).

d) **Collection period for trade receivables.**

This is also known as trade receivables turnover or the average collection period. It is the average amount of time that trade receivables take to pay their accounts.

It can be calculated using the following formula:

Debtors (Trade receivables) Turnover = $\dfrac{\text{Debtors (Trade Receivables)}}{\text{Credit Sales}} \times 365$ days …..in days

(or) = $\dfrac{\text{trade receivables}}{\text{credit sales}} \times 52$ ……. in weeks

(or) = $\dfrac{\text{trade receivables}}{\text{credit sales}} \times 12$ ….. in months

e) **Payment period for trade payables.**

This is also known as trade payables turnover or the average payment period. It is the average amount of time a business takes to pay its trade payables.

Payment period for trade payables = $\dfrac{\text{trade payables}}{\text{credit purchases}} \times 365$ ………in days

$$(or) = \frac{\text{trade payables x 52}}{\text{credit purchases}} \text{ .... in weeks}$$

$$(or) = \frac{\text{trade payables x 12}}{\text{credit purchases}} \text{ ......in months}$$

Q. Why is a current ratio between 2:1 and 1.5:1 considered desirable?
Ans. This indicates that the business has liquidity over and above what it needs to pay off its immediate liabilities to capitalize
on advantageous business opportunities, bargains etc., which require immediate liquidity.

Q What does a current ratio over 2:1 indicate?
Ans. A ratio over 2:1 indicates inefficient management of resources. It means that the business may have:
a) Too much inventory and this means over trading.
b) Too many trade receivables and the consequent risk of irrecoverable debts.
c) Too much money in the bank (in a current account) earning little or no interest.
d) Too much cash in hand and this indicates assets not being put to economic use.

Q. Why is over trading not desirable?
Ans. Too much inventory or over trading means:
a) Money tied up and this means the firm is not using its money to best effect.
b) The inventory requires a warehouse that indicates additional expenses by way of rent.
c) The inventory may expire or go out of fashion and be unsaleable.
d) The inventory may get stolen.
e) The inventory could get damaged.

Q. Why is inventory excluded from the Acid Test ratio?
Ans. Inventory is considered to be two steps away from being money and that is why it is not included in the Acid test ratio which measures immediate liquidity and the ability to pay off current liabilities immediately. The two steps are:
a) Inventory has to be sold.
b) Money has to be collected from debtors,
If inventory was included then the possibility of it having to be sold quickly, possibly at reduced prices, would arise.

Q. What would an Acid Test Ratio of more than 1:1 indicate?
Ans. An Acid Test Ratio of more than 1:1 indicates inefficient management of liquid assets. This would mean:
a) Too many debtors with a consequent risk of irrecoverable debts.
b) Too much money in the bank earning little or no interest.
c) Too much cash in hand which again is lying idle.

Q. What would an Acid Test Ratio of less than 1:1 indicate?
Ans. An Acid Test ratio of less than 1:1, 0.8:1, for instance, would be a very risky situation for the business. Many a business has had to close down due to its inability to pay off its creditors and thus being declared insolvent, even though it had a lot of money tied up in inventory that was not liquid.

Q. Which rate of inventory turnover is better: 53 times or 8 times?
Ans. The answer would depend on whether both figures refer to the similar businesses. If they do, then obviously, 53 times is better and indicates that the business is more efficient in selling its inventory. If 53 times represents business A that sells vegetables and 8 times represents business B that sells television sets then both rates are good. This is because the vegetable business should try to sell and replace its inventory almost every week television sets are more difficult to sell and hence, a rate of inventory turnover of 8 a year would mean

that it sells all its inventory and replaces it 8 times a year, an enviable accomplishment indeed!

Q. What would a higher trade receivables collection period indicate?
Ans. This would mean that debtors take longer to pay their debts, thus increasing the risk of irrecoverable debts and liquidity problems. It indicates an inefficient credit control policy.

Q. What are the ways of improving the trade receivables collection period?
Ans. The ways of improving the collection period are:
a) employing a factor.
b) offer cash discounts for early payment.
c) charge interest on overdue debts.
d) refuse further supplies until the overdue balance is paid.
e) improve credit control (by sending regular statements of accounts, reminders etc.)

Q. Who are factors?
Ans. Factors are firms or people who advance money against debts and then collect the debts themselves for a fee.

Q. What would a higher trade payables payment period indicate?
Ans. This would indicate that the firm is paying its creditors quickly and has enough liquidity to do so. However, a longer payment period is more advantageous for the firm since its liquidity improves and it enjoys interest free 'trade credit'. An efficient business would delay paying its creditors for as long it can without losing cash discounts for prompt payment and the goodwill of its suppliers.

Q. Why would the rate of inventory turnover vary from year to year?
Ans. The rate of inventory turnover may increase if the efficiency of the business increased. If the rate of inventory turnover has reduced, it may mean that the business has too much inventory or that sales are slowing down.

Q. Which ratio is known as the first or primary ratio?
Ans. The ROCE or return on capital employed is known as the first ratio. It relates profit for the year before tax to the capital employed in the business. The profit before tax is known as the 'bottom line'. Debentures and other long term loans are included in capital employed.

Q. How is profit before interest and tax as a % of sales revenue calculated?
Ans. Profit before interest and tax, or operating profit is calculated as a percentage of sales using the following formula:

Profit before interest and tax = $\frac{\text{profit before interest and tax}}{\text{sales revenue}} \times 100$

Q. List the ratios showing utilisation of resources.
Ans. The following ratios show utilisation of resources:

1. Sales as a percentage of capital employed = $\frac{\text{sales} \times 100}{\text{capital employed}}$

This is a secondary ratio.

2. Utilisation of total assets = $\frac{\text{sales revenue}}{\text{total assets}}$

This ratio is expressed in times and measures the number of times the sales cover the capital invested in the assets of a business.

3. Non-current asset turnover = $\frac{\text{sales revenue}}{\text{total non-current assets}}$

This ratio is expressed in times and relates the revenue earned through sales using the non-current assets that are bought with the intention to earn revenue.

4. Current asset turnover = $\dfrac{\text{sales}}{\text{total current assets}}$

This ratio is expressed in times.

5. Net current assets working capital) to sales = $\dfrac{\text{turnover}}{\text{net current assets}}$

Q. Name the financial ratios.

Ans. The financial ratios are:

1) Current ratio
2) Acid test or quick ratio, also known as the liquidity ratio
3) Trade receivables' ratio or trade receivables days
4) Rate of inventory turnover
5) Trade payables' ratio or trade payables' days

Q. What is meant by overtrading?

Ans. This is a situation where a business's turnover increases rapidly with a corresponding increase in trade receivables, trade payables and inventory. This situation may threaten the liquidity position of the business and the business could be in danger of being declared insolvent as they may not be in a position to pay their creditors.

Q. Explain the term 'The cash operating cycle'.

Ans. This cycle measures the time cash takes to circulate around the working capital system, the time between payment of creditors and receipt of cash from debtors. The interval marks the time when the company is paying its creditors with its own money.
The formula is:
Cash operating cycle = Inventory turnover in days + trade receivables days – trade payables days.

EXHIBIT

Merrick and company have arrived at the following figures:

	Inventory turnover	Trade receivables days	Trade payables days
20x4	20	29	37
20x5	19	37	43

Required:
Calculate the cash operating cycle for:
a) 20x4
b) 20x5
Solution:

Cash cycle for 20x4 = Inventory turnover + trade receivables' days – trade payables' days
= 20+ 29 – 37
= 12 days

Cash cycle for 20x5 = 19 + 37 – 43
= 13 days

Exercise 13.1

A business gives you the following information:

	Inventory Turnover	Trade receivables turnover	Trade payables turnover
20x2	22	25	34
20x3	24	28	34

Required:
Calculate the cash operating cycle for:
a) 20x2
b) 20x3

Exercise 13.2

	Inventory turnover	Trade receivables turnover	Trade payables turnover
20x0	25	27	39
20x1	21	26	38

Required:

Calculate the cash operating cycle for:

a) 20x0

b) 20x1

Q. Briefly explain: Net working assets to sales ratio.

Ans. With the increase in sales working assets requirements also rise. This ratio is considered a prime indicator of a company's ability to expand its operations without taking on additional debt.

The ratio provides an insight into the likely amount of additional working assets funding required from a given increase in sales. If the ratio is 20% this means that the company will require net working assets of 20 cents for every increase of $1 in sales. As increase in working assets requirements needs finance so management tries to minimise the level of net working assets in relation to sales.

This ratio is a useful measure of the amount of money that is tied up in funding the day-to-day trading activities of the business as it includes only those current assets and current liabilities that vary in direct proportion to sales turnover. It is possible to have a stable 'current' or 'quick' ratio while this ratio is falling. This would happen if sales were increasing rapidly without corresponding increase in net working assets. This low ratio may indicate 'overtrading' (excessive sales volume in relation to lower working assets investment in the business)'. This may also indicate that the business relies extensively upon credit granted by suppliers or the bank as a substitute for an adequate margin of operating funds.

Formula

Net working assets(Inventories plus Trade Receivables less Trade Payables) to sales	=	$\dfrac{\text{Net Working Assets}}{\text{Sales (Revenue)}} \times 100$

A lower ratio is usually preferred as it indicates that more of the working assets have been financed by short term funds resulting in lower amount of net working assets. On the other hand the larger the ratio, the more finance will be needed to fund larger requirements of net working assets in relation to sales.

Q. How is mark-up calculated?

Ans. The formula for Mark-up = $\dfrac{\text{Gross profit}}{\text{Cost of sales}} \times 100$

Q. How is the ratio of expenses to revenue calculated?

Ans. The formula is: $\dfrac{\text{expenses}}{\text{Revenue}} \times 100$

Q. Name the efficiency ratios.

Ans. The following ratios will measure the efficiency of a business:

1. Non-Current Asset Turnover = $\dfrac{\text{Net Revenue}}{\text{Total Net Book Value of Non-Current Assets}}$

2. Trade Receivables Turnover (also known as Average Collection Period)

3. Trade Payables Turnover (also known as Average Payment Period)

4. Inventory Turnover (in days) or Rate of Inventory Turnover (answer given in times)

Exhibit:

The final accounts of Mason for the year ended 31st December 20x7 are given below.

Mason's Income statement for the Year ended
31st December 20x7.

	$	$
Sales (all on credit)		130,000
Less Cost of sales:		
Inventory at 1st January 20x7	15,000	
Purchases of ordinary goods	65,000	
	80,000	
Inventory at 31st December 20x7	17,000	63,000
Gross profit		67,000
Less overheads -		
Selling and administration expenses		26,900
Profit for the year		40,100

Mason's Statement of Financial Position as at 31st December 20x7

	$	$
Non-current assets at net book value		65,780
Current Assets:		
Inventory	17,000	
Trade receivables	25,000	
Cash at bank	4,520	46,520
		112,300
Current liabilities		
Trade payables		24,300
Capital at 1st December 20x7	90,000	
Profit for the year	40,100	
	130,100	
Drawings	42,100	88,000
		112,300

Required:

a) Calculate the following :
1) Net profit as a percentage of sales (Profit margin)
2) Profit for the year as a percentage of capital employed.
3) Percentage of gross profit to sales
4) Current ratio
5) Quick ratio
6) Rate of inventory turnover
7) Collection period for trade receivables
8) Expenses to revenue ratio

b) Mason compared some of the accounting ratios for his business with those for other similar businesses. These were:

Net profit as a percentage of sales 16%
Percentage of gross profit to sales 40%
Quick ratio 1.1:1
Rate of inventory turnover 7 times

1) State whether each of Mason's four ratios is better or worse than that of other similar businesses.
2) Give a reason for each of your answers to (b) (1).
3) State whether or not Mason should be satisfied with the ratios for his business.

Solution:

a) 1) Net profit as a percentage of sales = $\dfrac{\text{Net profit}}{\text{sales revenue}} \times 100 = \dfrac{40,100 \times 100}{130000} = 30.8\%$

2) Net profit as a percentage of capital employed = $\dfrac{\text{Net profit}}{\text{capital employed}} \times 100 = \dfrac{40,100 \times 100}{88000} = 45.6\%$

3) Percentage of Gross profit to sales = $\dfrac{\text{Gross profit}}{\text{sales revenue}} \times 100 = \dfrac{67,000 \times 100}{130000} = 51.5\%$

4) Current ratio = $\dfrac{\text{Current Assets}}{\text{Current liabilities}} = \dfrac{46,520}{24300}$ 1.9:1

5) Quick ratio = $\dfrac{\text{Current assets} - \text{inventory}}{\text{Current liabilities}} = \dfrac{46,520 - 17,000}{24300}$ 1.2:1

6) Rate of inventory turnover = $\dfrac{\text{Cost of sales}}{\text{average inventory}} = \dfrac{63,000}{(15000+17000)/2} = 3.9$ times

7) Collection period for trade receivables = $\dfrac{\text{Trade receivables}}{\text{Sales revenue}} \times 365 = \dfrac{25,000}{130000} \times 365$
= 70 days (approx.)

b) 1) Mason's Net profit as a percentage of sales at 30.8% is better than those of similar businesses at 16%.
Mason's Gross profit as a percentage of sales at 51.5% is better than those of similar businesses at 40%.
Mason's quick ratio at 1.2:1 is worse than those of similar businesses at 1.1:1.
Mason's rate of inventory turnover at 2 times is worse than those of similar businesses at 7 times.

2) Reasons:
Mason has made $30.8 net profit for every $100 of sales compared to $16 made by similar businesses.
Mason has made $51.5 gross profit for every $100 of sales compared to $40 made by similar businesses.
Mason has a slightly higher quick ratio (1.2:1) than those of similar businesses (1.1:1). The ideal ratio is 1:1 and all the businesses in the industry seem to be more liquid than the ideal. A business should have immediate liquidity of a value equal to its current liabilities to be considered efficient in managing its current assets.
Mason has sold and replaced his inventory only twice this year. Similar businesses have sold and replaced their inventory seven times, thus displaying strong salesmanship. Either Mason has too much inventory compared to the rest of the industry or his sales are too slow.

3) Comments:
Profitability: Mason's gross profit as a percentage of sales is excellent compared to that of the rest of the industry. It is possible that he has good suppliers or that he is able to nose out bargains and buy goods more cheaply. Also, he might not be passing on his price increases to his customers. His net profit as a percentage of sales is also almost double that of a similar business. This indicates efficiency in managing expenses.
Liquidity: Mason is quite good at managing his liquidity too. Though his quick ratio is slightly over the industry's and also more than the ideal, it is not very much so. Mason has enough liquidity to pay off his creditors in an emergency and does not have a liquidity problem. He is therefore in no danger of being declared insolvent if faced with immediate payment of debts.
His rate of inventory turnover, however, is dismal compared to his competitors. He needs to revamp his sales policies and strategies. More promotions and advertising is recommended.

Tip √
1) Always give the formula in your answer, even though it seems repetitive. That way, even if your calculation is wrong, you will get almost half the total marks for that question for a right formula.
2) The inventory included in the quick ratio is closing inventory...from the Statement of financial position.

Exercise 13.3
Leela purchased Song's business on 1st December 20x4.
Song's assets and liabilities at 1st December 20x4 were as follows;

	$
Machinery	12,000
Motor van	6,000
Equipment	4,800
Inventory	10,000
Trade receivables	4,500
Other receivables	650
Bank overdraft	3,250
Trade payables	1,900
Other payables	340

Leela took over all the assets and liabilities at the values shown above. Leela paid $ 40,000 for the business including goodwill.
Required:
a) Prepare the Statement of financial position of the business as it appeared on 1st December 20x4 immediately after Leela had purchased it.
b) Calculate for the business:
1) the current ratio
2) the quick ratio
c) Leela hopes to earn 12% return on her capital. Calculate the profit she must earn.

Exercise 13.4
You are given the following table:

Ratio Average for:	the trade	Kelsey's ratios
Gross profit margin	53%	56%
Net profit percentage	25%	19%
Current ratio	2.3:1	3.3:1
Quick ratio	1:1	0.9:1
Collection period for trade receivables	56 days	69 days
Payment period for trade payables	35 days	25 days

Required:
Comment on the following:
Kelsey's comparative profitability
Kelsey's comparative efficiency

Exercise 13.5
The opening inventory of a business is $12,000 and the cost of sales is $240,000.
Using the average figure of opening and closing inventory, what value of closing inventory is needed to give an inventory turnover of 10

Exercise 13.6

The following items appear in a Statement of financial position:

	$
Inventory	14,000
Provision for doubtful debts	2,000
Cash at bank	500
Trade payables	10,000
The current ratio of	2:1

Required:
Calculate the closing trade receivables.

Q. What is meant by the term 'gearing'?

Ans. Simply put, gearing is the relationship between borrowings (interest bearing debt) and equity (the shareholders interest in the company). Gearing is a measure of financial leverage, demonstrating the degree to which a firm's activities are funded by owner's funds versus creditor's funds.

Gearing = $\dfrac{\text{fixed cost capital}}{\text{Total capital}}$

= $\dfrac{\text{non-current liabilities + preference share capital}}{\text{Issued Ordinary Share Capital + All Reserves + Non-Current Liabilities + Preference Shares}}$

The ratio indicates the financial risk to which a business is subjected, since excessive debt can lead to financial difficulties. A company is described as highly geared if the gearing is more than 0.5. If the ratio is less than 0.5, then the company is lowly geared. A high gearing ratio is indicative of a great deal of leverage, where a company is using debt to pay for its continuing operations. In a business downturn, such companies may have trouble meeting their debt repayment schedules, and could risk bankruptcy. The situation is especially dangerous when a company has engaged in debt arrangements with variable interest rates, where a sudden increase in rates could cause serious interest payment problems. A high gearing ratio is less of a concern in a regulated industry, such as a utility, where a business is in a monopoly situation and its regulators are likely to approve rate increases that will guarantee its continued survival. Lenders are particularly concerned about the gearing ratio, since an excessively high gearing ratio will put their loans at risk of not being repaid. Those industries with large and ongoing fixed asset requirements typically have high gearing ratios.

A low gearing ratio may be indicative of conservative financial management, but may also mean that a company is located in a highly cyclical industry, and so cannot afford to become overextended in the face of an inevitable downturn in sales and profits.

However, these figures are rather arbitrary. More importantly, the analyst should consider the movements in the ratio year-on-year.

Q. How can a company reduce its gearing?

Ans. There are a number of methods available for reducing a company's gearing ratio, including:

- *Sell shares.* The board of directors could authorize the sale of shares in the company, which could be used to pay down debt.
- *Convert loans.* Negotiate with lenders to swap existing debt for shares in the company.

- *Reduce working capital.* Increase the speed of accounts receivable collections, reduce inventory levels, and/or lengthen the days required to pay accounts payable, any of which produces cash that can be used to pay down debt.
- *Increase profits.* Use any methods available to increase profits, which should generate more cash with which to pay down debt.

Q. Explain: Income gearing

Ans. The gearing ratio gives an indication of the level of gearing. The income gearing ratio gives an indication on whether a company can afford that level of gearing. Income gearing is the proportion of the annual income streams devoted to the prior claims of debt holders. The reciprocal of income gearing is the interest cover. The rule-of-thumb for the interest cover ratio is that interest payments should be covered by profits before taxation and interest, at least four times. For our income gearing ratio this translates to 25% being the benchmark.

Income gearing = $\dfrac{\text{interest expenses}}{\text{Profit before interest and tax (PBIT)}}$

Q. List the investment (stock exchange) ratios.

Ans. There are five main ratios that can be used by shareholders in order to assess the worth of a particular company and their shares: They are:

1. Earnings per share = $\dfrac{\text{Net Profit} - \text{Preference Share Dividend}}{\text{Number of issued Ordinary Shares}}$

2. Price Earnings Ratio = $\dfrac{\text{Market Price per share}}{\text{Earnings per share}}$

3. Dividend yield = $\dfrac{\text{Dividend paid and proposed}}{\text{Market Price of share}}$

4. Dividend cover = $\dfrac{\text{Profit available to pay ordinary dividend}}{\text{Ordinary dividend paid}}$

5. Dividend per share = $\dfrac{\text{Ordinary dividend paid}}{\text{Number of issued Ordinary Shares}}$

Q. Explain 'Earnings per share ratio (EPS)'.

Ans. This measures the company's potential dividends that it could pay to shareholders. It is calculated using the following formula: $\dfrac{\text{Net Profit} - \text{Preference Share Dividend}}{\text{Number of issued Ordinary Shares}}$

For example, if a company has profit after tax of $12m and it has issued 40 million ordinary shares, then its E.P.S. would be: $\dfrac{12}{40} = 0.3$

This means that every ordinary share could pay a dividend of 30 pence IF all the profit after tax is distributed as dividends. However, it is most likely that some of the profit after tax will be kept in the company for re-investment (this is called retained profit). Clearly the shareholders would want as much of the profit after tax as possible to be payable to themselves

Q. Explain: 'Price Earnings Ratio (P/E)'

Ans. This measures the market price of the share as a proportion of the earnings per share calculated above. It is calculated using the following formula:

P/E ratio = $\dfrac{\text{Market Price per share}}{\text{Earnings per share}}$

For example , if the current market price for a company's share is $1.50, and the earnings per share is 30 cents, then the P/E ratio would be:

P/E ratio = $\dfrac{1.50}{30} = 5$

This answer indicates that it would take an investor 5 years to recover the cost of the share. This figure would need to be compared to other companies' P/E ratios before a judgment could be made.

In general, the higher the P/E ratio, then the better the expectations of the company's future profitability. However, the share price of the company is likely to fluctuate frequently, and therefore the P/E ratio of the share will not be the same for very long - this can make it difficult to compare the P/E ratio with other companies.

Q. Illustrate with the help of an example, the importance of the ratio 'Dividends per share.

Ans. This ratio measures the size of the dividends that the company actually pays to its shareholders. It is calculated using the following formula:

Dividends per share =   Total dividends paid/Number of ordinary shares

For example, if a company has profit after tax of $12m (and issues 25% of this as dividends) and it has issued 40 million ordinary shares, then its dividend per share would be:

Dividend per share = 3/40 = $0.075

This means that every ordinary share would pay a dividend of 7.5 cents. The remaining $9m of profit after tax would be retained for future investment. Clearly, the shareholders would want the dividend per share to be as high as possible, in order to maximise their return on their investment.

Q. Explain, with the help of an example: Dividend yield.

Ans. This shows the dividend per share expressed as a percentage of the market price of the share. It is calculated using the following formula:

Dividend yield = d<u>ividend per share x 100</u>

               Market price per share

For example, if a company had a dividend per share of 7.5 cents, and a market price of $1.50,

The dividend yield = <u>0.075 </u>x 100 = 5%

                1.50

This is **not a very high return** for the risk involved in investing money in shares. This figure would need to be compared to other investments (e.g. other companies, banks, etc.) to see if it is providing a competitive return.

Q. Explain, with the help of an example: Dividend cover.

Ans. This measures how many more times the dividends could have been paid out of the profit after tax. It is calculated using the following formula:

Dividend cover =   <u>Profit after tax</u>

               Total dividends paid

For example, if a business had profit after tax of $12m and it paid total dividends of $3m,

The dividend cover = 12/3= 4 times

This means that the company did not pay the shareholders a significant proportion of the profit after tax in the form of dividends - the company has actually only paid a quarter of their profit after tax as dividends. This means that the company kept much of the profit after tax as retained profit for re-investment.

Exercise 13.7

The summarised statement of financial position of Pelico Ltd at 31 December 2012 was as follows:

	$000
Non-current assets	1,900
Net current assets	80
	1980
Ordinary shares of $1	1,000
Share premium account	960
Revenue reserves	20
	1,980

The ordinary shares were quoted at $3.84. Profit before interest and tax was $600,000. A dividend of $0.40 was paid on its ordinary shares for the year.

Required: Calculate the following ratios for the year ended 31 December 2012

a. **Gearing**
b. **Dividend cover**
c. **Earnings per share**
d. **Price earnings ratio**
e. **Dividend yield**

Exercise 13.8

You are given the following information for the year ended 31 March 20x7:

Rate of inventory turnover	20 days
(calculated using average inventory)	
Gross profit margin	50%
Net profit margin	15%
Dividend paid as a % of net profit	25%
Trade payables payment period	32 days

Trade receivables collection period   28 days

Current ratio   3:1

Issued share capital   500,000 ordinary shares of $0.50 each

Income statement balance at 1 April 20x6 $73,424

Inventory at 31 March 20x7 $14,000

Market price of ordinary share at 31 March 20x7 $0.80

Required:

    a. **Prepare an Income Statement for the year ended 31 March 20x7 in as much detail as possible.**
    b. **Prepare a Statement of financial position at 31 March 20x7 in as much detail as possible.**

Note: 1. Figures to be expressed to the nearest $

      2. Non-current assets and balance at bank are balancing figures.

The following statistics have been prepared by a local bank. They relate to similar businesses in the same district as the company.

Dividend yield   5.6%

Dividend cover   3 times

Dividend per share   10.7 cents

Earnings per share   32 cents

Price earnings ratio (PER) 5.9

Required:

    c. **Explain what each of the 5 ratios indicates.**
    d. **Calculate the same five ratios for the company.**
    e. **Discuss the five ratios calculate and comment on what they show about the company.**

TEST YOURSELF

13.1 | MULTIPLE CHOICE QUESTIONS
i) The closing inventory of a business was $12,000 and the cost of goods sold was $75,000. If the inventory turnover was 10 times,
what was the opening inventory?
A) $6,000 B) $5,000 C) $ 3,000 D) $7,500

ii) With the following information, calculate the cash operating cycle:
Trade payables' days: 37
Trade receivables' days: 25
Inventory was turned over 14 times that year.
A) 14 days B) 2 days C) 12 days D) 11 days

iii) You are given the following information:

	Gross profit	Sales
20x1	$ 412,000	$ 1,200,000
20x2	$ 480,000	$ 1,600,000

Which of the following is not the reason for the gross profit margin decreasing?
A) A rise in the price of good purchased may have been passed on to customers.
B) The goods were purchased from a different supplier at a lower price
C) The cost of sales may have been increased by the theft of stock.
D) The margin on sales may have been cut to increase volume of sales.

iv) The following information has been extracted from the books of a company:

	$
Trade receivables at the end of the year	20,000
Trade receivables at the start of the year	15,000
Credit sales for the year	120,000
Cash sales for the year	30,000

What is the Trade receivables collection period?
A) 61 days B) 49 days C) 37 days D) 46 days

v. Moneybags and company give you the following information:

	$000
10% debentures	100
Ordinary shares of $1 each	300
10% preference shares of $1 each	60
General reserve	100
Retained profit	104
Authorised share capital	500
Profit before interest and tax	180
Profit after interest and tax	100

What is the Return on Capital Employed?
A) 8.59% B) 15.46% C) 27.11% D) 15.06%

vi. If inventory is sold on credit, what would that result in?
A. Current ratio decreases
B. Acid test ratio increases
C. Current ratio increases
D. Acid test ratio decreases

vii. If the market price of a share is $2.41 and the dividends per share is 9c, then what is the dividend yield?
A. 3.5%   B. 9%   C. 3.37% D. 3.73%

viii. If the EPS is 12c and the market price of the share is $3.60, then the Price/Earnings ratio would be:
A. 3.33%   B. 0.30   C. 3 times D. 30

ix. If the market price of a share is $3.78 and the dividends per share is 12c, then the dividend yield is:
A. 37.8% B. 12%   C. 32% D. 3.2%

x. Which item would NOT be included in the calculation of the Price/ Earnings ratio?
A. Profit available to ordinary shareholders
B. Number of ordinary shares outstanding
C. Market price of the share
D. Total dividends distributed

13.2 A business has cash sales of $70,890 and credit sales of $1,500,000 in a year (360 days).
The trade receivables' collection period is 12 days (approx).
Required:
Calculate the closing trade receivables' balance.

13.3 The table shows an extract from a company's final accounts:

	$
Purchases	30,000
Cost of sales	25,000
Trade payables	5,000
Other payables	1,200

Required:
Calculate the trade payables' payment period for the year.

13.4. A firm has $15,000 in the bank and buys inventory for $ 2,000 paying by cheque.
a) What is the effect of this on the current ratio?
b) What is the effect of this on the quick (acid test) ratio?

13.5 A business has a current ratio of 1.25:1 and a quick (acid test) ratio of 1:1. The business sells inventory on credit at its usual mark-up.
What is the effect of this on the current and quick (acid test) ratio?

13.6 A company's income statement showed a profit before interest of $125,000. Interest paid was $5,000.
The table shows amounts included in the company's Statement of financial position:

	$
Non-current assets	480,000
Net current assets	30,000
10% Debentures	70,000

Calculate: **the return on the total capital employed?**

13.7 The following information has been calculated from the accounts of a business:
Days taken to pay creditors 40
Days taken by debtors to pay 56
Inventory turnover in days 14
Required:
Calculate the cash operating cycle.

13.9 You are given the following information about Hyatt plc.

	2009	2010	2011	2012
Gearing	0.24	0.55	0.63	1.22
Income gearing	5.5%	9.4%	19.8%	122.5%

Required:
Comment on the ratios

13.10

Chandra is considering investing in ordinary shares. He has obtained the summarised financial statements of two companies, Richards Limited and Sobers Limited.

The following data is available.	Richards Limited	Sobers Limited
Income Statements (extracts)	$	$
Gross profit	85 000	65 000
Profit from operations	66 000	48 000
Finance charges	(6 000)	(8 000)
Profit before tax	60 000	40 000
Tax	(30 000)	(20 000)
Profit after tax	30 000	20 000
Statements of Financial Position		
Total assets	500 000	400 000
Equity		
$1 ordinary shares	150 000	100 000
Share premium	15 000	20 000
Retained earnings	105 000	85 000
	270 000	205 000
Non-current liabilities		
8% debentures (2022)	75 000	100 000
Current liabilities	155 000	95 000
Total equity and liabilities	500 000	400 000

Both companies have non-current assets equal in value to their current assets.

The market value of an ordinary share in Richards Limited is $1.80.

The market value of an ordinary share in Sobers Limited is $2.40.

Neither company has paid any dividends during the year.

Richards Limited proposes a final dividend of $0.06 per ordinary share and Sobers Limited $0.09 per ordinary share.

REQUIRED

a. Calculate the following ratios for both companies

(i) Current ratio

(ii) Return on capital employed

(iii) Gearing ratio

(iv) Income gearing

(v) Earnings per share

(vi) Price earnings ratio

(vii) Dividend yield.

b. Advise Chandra which company he should invest in. Base your answer on your calculations for the return on capital employed, gearing ratio and income gearing only.

(UCLES, 2015, AS/A Level Accounting, Syllabus 9706/43, May/June)

CHAPTER 14
COMPUTERISED ACCOUNTING SYSTEMS

Q. How is manual accounting different from computerised accounting?

Ans. Ways in which manual accounting is different from computerised accounting can be examined as follows:

1. Speed and accuracy: The main difference between manual and computerised systems is speed. Accounting software processes data and creates reposts much faster than manual systems. Calculations are done automatically in software programmes, minimising errors and increasing efficiency. Once data is input, you can create reports literally by pressing a button in a computerised system.

2. Cost: Manual accounting with paper and pencil is much cheaper than a computerised system, which requires a machine and software. Other expenses associated with accounting software include training and programme maintenance. Expenses can add up fast with costs for printers, paper, ink and other supplies.

3. Backup: A third difference is the ease of backup of a computerised system. All transactions can be saved and backed up in case of fire or other mishap. You cannot do this with paper records, unless you make copies of all pages – a long and inefficient process.

4. End-of-period reports: Computerised accounting packages will automatically put all relevant ledger entries for period reports. Manual accounting takes longer, but can help a bookkeeper better understand the posting and end-of-period processes.

5. Data Manipulation: With a computerised system, information for a particular period of time can be compiled quickly. With a manual system, it can take time to locate the information from each book and compile it into a report.

Q. What is the difference between hardware and software?

Ans. The major differences between computer hardware and software are:

HARDWARE	SOFTWARE
1. Physical parts of the computer are called hardware.	1. A set of instructions given to the computer is called software.
2. You can touch, see and feel hardware.	2. You cannot touch and feel software.
3. Hardware is constructed using physical materials or components.	3. Software is developed by writing instructions in programming language.
4. A computer is hardware, which operates under the control of software.	4. The operations of computer are controlled through software.
5. If hardware is damaged, it should be replaced with new one.	5. If software is damaged or corrupted, its backup copy can be reinstalled.
6. Hardware is not affected by computer viruses.	6. Software is affected by computer viruses.
7. Hardware cannot be transferred from one place to another electronically through a network.	7. Software can be transferred from one place to another electronically through a network.
8. Users cannot make new duplicate copies of the hardware.	8. Users can make many new duplicate copies of the software.

Q. What is the difference between large systems and small systems?

Ans. Small firms can handle their accounting with the use of a personal computer using basic accounting software as the volume of their transactions is not large. However, a large business, with a consequent large number of transactions, involving a number of parties and accounts will need the support of a database. A database is a collection of all information about the customer, supplier, asset etc. at one place, from where it is retrieved at the time of recording a transaction or generating a report. The data collected is processed to eliminate duplicate or redundant data, also known as a normalisation of data. Small and medium-sized businesses may use 'off-the- shelf' packages that are flexible enough to be adapted to most businesses.

Very large businesses may use a mainframe for handling bulk data with personal computers for departmental accounts and the like (workstations). These workstations will be networked using LANs (Local area networks) that are internal to the location and WANs (wide areas networks) that connect with computers located outside the location, for example, a company's head office. Network technology is constantly improving and becoming more flexible, through the use of wireless LANs and the ability to send data across mobile phone networks.

Computer programmes may be developed 'in house' or written under contract with an outside firm. These systems are tailored to the business' needs. A supermarket, for example may incorporate EPOS (Electronic point of sale) that keep an accurate check on what is sold, inventory levels, reordering and cash sales. Such 'bespoke' computer systems will normally be used by large businesses.

While accounting solutions have traditionally been packaged as insulated, on-premise software, many providers now offer cloud-based solutions. SaaS (Software as a service or on-demand software) accounting software solutions usually include all the features of more traditional systems, with the added benefit of anytime, anywhere accessibility and seamless updating. SaaS solutions tend to be more cost-effective and easier to implement, and are a great option for small businesses. Businesses in certain sectors with unique financial requirements, including construction and non-profit work, should look for industry-specific solutions that cater to their specific needs.

Q. List the ways in which computers can be used in accounting.

Ans. Accurate record keeping is critical in the fast-paced world of finance. Computers help increase the efficiency of a business as financial statements and reports can be generated at a moment's notice. A typical integrated double entry accounting system will contain some or all of the following components:

1. Spreadsheets
2. General ledgers
3. Accounts payable
4. Accounts receivable
5. Inventory control
6. Point of sale
7. Purchasing and receiving
8. Time and billing modules, to name a few.

Q. What is a spreadsheet?

Ans. Also referred to as a worksheet, a spreadsheet is a file made of rows and columns that help sort data, arrange data easily and calculate numerical data. A spreadsheet software programme has the unique ability to calculate values using mathematical formulae and the data in cells. Electronic spreadsheets allow you to do anything that you would normally do with a calculator, pencil and columnar scratch pad. Spreadsheets were primarily designed for managers who in the process of planning must do 'what if?' calculations. Examples of spreadsheets are Excel, Quattro Pro, Lotus 1-2-3.

Q. Describe how electronic spreadsheets can be used in businesses.

Ans. With spreadsheet software, business managers and administrators can capture, manipulate, analyze and present valuable data related to particular areas of their operation. This includes budget management such as tracking income and expenses.

Spreadsheets include automated formatting options for currency as well as the option to display negative numbers in red, providing a clear representation of a financial situation. Some organizations also use spreadsheets to manage specific aspects of income and expenses in detail, for example with a dedicated worksheet for payroll expenses. Most spreadsheet programs allow multiple worksheets to work in conjunction with one another. Spreadsheet data sets can be used to inform the process of making future plans for a business. As well as including graphs or tables representing historical business data within business plans, spreadsheets can be created specifically for the purposes of projection. Spreadsheets can play a role in project management tasks within certain organizations. With a project-tracking spreadsheet you can record and track tasks or activities associated with particular projects.

In third generation integrated business software, spreadsheet, graphics, and data management capabilities are supplemented by word processing and communications capabilities. With such comprehensive programs, it is possible to create multiple windows on the computer display. Each window could contain a different application: a graph in one, a spreadsheet in another, and word processing in a third. The window capabilities of integrated programs such as Symphony and Framework make it easy, for example, to transfer a spreadsheet or a data-base report to word processing for styling and formatting before printing.

Q. How useful are computerised general ledgers in a business?

Ans. Computerised general ledgers are labour – saving devices that facilitate the preparation of financial statements and help establish multiple income and cost entries. Posting to the General Ledger is done behind the scenes by the accounting software. One can also view transactions right on the screen.

Q. Explain the use of computerised accounts receivable.

Ans. Accounts receivable, when computerized, can get a business' bills out the same day that they performed a service. An accounts receivable module prepares invoices and customer accounts, adds credit charges where appropriate, handles incoming payments, flags a manager's attention to customers that are delinquent, and produces dunning notices. Daily cash control is enabled. Bills go out on time, while errors such as billing a customer twice for the same item are avoided. A further advantage is that debits and credits are posted automatically to the general ledger, order entry, and in some instances inventory, once they are entered in accounts receivable.

Q. Explain the use of computerised accounts payable.

Ans. Accounts payable, when computerized, will provide for purchase order control, invoice processing, payment selection and handling, payment control, cash-requirements, forecasting, and tax returns. It will also double-check the accuracy of the vendors' invoices.

Some software systems have the added capability of cross-checking invoices against the purchase order and the inventory module.

Q. What are the functions of a computerised inventory control module?

Ans. An Inventory Control module has multiple functions, including tracking inventory for both costing and tax purposes, controlling purchasing (and the overall level of expenditure) and minimizing the investment in inventory (and subsequent loss of cash flow).

Q. What does a computerised payroll module do?

Ans. The payroll module prepares and prints payroll statements, including all itemized deductions. It is integrated with the general ledger so that the accountant can prepare tax returns with ease.

Q. How does a computerised Point of Sale module work?

Ans. The Point of Sale module captures all sales information at (or in place of) the cash register, including the salesperson's name, the date, customer, credit information and items and quantity sold. It can produce sales slips or sales invoices. In addition, it reports on items, customer, and salesperson activity.

Q. Why is a Purchasing and Receiving module invaluable?

Ans. A Purchasing and Receiving module can be an invaluable addition as it can generate purchase orders and track their fulfilment. The business can find out which vendors are delivering on time thus saving one the expense of having to follow up on partial and incomplete orders.

Q. How is a Time and Billing module useful?

Ans. A Time and Billing module reduces manual and clerical work, simplifies the billing process, prompts the business and its partners to bill on time, reduces unbilled work-in progress, minimizes unreported time, reduces unbilled time, measures and analyses non-chargeable time and provides the criteria to analyse staff performance. Because a computerized accounting system is basically a computerized data management system, the disposition of labour is almost the same. One staff member must serve as a data-base manager and be in charge of setting up the chart of accounts, establishing the interrelationships among the files and establishing and maintaining an audit trail.

Q. What are the disadvantages of using a computerised accounting system?

Ans. The disadvantages can be examined as follows:

Security: It is easy for someone to make changes that alter a business' financial transactions and possibly cause serious harm. For example, bills to customers could be altered thus reducing the amount due a customer. In order to avoid this, a secure password access should be set up and trustworthy employees only should have access to the system. There will always be some risks that are best shared through insurance, rather than prevented or avoided.

Ease of use: Computerized accounting is by no means a be-all, end-all solution. Accounting software can create difficult situations for accountants needing to correct data entry errors. Instead of erasing numbers and entering them into the correct column, accountants must carefully prepare adjusting journal entries to correct information. These entries can create more errors if posted incorrectly. Creating additional errors requires accountants to spend even more time correcting financial information.

Loss of information: When you use a computer, it is possible that data can be lost because of hardware or software damage. There can be loss of data due to accidents like fire etc. There can be loss of data or change of data due to fraud or embezzlement. There can be loss or unavailability of data due to loss of staff or a breakdown in the system. Inaccurate data may be due to clerical error or mistakes in programming.

Errors: Since the computer has no judgement of its own, it does not pick up on errors as a human being does.

Computer-related crime: Most computer-related crime is opportunistic. Copies of computer printouts get misdirected, or thrown in a waste paper basket in a public place. Magnetic tapes from bankrupt companies have been sold with data still on them. Often a programming error reveals a system flaw: someone who by chance reads a magnetic tape file that he should have been writing discovers interesting data on it and misappropriates it. Wherever a computer is used to handle an organization's accounts, it can be used as a means of attacking the funds it controls.

Reliability: Manual accounting can function independently of machines so that work continues when "the system" isn't working.

Cost: Costs include developing compatible software, introduction of the system, training staff, recruiting specialised staff, hardware, on-going maintenance and upgrading. With rapid technological advances, computer systems and equipment can also fast become outdated and have to be replaced.

Creativity in analysis: Although computerized accounting systems are adept at rapidly computing complex analyses of accounting transactions and reports, the subtlety and focus of an analysis' conjecture or hypothesis depends on the person operating the system. In this view, manual accounting may have an advantage over computerized accounting systems. Without the nuance and experience of an actual person, computerized accounting systems lose their potential for sophisticated analysis. Additionally, analysis may be hampered or obstructed by software design.

Q. How can a business ensure that these disadvantages are minimised?

Ans. There are various measures that can be taken:

- Dispersion, which is designed to minimize losses in the event of deliberate or accidental threat, can be used.
- Duplication is designed to ensure that the system survives damage to any individual part. Duplication is also the fundamental method of detecting errors in processing.
- Defence in depth is designed to make the attacker overcome a series of barriers before he can damage any vital part of the system.
- With modern backup systems and increased functionality, the disadvantage of reliability in computerized accounting may be lessened.

In addition, most companies have computer auditors who ensure the integrity and accuracy of the organizations records, protect and conserve the organization's assets and prevent fraud, theft and error. These auditors also ensure that systems will survive the hazards to which they are exposed.

Q. What are the advantages of computerised accounting systems?

Ans. The advantages can be examined as follows:

Time: Traditional manual accounting was a tedious process requiring accountants to spend copious amounts of time mathematically checking numbers in the company's accounting information. Simple mistakes such as transposing numbers or entering information into the incorrect column could create significant errors. Computerized accounting systems allow accountants to process more information than before by creating easier review processes.

Increased productivity and job satisfaction: Accountants can potentially spend less time looking for errors and more time analyzing information for decision purposes.

Speed: The most important advantage of using the computer is the speed with which we can record data, post it and then generate financial statements and reports. For example, with an accounts receivable module, you just need to enter the actual cash totals of items purchased and the software distributes these amounts to the general ledger so they become credits to corresponding revenue accounts. At the same time, an offsetting entry is made automatically to the accounts receivable account. With a computer, one can receive a statement of financial position, income statement or other accounting reports at a moment's notice.

Unskilled work: Some day to day data entries can be turned over to relatively unskilled workers.

Increased accuracy: Computerized accounting has the advantage of higher accuracy when compared with manual accounting. The potential for human error is greater when employees are manually completing accounting procedures. This may be particularly true when dealing with multiple currencies, for example, since computerized programs can instantly convert exchange rates.

Reporting & Decision-making: The advantages of computerized accounting include fast, complex reporting. Computerized systems can produce invoices, purchase orders and other documents more quickly. Many reports are automatically updated and instantly available. This helps improve the decision-making process within a business.

Automation: Since all the calculations are handled by the software, computerized accounting eliminates many of the mundane and time-consuming processes associated with manual accounting. For example, once issued, invoices are processed automatically making accounting less time-consuming. Here are a number of steps in the manual accounting cycle that will be automated by a reliable accounting software program such as QuickBooks:

- Posting to Ledger accounts
- Preparation of Unadjusted Trial Balance
- Posting of adjusting entries
- Preparation of adjusted Trial Balance
- Journalising closing entries
- Posting of closing entries
- Prepare a post-closing Trial Balance
- Preparation of financial statements

Data Access: Using accounting software, it becomes much easier for different individuals to access accounting data outside of the office, securely. This is particularly true if an online accounting solution is being used.

Reliability: Because the calculations are so accurate, the financial statements prepared by computers are highly reliable.

Scalable: When the business grows, accounting increases and becomes more complex. With computerized accounting, this does not pose a problem as it is easier to sift through data using software than through paper records.

Security: The latest data can be saved and stored in offsite locations so it is safe from natural and man-made disasters like earthquakes, fires, floods, arson and terrorist attacks. In case of a disasters, the system can be quickly restored on other computers.

Q. Discuss ways in which the integrity of the accounting data can be ensured during the transfer to a computerised accounting system.

Ans. Enough time should be set aside when converting a manual bookkeeping system to a computerized system as it is important to ensure that the new system starts with information that matches the current books. The steps recommended are:

- **Assess needs:** What will the software be used for: preparing financial statements, preparing reports, handling payroll or accounts receivable and payable? Is the software required to connect to business' bank's website? It is essential to make a list of what the software will be handling before starting to look for the package that will suit the business.

- **Research:** time should be spent looking for the right package, assessing the cost, functionality and user-friendliness of each accounting package. For a small business, off-the- shelf products that are flexible and adaptable to the needs of the business would be a good, reasonably-priced option. It is vital to ensure that the software be compliant with the reporting standards for the country the business operates in, and that the product uses double entry, not single entry. It would be an added benefit if the provider offers free, on-going support and seamless automatic upgrades.

- **Trial versions:** Most accounting programmes will offer a trial version that can be downloaded from the manufacturer's website. Time should be spent with the program to see if it meets the needs of the business. Only when a suitable programme is found should the business purchase and install it.

- **Gather paper accounting records:** To set up the accounting software, all information is to be moved from paper records onto the computer. This includes journals, ledgers, invoices, etc. The new system should start with information that matches the current books.

- **Create templates:** any accounting programme will have templates already set up for common accounting tasks. Start by setting up new templates to match the way things have been set up on paper in the past, before entering any data.

- **Enter data:** From this point on, all data should be entered in both the computer software and in the business' paper records for a while. This is in order to get used to using the software and to ensure that all the tasks done previously are being carried out using the software.

- **Back up data:** One concern with using software for accounting is that data can be lost if something goes wrong with the computer. Hence it is important to ensure that accounting records are backed up regularly on disks or online.

In order to establish a reasonable degree of confidence in data generated by an accounting system, the hardware, software, communications and human operating procedures must operate in concert. Integrity of data can be compromised in any one of the several phases of the "life cycle" of accounting data. The basic stages in this life cycle might be characterized as follows:

1. **Measurement and classification:** The process for entering initial data varies depending on the software chosen. It is important to use the information that comes with the software by reading through the manual, reviewing the startup suggestions made, and subsequently picking the methods that best match the business' operating style.

2. **Transcription, validation and storage:** The best time to convert is at the end of an accounting period: at the end of a calendar or fiscal year. This is to avoid a lot of extra work of adding transactions that already occurred during a period.

It is suggested that the data from the trial balance used to close the books at the end of most recent accounting period should be entered in the computerized system. Asset, liability, and equity accounts should have carry-over balances, but income and expense accounts should have zero balances.

3. **Processing, updating and recovery:** After all the appropriate data is entered, it is important to run a series of financial reports, such as an income statement and statement of financial position, to be sure the data is entered and formatted in the way the business wants. It is a lot easier to change formatting when the system is not full of data.

A Check should be carried out to see if the right numbers have been entered by verifying that the new accounting system's financial reports match what was created manually. If the numbers are different, it is important to find out why. Otherwise the reports at the end of the accounting period will be wrong. If the numbers don't match, the error could be in the data entered or in the reports developed manually. Hence entries should be rechecked. If the income statement and statement of financial position still don't look right, then the trial balance should be rechecked as well.

TEST YOURSELF

14.1. Multiple choice questions:

i. Accounting software is applicable to which area of accounting?

A. tax accounting B. Public accounting C. Management consulting D. all of these

ii. Which of the following does not influence the organisation of a computerised system of accounting:

A. organisational culture
B. Information technology
C. Business strategy
D. Legal environment

iii. What is data?

A   all of the facts that are collected, stored and processed by a computerised system
B   all of the debit and credit information about each transaction
C   the output that results from an input of information
D   the same thing as information

iv. Reliability refers the characteristic of information whereby:

A. uncertainty is reduced
B. information is free from error or bias
C. timely
D. verifiable

v. Timely, accurate information can improve decision-making in what way?

A. It identifies situations requiring management action
B. It provides a basis for choosing from alternative actions
C. It provides feedback that can be used to improve future decisions
D. All of the above

14.2. List the advantages of a computerised accounting system.

14.3. What are the disadvantages of a computerised accounting system?

14.4. Discuss ways in which the integrity of the accounting data can be ensured during a transfer to a computerised accounting system.

14.5. Discuss the process of computerising the business accounts.

CHAPTER 15
ACTIVITY BASED COSTING

Q. What is meant by 'Activity based costing'?

Ans. Activity based costing (ABC) assigns manufacturing overhead costs to products in a more logical manner than the traditional approach of simply allocating costs on the basis of machine or labour hours. Activity based costing first assigns costs to the activities that are the real cause of the overhead. It then assigns the cost of those activities only to the products that are actually demanding the activities. ABC therefore focuses on activities. A key assumption in activity-based costing is that overhead costs are caused by a variety of activities, and that different products utilize these activities in a non-homogeneous fashion. Sometimes, however, the activity itself is the cost object of interest. For example, managers at a jeans' manufacturer might want to know how much the company spends to acquire denim fabric, as input in a sourcing decision. The "activity" of acquiring fabric incurs costs associated with negotiating prices with suppliers, issuing purchase orders, receiving fabric, inspecting fabric, and processing payments and returns.

Q. Explain, by citing an example, how ABC can be used?

Ans. A product 'Queses' is a low volume product which requires the following activities: engineering, testing and numerous machine setups as it is ordered in small quantities. Another product made by the company is 'Treses' which is a high volume product that runs continuously requiring little attention and only some engineering. If the company uses traditional costing methods, the overheads incurred would be allocated over both products based on the number of machine hours, then Queses will have little overhead costs allocated to it. Treses, on the other hand, will be allocated a major part of the overhead costs even though it demanded very little overhead activity. This will result in a miscalculation of each product's true cost. Activity based costing will rectify this by assigning overheads on more than just one activity such as engineering, testing and multiple machine setups – not just the single activity of running the machine.

Q. Why has the importance of ABC grown in recent years?

Ans. Activity based costing has grown in importance due to the following reasons:
1) manufacturing overhead costs have increased significantly,
2) manufacturing overhead costs no longer correlate with the productive machine hours or direct labor hours,
3) the diversity of products and the diversity in customers' demands have grown, and
4) some products are produced in large batches, while others are produced in small batches.

Q. Define:

a. Cost drivers

b. Cost pools

Ans. a. Cost drivers: An activity cost driver is associated with activities undertaken in a department. A factory, for example, may have running machinery as an activity. The activity cost driver associated with running the machinery could be machine operating hours, which would drive the costs of labour, maintenance and power consumption of running the machinery activity.

In activity-based costing systems, the most significant cost drivers are identified. Then a database is created that shows how these cost drivers are distributed across products. This database is used to assign costs to the various products depending on the extent to which they use each cost driver.

b. Cost pools are a grouping of individual costs, typically by department or service center.

Cost allocations are then made from a cost pool. For example, the cost of the repair & maintenance department is accumulated in a cost pool and then allocated to those departments using its services.

Q. Explain in detail the uses of ABC.

Ans. The fundamental advantage of using an ABC system is to more precisely determine how overhead is used. Once you have an ABC system, you can obtain better information about the following issues:

- *Activity costs.* ABC is designed to track the cost of activities, so you can use it to see if activity costs are in line with industry standards. If not, ABC is an excellent feedback tool for measuring the ongoing cost of specific services as management focuses on cost reduction.
- *Customer profitability.* Though most of the costs incurred for individual customers are simply product costs, there is also an overhead component, such as unusually high customer service levels, product return handling, and cooperative marketing agreements. An ABC system can sort through these additional overhead costs and help you determine which customers are actually earning you a reasonable profit. This analysis may result in some unprofitable customers being turned away, or more emphasis being placed on those customers who are earning the company its largest profits.
- *Distribution cost.* The typical company uses a variety of distribution channels to sell its products, such as retail, Internet, distributors, and mail order catalogs. Most of the structural cost of maintaining a distribution channel is overhead, so if you can make a reasonable determination of which distribution channels are using overhead, you can make decisions to alter how distribution channels are used, or even to drop unprofitable channels.
- *Make or buy.* ABC provides a comprehensive view of every cost associated with the in-house manufacture of a product, so that you can see precisely which costs will be eliminated if an item is outsourced, versus which costs will remain.
- *Margins.* With proper overhead allocation from an ABC system, you can determine the margins of various products, product lines, and entire subsidiaries. This can be quite useful for determining where to position company resources to earn the largest margins.
- *Minimum price.* Product pricing is really based on the price that the market will bear, but the marketing manager should know what the cost of the product is, in order to avoid selling a product that will lose a company money on every sale. ABC is very good for determining which overhead costs should be included in this minimum cost, depending upon the circumstances under which products are being sold.
- *Production facility cost.* It is usually quite easy to segregate overhead costs at the plant-wide level, so you can compare the costs of production between different facilities.

Clearly, there are many valuable uses for the information provided by an ABC system. However, this information will only be available if you design the system to provide the specific set of data needed for each decision. If you install a generic ABC system and then use it for the above decisions, you may find that it does not provide the information that you need. Ultimately, the design of the system is determined by a cost-benefit analysis of which decisions you want it to assist with, and whether the cost of the system is worth the benefit of the resulting information.

Q. Explain the problems that businesses encounter with ABC.

Ans. Many companies initiate ABC projects with the best of intentions, only to see a very high proportion of the projects either fail, or eventually lapse into disuse. There are several reasons for these issues, which are:

- *Cost pool volume.* The advantage of an ABC system is the high quality of information that it produces, but this comes at the cost of using a large number of cost pools – and the more cost pools there are, the greater the cost of managing the system. To reduce this cost, run an ongoing analysis of the cost to maintain each cost pool, in comparison to the utility of the resulting information. Doing so should keep the number of cost pools down to manageable proportions.

- *Installation time.* ABC systems are notoriously difficult to install, with multi-year installations being the norm when a company attempts to install it across all product lines and facilities. For such comprehensive installations, it is difficult to maintain a high level of management and budgetary support as the months roll by without installation being completed. Success rates are much higher for smaller, more targeted ABC installations.

- *Multi-department data sources.* An ABC system may require data input from multiple departments, and each of those departments may have greater priorities than the ABC system. Thus, the larger the number of departments involved in the system, the greater the risk that data inputs will fail over time. This problem can be avoided by designing the system to only need information from the most supportive managers.

- *Project basis.* Many ABC projects are authorized on a project basis, so that information is only collected once; the information is useful for a company's current operational situation, and it gradually declines in usefulness as the operational structure changes over time. Management may not authorize funding for additional ABC projects later on, so ABC tends to be "done" once and then discarded. To mitigate this issue, build as much of the ABC data collection structure into the existing accounting system, so that the cost of these projects is reduced; at a lower cost, it is more likely that additional ABC projects will be authorized in the future.

- *Reporting of unused time.* When a company asks its employees to report on the time spent on various activities, they have a strong tendency to make sure that the reported amounts equal 100% of their time. However, there is a large amount of slack time in anyone's work day that may involve breaks, administrative meetings, playing games on the Internet, and so forth. Employees usually mask these activities by apportioning more time to other activities. These inflated numbers represent misallocations of costs in the ABC system, sometimes by quite substantial amounts.

- *Separate data set.* An ABC system rarely can be constructed to pull all of the information it needs directly from the general ledger. Instead, it requires a separate database that pulls in information from several sources, only one of which is existing general ledger accounts. It can be quite difficult to maintain this extra database, since it calls for significant extra staff time for which there may not be an adequate budget. The best work-around is to design the system to require the minimum amount of additional information other than that which is already available in the general ledger.

- *Targeted usage.* The benefits of ABC are most apparent when cost accounting information is difficult to discern, due to the presence of multiple product lines, machines being used for the production of many products, numerous machine setups, and so forth – in other words, in complex production environments. If a company does not operate in such an environment, then it may spend a great deal of money on an ABC installation, only to find that the resulting information is not overly valuable.

The broad range of issues noted here should make it clear that ABC tends to follow a bumpy path in many organizations, with a tendency for its usefulness to decline over time. Of the problem mitigation suggestions noted here, the key point is to construct a highly targeted ABC system that produces the most critical information at a reasonable cost. If that system takes root in your company, then consider a gradual expansion, during which you only expand further if there is a clear and demonstrable benefit in doing so. The worst thing you can do is to install a large and comprehensive ABC system, since it is expensive, meets with the most resistance, and is the most likely to fail over the long term.

Q. What are the four broad categories of activities identified in an activity-based costing system?

Ans. The four broad categories of activities identified in an activity-based costing system are as follows:

(a) Unit-level activities: Must be done for each unit of production. This activity or cost occurs every time a unit is produced. An example is the utility cost for production equipment. This level of activity usually relates directly to production volume.

(b) Batch-level activities: Must be performed for each batch of products. Examples include moving raw material between the stock room and production line or setting up a machine for a run.

(c) Product-sustaining activities: This activity is performed to maintain product designs, processes, models, and parts. Examples include expediting purchasing, maintaining tools and dies, or assuring quality. Sustaining activities are required for supporting a key manufacturing capability or process.

(d) Facility-level (or general-operations-level) activities: Required for the entire production process to occur. They are fundamental to supporting the business entity at the most basic level. Examples are managing or cleaning the building. Depreciation is also a facility-level account because depreciation on plant and equipment represents the cost of providing production facilities in which manufacturing can take place.

Q. How can the cost of each activity be calculated?

Ans. The cost of each activity = $\dfrac{\text{cost of activity}}{\text{Number of times that activity is performed}}$

Q. Outline the difference in Absorption costing and Activity Based Costing.

Ans. The stages in calculating the cost of a product using Absorption costing are:

1. Identify the cost centres
2. Identify the direct costs associated with the cost object
3. Identify overhead cost attributable to each cost centre
4. Select the cost allocation basis for assigning overhead costs to the cost object (e.g. machine or labour hours)
5. Develop an overhead absorption rate per unit for each cost centre in order to allocate them to the cost object.

Activity-based costing refines steps 3 and 4 by dividing large heterogeneous cost centers into multiple smaller, homogeneous cost pools. ABC then attempts to select, as the cost allocation base for each overhead cost pool, a cost driver that best captures the *cause and effect relationship* between the cost object and the incurrence of overhead costs. Often, the best cost driver is a nonfinancial variable.

Hence the stages in calculating the cost of a product using Activity Based Costing are:

1. Classify costs – direct and overheads
2. Identify the activities responsible for the overhead cost.
3. Identify the cost drivers.
4. Apportion appropriate overheads to the cost drivers.
5. Calculate the cost driver rate.

6. Absorb both indirect and direct costs into the product or service.

Product-costing systems based on a single, volume-based cost driver (Absorption costing) tend to over-cost high-volume products, because all overhead costs are combined into one pool and distributed across all products on the basis of only one cost driver. This simple averaging process fails to recognize the fact that a disproportionate amount of costs often is associated with low-volume or complex products. The result is that low-volume products are assigned less than their share of manufacturing costs, and high-volume products are assigned more than their share of the costs.

In traditional, volume-based costing systems, only direct material and direct labour are considered direct costs. In contrast, under an activity-based costing system, an effort is made to account for as many costs as possible as direct costs of production. Any cost that can possibly be traced to a particular product line is treated as a direct cost of that product.

Q. What are the advantages of using activity-based costing?

Ans. Activity-based costing results in improved costing accuracy for the following reasons.

1. Companies that use ABC are not limited to a single driver when allocating costs to products and activities. Not all costs vary with units, and ABC allows users to select a host of non-unit-level cost drivers.
2. Consumption ratios often differ greatly among activities. No single cost driver will accurately assign costs for all activities in this situation.
3. Activity-based costing increases the number of cost pools used to accumulate overhead costs. Rather than accumulating all overhead costs in a single, plant-wide pool, or accumulating them in departmental pools, costs are accumulated for each major activity.
4. The activity cost pools are more homogeneous than departmental cost pools. In principle, all of the costs in an activity cost pool pertain to a single activity. In contrast, departmental cost pools contain the costs of many different activities carried out in the department.
5. Activity-based costing changes the bases used to assign overhead costs to products. Rather than assigning costs on the basis of direct labor or some other measure of volume, costs are assigned on the basis of activity measures that gauge how much of the overhead resource has been consumed by a particular activity.
6. ABC improves product costing accuracy and decision making.
7. ABC allows managers to exert more control over the activities that cause the costs.
8. ABC allows managers to identify which of the activities add value and which do not

Q. What are the disadvantages of activity-based costing?

Ans. The disadvantages are:

1. Activity-based costing assumes that costs are proportional to activity. In reality, costs appear to increase less than in proportion to increases in activity. This implies that activity-based product costs will be overstated for purposes of making decisions. (The same criticism can be levelled at conventional product costs.)
2. The costs of implementing and maintaining an activity-based costing system can be high and the benefits may not justify this cost.

Exerise15.1

Determine whether the following are product-level, batch-level or facility level activities.

1. Various individuals manage the parts inventories.
2. A clerk in the factory issues purchase orders for a job.
3. The personnel department trains new production workers.
4. The factory's general manager uses her office in the factory building.
5. Direct labor workers assemble products.

6. Engineers design new products.
7. The materials storekeeper issues raw materials to be used in jobs.
8. The maintenance department performs periodic preventative maintenance on general-use equipment.

EXHIBIT

Company ABC has 2 fixed price contracts for 2 different clients. The company has enough capacity for both contracts but is uncertain whether they will be profitable.
Data as follows:

Customer	A	B
Component Type	A999	B999
Contract Value($)	$27,000	$100,000
Contract Quantity	1,000 units	2,000 units
Material cost/unit	$15	$20
Moulding time/batch	5 hours	7.5 hours
Batch Size	100 units	50 units

Annual Budgeted overheads as follows:

Activity	Cost Driver	Cost driver volume/yr	Cost pool
Moulding	Moulding hours	2,000	$150,000
Inspection	Batches	150	$75,000
Production Management	Contracts	20	$125,000

Required:
(a) Calculate the activity based costs and profits for each contract
(b) Calculate the profit for each job using Absorption costing. Absorb overheads using moulding hours.
(c) Compare the two methods.

Solution:

(a) Computation of the activity based costs and profits for each contract.
Step 1: Cost per unit of cost driver = Cost pool / cost driver volume

Activity	Cost pool A	Cost driver/yr B	Cost/unit of cost driver A/B
Moulding	$150,000	2,000	$75/moulding hour
Inspection	$75,000	150	$500/batch
Production Management	$125,000	20	$6,250/contract

Step 2: Compute the cost drivers consumed by each contract

Cost driver	Customer A	Customer B
Batches	1,000 unit/100 =10	2,000unts/50=40
Moulding hours	10 batches x 5=50	40 batches x 7.5=300
Contracts	1	1

3: Finally, compute the costs and profit for each contract

	Contract A	Contract B
Selling price	$27,000	$100,000
Materials	1,000 x $15=$15,000	2,000 x$20=$40,000
Moulding	50 hours x$75=$3,750	300hours x$75=$22,500
Inspection	10 batches x $500=$5,000	40 batches x $500=$20,000
Management	$6,250	$6,250

| Total cost | $30,000 | $88,750 |
| Profit/(Loss) | ($3,000) | $11,250 |

(b) Computation of profit based on absorption costing using moulding hour

Overhead absorption rate =Total annual overheads/annual moulding hour

= ($150,000+$125,000)/2,000 =$175 per moulding hour.

Costs and profits for each contract

	Contract A	Contract B
Selling price	$27,000	$100,000
Materials	1,000 x $15=$15,000	2,000 x $20 =$40,000
Overheads	50 hours x$175=$8,750	300 hours x$175=$52,500
Total cost	$23,750	$92,500
Profit/(Loss)	$3,250	$7,500

(c) Conclusion

1. Based on activity based costing, Customer A's contract would be unprofitable while Customer B's contract is worth accepting.

2. If we use the traditional costing accounting/method which is the absorption costing basis, the management will think that both contracts were profitable.

3. Using activity based costing, the management should only accept only 1 contract which is Customer A's contract.

Exercise 15.2

Company XYZ has 6 standard products from stainless steel and brass. The company's most popular product is Product Packie

The following are Product's data for next year budget:

Activity	Cost Driver	Cost driver volume/yr	Cost pool
Purchasing	Purchase orders	1,500	$75,000
Setting	Batches produced	2,800	$112,000
Materials handling	Materials movements	8,000	$96,000
Inspection	Batches produced	2,800	$70,000
Machining costs	Machine hours	50,000	$150,000

Additional information:

Purchase orders: 25

Output: 15,000 units

Production batch size: 100 units

Materials movements per batch: 6

Machine hours per unit: 0.1

Required:

(a) Calculate the budgeted overhead costs using activity based costing principles

(b) Calculate the budgeted overhead costs using absorption costing (absorb overhead using machine hours)

(c) How can the company reduce the ABC for Product Packie

Exercise 15.3

(a) Refer to table below and fill up the following values:

(i) Overhead per cost driver unit

(ii) Total overhead per product per activity

(iii) Cost per item

Activity	Total over heads $	Total cost driver units	Over head per cost driver unit	Cost driver units per product			Total overhead per product per activity		
				M	N	O	M	N	O
Machinery set-ups	20,000	230		140	80	100			
Materials handling	12,000	90		12	14	14			
Quality control	24,000	120		75	55	70			
Supervision	6,000	40		10	15	25			
Maintenance	6,450	25		4	6	5			
				Number of units produced			1,100	450	450
				Cost per item ($)					

Required
  (b) What is a cost driver unit?
  (c) What do you understand by the term "cost driver unit".
  (d) Give an example for each activity listed in the above table.

Exercise 15.4
A company manufactures two products, X and Y, using the same equipment and similar processes. Data for the production of these items in one period is shown below:
Data:

	A	B
Quantity produced per period		
Material cost per unit	20,000	10,000
Direct labour hours per unit		$20
Machine hours per unit		½
Set-ups per period		4
Orders handled per period		70
Cost per direct labour hour		160

Overhead costs	$
Relating to machine activity	300,000
Relating to set-ups of production runs	50,000
Relating to handling of orders	70,000

Required:
Using activity-based costing, what is the full production cost per unit A?

Exercise15.5
Ahmed manufactures two products. He has recently started using Activity Based Costing (ABC) for allocating the overhead costs to these products. The budgeted data for one month is available as follows:

	Product X	Product Y
Demand (units)	10 000	14 000
Number of orders	20	60
Number of production runs	12	36

	Per unit	Per unit
Direct labour hours	0.75	1.5
Machine hours	2.5	0.5
Direct costs ($)	100	50

Total factory overhead costs	$
Machine maintenance costs	264 000
Ordering costs	54 000
Production run costs	24 000
	342 000

REQUIRED

(a) Calculate the full cost per unit for Product X and Product Y using ABC.

Additional information

Ahmed previously used direct labour hours as a basis to charge overheads to each product.

REQUIRED

(b) Calculate the overhead charged to each product using the direct labour hour rate.

(c) Explain the effect that changing the method has had on the overhead cost of each product.

Additional information

A customer requires 50 units of Product X and has offered to pay Ahmed a total of $8450 for them. Ahmed uses 40% mark-up on all his products.

REQUIRED

(d) Recommend whether or not Ahmed should accept the offer. Justify your decision using appropriate calculations and considering both financial and non-financial factors.

(e) State two reasons why a business may use ABC for allocating overhead costs.

(UCLES, 2017, AS/A Level Accounting, Syllabus 9706/33, May/June)

Exercise 15.6

"The idea behind this method of costing is that it is the cause of a cost which is important and not whether it is fixed or variable."

REQUIRED

(a) Identify the costing method described in the quotation.

Additional information

Haruka Limited produces a single product. The factory is operational 5 days a week for 50 weeks a year. It produces one batch of 200 units each day.

Overheads amount to $79 000 a year.

REQUIRED

(b) Calculate the overhead cost per unit to two decimal places.

Additional information

These overheads comprised:

	$
Machine set-up costs	2 000
Production quality inspections	5 000
Production stoppage costs	4 000
Machine maintenance	8 000
Machine running costs	60 000

The machines were set up at the start of each working day.

There was a quality inspection every week.

The machines were maintained each day.

Production was stopped on average once every 4 weeks for unexpected maintenance.

Samir, the finance director, asks Sara, the factory accountant, to analyse the overhead cost per unit across each of the five overheads incurred.

 REQUIRED

 (c) Prepare an analysis showing how the total overhead cost per unit (from part b) is split between each of the individual overheads.

Additional information

Sara has complained to Samir that producing this analysis is not worthwhile.

 REQUIRED

 (d) Advise Samir whether or not he should continue to ask for this analysis in the future years. Justify your answer by considering the benefits and drawbacks of this costing method.

(UCLES, 2016, AS/A Level Accounting, Syllabus 9706/32, Oct/Nov)

TEST YOURSELF

Q1. Multiple choice questions:

i. In a "pure" ABC system, which of the following would *not* be assigned to products?

 A. batch-level activities

 B. facility-level activities

 C. process-level activities

 C. product-level activities

ii. Which of the following would be classified as a product-level activity?

 A. plant management

 B. production scheduling

 C. engineering changes

 D. material handling

iii. Which of the following statements is correct?

 A. Activity-based costing uses a number of activity cost pools, each of which is allocated to products on the basis of direct labour-hours.

 B. Activity rates in activity-based costing are computed by dividing costs from the first-stage allocations by the activity measure for each activity cost pool.

 C. An activity-based costing system is generally easier to implement and maintain than traditional costing system.

 D. One of the goals of activity-based management is the elimination of waste by allocating costs to products that waste resources.

iv. Bangayan Company uses activity-based costing to determine the costs of its two products: A and B. The estimated total cost and expected activity for one of the company's three activity cost pools are as follows.

Estimated cost = $14,000

Estimated Activity:	Product A	Product B
	400	300

The overhead cost for this activity is closest to:

 A. $4.00   **B.** $8.59   **C.** $18.00   **D.** $ 20.00

v. A company uses ABC to compute product costs for external reports. The company has 3 activity cost pools and applies overheads using predetermined overhead rates for each activity cost pool. Estimated costs totaled $40,000 and expected activity equals 2,500 for this activity cost pool. Actual activity for the current year was 2,490. The amount of overhead applied for this activity during the year was closest to:

    A. $ 36,300   **B.** $39,840   **C.** $40,000   **D.** $ 96,910

15.2 B Limited manufactures two products Alpha and Omega. The following budgeted figures are available.

Alpha Omega Budgeted production and sales units 20 000 8 000 Direct materials used per unit 5 kilo 11 kilo Direct materials cost per kilo $20 $11 Labour hours per unit 2 1 Direct labour cost per hour $12 $6

The fixed overheads are forecast as $396 000 and are allocated on the basis of labour hours.

Answer the following questions in the Question Paper. Questions are printed here for reference only.

  (a) Calculate for each product: (i) the total production costs

                                     (ii) the production cost per unit

Additional information
The sales price per unit is calculated by adding 50% to the cost.
 (b) Calculate the selling price per unit for each product.

Additional information
The directors of the company have been advised that they should adopt activity based costing to allocate the production overheads. They have identified the four major activities involved in the production cycle as machine set-up, materials handling, maintenance of machinery and production inspection and packing. The costs of each activity have been established and the overheads apportioned between the activities as follows:

Production Overheads	$	Alpha	Omega
Machine set-up	90 000	15 times	10 times
Materials handling	80 000	6 receipts	14 receipts
Machine maintenance	46 000	130 hours	100 hours
Inspection and packing	180 000	40 hours	20 hours
	396 000		

 (c) State two disadvantages to a business of adopting activity based costing.
 (d) Calculate the total production overhead to be allocated to each product using activity based costing.
 (e) Recalculate the cost per unit and selling price of each product maintaining the 50% mark-up.
 (f) Explain three reasons why B Limited should change the method of allocating overheads to using activity based costing.
Additional information
It has been suggested that customers will not accept the increase in price of Omega. The directors are therefore considering changing the profit margins to 60% on Alpha and 30% on Omega.
 (g) (i) Calculate the new total profit for each product if this change is adopted.
    (ii) Give two reasons why B Limited should adopt this change.
(UCLES, 2018, AS/A Level Accounting, Syllabus 9706/33, May/June)

CHAPTER 16
STANDARD COSTING

Q. Explain 'Standard costing'.

Ans. Standard costs are estimated, expected costs, usually associated with a manufacturing company's costs of direct material, direct labor, and manufacturing overheads. Rather than assigning the actual costs of direct material, direct labor, and manufacturing overheads to a product, many manufacturers assign the expected or standard cost. This means that a manufacturer's inventories and cost of goods sold will begin with amounts reflecting the standard costs, not the actual costs, of a product. Manufacturers, of course, still have to pay the actual costs. As a result there are almost always differences between the actual costs and the standard costs, and those differences are known as variances. The core reason for using standard costs is that there are a number of applications where it is too time-consuming to collect actual costs, so standard costs are used as a close approximation to actual costs. Many companies use standard cost calculations to derive product prices. Standard costing and the related variances are valuable management tools.

Q. Why is standard costing considered to be a valuable management tool?

Ans. Standard costs are set with a view to measuring actual performance against the standard and reporting variances to the managers responsible. Variances are tools to control costs, improve efficiencies and should be used positively. Here are some potential uses:

1. **Budgeting** A budget is always composed of standard costs, since it would be impossible to include in it the exact actual cost of an item on the day the budget is finalized. Also, since a key application of the budget is to compare it to actual results in subsequent periods, the standards used within it continue to appear in financial reports through the budget period.

2. **Inventory costing** It is extremely easy to print a report showing the period-end inventory balances (if you are using a perpetual inventory system), multiply it by the standard cost of each item, and instantly generate an ending inventory valuation. The result does not exactly match the actual cost of inventory, but it is close. However, it may be necessary to update standard costs frequently, if actual costs are continually changing. It is easiest to update costs for the highest-dollar components of inventory on a frequent basis, and leave lower-value items for occasional cost reviews.

3. **Overhead application** If it takes too long to aggregate actual costs into cost pools for allocation to inventory, then you may use a standard overhead application rate instead, and adjust this rate every few months to keep it close to actual costs.

4. **Price formulation** If a company deals with custom products, then it uses standard costs to compile the projected cost of a customer's requirements, after which it adds on a margin. This may be quite a complex system, where the sales department uses a database of component costs that change depending upon the unit quantity that the customer wants to order. This system may also account for changes in the company's production costs at different volume levels, since this may call for the use of longer production runs that are less expensive

Q. List the disadvantages of standard costing.

Ans. Some problem areas are:

- *Cost-plus contracts.* If you have a contract with a customer under which the customer pays you for your costs incurred, plus a profit (known as a cost-plus contract), then you must use actual costs, as per the terms of the contract. Standard costing is not allowed.
- *Drives inappropriate activities.* A number of the variances reported under a standard costing system will drive management to take incorrect actions to create favorable variances. For example, they may buy raw materials in larger quantities in order to improve the purchase price variance, even though this increases the investment in inventory. Similarly, management may schedule longer production runs in order to improve the labor efficiency variance, even though it is better to produce in smaller quantities and accept less labour efficiency in exchange.
- *Fast-paced environment.* A standard costing system assumes that costs do not change much in the near term, so that you can rely on standards for a number of months or even a year, before updating the costs. However, in an environment where product lives are short or continuous improvement is driving down costs, a standard cost may become out-of-date within a month or two.
- *Slow feedback.* A complex system of variance calculations is an integral part of a standard costing system, which the accounting staff completes at the end of each reporting period. If the production department is focused on immediate feedback of problems for instant correction, the reporting of these variances is much too late to be useful.
- *Unit-level information.* The variance calculations that typically accompany a standard costing report are accumulated in aggregate for a company's entire production department, and so are unable to provide information about discrepancies at a lower level, such as the individual work cell, batch, or unit.

Q. What are the different types of standards?

Ans. A standard is predetermined or planned and managers normally wish that actual results equate to standards. The different types of standards are:

- Basic
- Ideal
- Attainable

Q. Explain: Basic standards

Ans. These are standards established considering those factors that remain unchanged over a long period of time and are altered only when the business operations change significantly. These standards help compare business operations over a longer period of time. As basic standards are not updated according to latest circumstances, they are not used often as they cannot help in short term period variance analysis.

Q. Explain: Ideal standards

Ans. These standards are possible using optimum production conditions signifying the achievement of maximum efficiency at a minimum cost. They are rarely used as they are almost impossible to achieve and can therefore be very demotivating to the workforce. However, JIT and TQM businesses often use an ideal standard due to their emphasis on continuous improvement and high quality.

Q. Explain: Attainable standards

Ans. These standards are based on current circumstances and are achievable given efficient production conditions and allowing for unavoidable production problems such as fatigue, wastage, breakdowns in machinery etc. Current standards may be set lower or easier than expected standards but good managers always try to achieve what is attainable so that no resource is left unused.

Q. Define:

a. A variance

b. Standard hour

c. Sub-variances

d. Favourable variances

e. Adverse variances

Ans. a. A variance is the difference between a budgeted, planned or standard cost or revenue and the actual amount incurred/sold. Variances can be calculated for sales, material, labour, variable overheads and fixed overheads.

b. A standard hour is the amount of work achievable, at the expected level of efficiency, in an hour.

c. A sub-variance: It is a part of a total variance. When sub-variances are added together, they equal the total variance.

d. Favourable variances: These are when standard costs are more than actual costs or standard revenue is less than actual revenue.

e. Adverse variances: These are when actual costs are more than standard costs or actual revenue is less than standard revenue.

Q. Define: Total direct materials variance

Ans. This variance identifies the difference between the expected expenditure and the actual expenditure on direct materials.

EXHIBIT

Ice & co have budgeted $45,000 for direct materials in the month of June. It was confirmed that the expenditure for direct materials was:

   a. $50,000.
   b. $36,000
Required:
Calculate the total direct materials variance.

Solution:

  a. Total direct material variance = 50,000 – 45,000 = $5,000 (adverse)
  b. Total direct material variance = 50,000 – 36,000 = $14,000 (favourable)

Q. Name the materials sub-variances.

Ans. Materials sub-variance are:

  a. Materials usage variance: If actual production used more or less units of material than expected.
  b. Materials price variance: If each unit of material cost more or less than expected.

Q. What is the formula for each materials sub-variance?

Ans. Material usage variance = SP (SQ – AQ)

      Materials price variance = AQ (SP – AP)

Where SP = Standard price, SQ = standard quantity, AQ= Actual quantity, AP = actual price.

EXHIBIT

You are given the following information:

	STANDARD	ACTUAL
Quantity of materials	59,850	60,000
Cost per kg	1.10	1.05

Required:

Calculate:

  a. Materials price variance
  b. Materials usage variance
  c. Total material variance

Solution:

  a. Materials price variance = 60,000 (1.10 – 1.05)   = $3,000 (favourable).
     This is due to the materials costing less than expected.
  b. Materials usage variance = 1.10 (60,000 – 59,850) = $165 (adverse).
     This is due to usage being more than expected.
  c. Total materials variance   = $2,835 (favourable)

Exercise 16.1

P&G produces large size suitcases for the use of tourists. The company uses a standard costing system to control costs. The standards for materials and labour costs to manufacture 1 suitcase are as follows:

Direct materials: 7.2 lbs. @ $5 per kg. $36.00

Direct labour: 0.4 hours @ $20 per hour $8.00

During the last month, P&G produced 2,500 large suitcases. 20,000 kg of direct materials were purchased @ $4.8 per kg. There was no direct materials inventory at the beginning and end of the month. 900 direct labour hours were recorded @ $24 per hour.

Required:

Calculate:

    a. **direct materials price variance**

    b. **direct materials quantity variance.**

Exercise 16.2

The standard requirements to manufacture one chair are as follows:

Direct materials: 5 metres wood @ $0.60 per metre

Direct labour: 1.2 hours @ $14 per hour

During the last month, Jason manufactured 4,000 chairs. 50,000 metres of wood was purchased @ 0.56 per metre. 20,000 metres of wood was in stock at the end of the month. 6,400 direct labour hours were worked @ $15 per hour.

Required:

Calculate:

    a. **direct materials price variance**

    b. **direct materials quantity variances**

Q. Why do direct material variances arise?

Ans. The reasons for direct materials price variances are:

A favourable or unfavourable material price variance may occur due to one or more of the following reasons:

1. **Order size:** Some suppliers allow discounts on large orders. Materials purchased in large quantities may reduce the unit price and a favourable price variance may occur.

2. **Rise in price :** The rise in the general price level may increase the input costs of the vendor and as a result the vendor may increase the price of the materials. The rise in price is very common reason of an unfavourable variance.

3. **Urgent needs :** If production department does not indicate the need of materials on time, the purchasing department may have to order on urgent basis. This may increase the price of materials and other expenses associated with the order.

4. **Quality :** A favourable price variance may be the result of purchasing low quality materials and an unfavourable variance may be the result of purchasing high quality materials.

5. **Inefficient standard setting:** Inefficiencies in terms of forecasting and environmental scanning during the standard setting process can be a reason for huge variances.

6. **Transportation:** Transportation is a part of total direct materials cost. Any change in the transportation expenses can change the total and per unit cost of direct materials available for use and can become the reason of favourable or unfavourable direct materials price variance.

7. **The role of just-in-time manufacturing :** A company that operates under a just-in-time (JIT) manufacturing system may have to face a shortage of direct materials due to a sudden increase in demand for the product. Rush orders normally increase costs. In this case the company will have to either accept an unfavourable materials price variance or lose sales.

8. **Inefficient or unreliable Suppliers:** A deviation from standard material costs may be the result of inefficient or unreliable vendors. For example, if suppliers of raw materials are unable to meet the demand, the company may have to look for another supplier who may be more costly.

Q. Define: Total direct labour variance

Ans. Total direct labour variance is the difference between the budgeted (standard) cost of direct labour to produce a specific number of units and the actual cost that was incurred to produce those units. e.g. If a company expected to pay $40,000 for direct labour for the month of June and the actual costs were $34,000, then the total direct labour variance for the month of June was $6,000 (favourable).

Q. Define: Direct labour efficiency variance

Ans. This is a sub-variance. The difference between the actual time taken to manufacture a certain number of units and the time allocated by standards to manufacture these units, multiplied by the standard direct labour rate is called the direct labour efficiency variance or direct labour quantity variance. It could be favourable or unfavourable. If the workers manufacture a certain number of units in an amount of time that is less than that allowed by the standards, the variance is known as a favourable direct labour efficiency variance. However, if the workers take more time than that allocated by the standards, the variance is known as an unfavourable direct labour efficiency variance.

Q. What are the reasons for unfavourable labour efficiency variances?

Ans. Some common reasons for an unfavourable labour efficiency variance are:
1. Inexperienced workers
2. Poorly motivated workers
3. Old or faulty equipment
4. Purchase of low quality or unsuitable direct materials
5. Poor supervision
6. Insufficient demand for the company's product
7. Frequent breakdowns
8. Shortage of raw materials
9. A Just-in-time manufacturing system

Q. Discuss the reasons for an unfavourable labour rate variance.

Ans. Usually, a labour rate variance does not occur due to a change in the labour rates because they are normally predictable. The common reason of an unfavourable labour rate variance is inappropriate use of labour by production supervisors.

All tasks do not require equally skilled workers. Some tasks are more complicated and require more experienced workers than others. This should be kept in mind when tasks are assigned to workers. If simple, unskilled tasks are assigned to very experienced workers, an unfavourable labour rate variance may be the result, as highly experienced workers are paid higher wages. On the other hand, if poorly trained workers are assigned tasks that require a high level of expertise, a favourable labour rate variance may be the result. Because such workers are usually paid low wages. But inexperienced workers may not be as efficient and due to wastage of materials, the result could be an unfavourable materials usage variance.

Q. How would you calculate the following sub-variances:
a. direct labour efficiency variance
b. direct labour rate variance?

Ans. Labour efficiency variance is calculated as follows:
a. SH x SR – AH x SR = Labour efficiency variance (Standard wage rate remains constant.
b. AH x SR – AS x AR = Labour wage rate variance (Actual hours worked remains constant)
Where SQ = Standard hours, SR = Standard rate, AH = Actual hours, AR = Actual rate.

EXHIBIT

A furniture manufacturing company presents the following data for the month of July 2015.

Standard direct labour rate per hour	$6.50
Actual direct labour rate per hour	$6.75
Standard time to produce on unit of product	3 hours

| Production during the month of July 2015 | 600 units |
| Hours worked during the month of July | 1850 hours |

Required:
 a. **Calculate the direct labour efficiency variance**
b. **Indicate whether the variance is favourable/unfavourable**

Solution:
a. Direct labour efficiency variance = SR × (AH – SH)

$$= \$6.50 \times (1{,}850 \text{ hours} - 1{,}800 \text{ hours }^*)$$

$$= \$6.50 \times 50 \text{ hours}$$

$$= \$325 \text{ (Unfavourable)}$$

Standard hours allowed to manufacture 600 units =600 units × 3 hours = 1,800 hours

Note: The actual direct labour rate is not used to compute this variance.

b. The variance is unfavourable because labour worked 50 hours more than what was allowed by standard.

Exhibit
A labour-intensive manufacturing company that uses a standard costing system gives you the following information: The standard time to manufacture a product 2.5 direct labour hours.
 The standard wage rate is $7.80 per hour.
 Last month, 600 hours were worked to manufacture 1,700 units.
 Workers were paid @ $7.95 per direct labour hour.

Required:
Calculate direct labour rate variance.
Solution
Direct labour rate variance = AH(SR –AR)
 = $600 × ($7.80 – $7.95)
 = $90 (unfavourable)
In this example, the company has an unfavourable labour rate variance of $90 because it has paid a higher hourly rate ($7.95) compared to the standard hourly rate ($7.80).

Exercise 16.3
You are given the following information:
 Budgeted: 48,250 hours at $6.50 per hour
 Actual: 50,000 hours at $7.00 per hour
Required:
Calculate the direct labour rate variance.

Exercise 16.4
100 unites of a product are produced for which the material costs are:
Standard: 1,500 Kgs; cost per unit $5.50
Actual: 1,650 kgs; Total cost $9,570
Required:
Calculate the raw material price variance.

Exercise 16.5

10,000 units of a product are produced per annum. You are given the following information:

	Direct material	Direct labour
Actual cost	$22,000	$32,000
Total variance	$2,000 (adverse)	$4,000 (favourable)

Required:

Calculate the standard prime cost (direct material + direct labour) per unit.

Exercise 16.6

A manufacturing company produced 540 units in 4,300 hours at a total direct labour cost of $26,660.

Its standard labour cost for one unit of 8 hours of direct labour was $6 per hour.

Required:

Calculate the labour efficiency variance for the period.

Q. What is a flexed budget?

Ans. A flexed budget is a budget that has been adapted to reflect changes in activity levels. This is done so that when making a comparison between standard costs and actual costs, like is compared to like and the budget is specific to the inputs. Flexed budgets are prepared at the end of the period, once the actual output is known. Variances yielded are more relevant than those generated under a static budget as both the budgeted (standard) and actual expenses are based on the same activity measure. These variances will likely be less than when using a static budget and lend themselves to better decision making.

Q. What is a static budget?

Ans. A static budget contains fixed amounts that do not vary with actual activity levels. It is based on the projected level of output, prior to the start of the period. In other words, it is the 'original budget'.

EXHIBIT

Income statement line item	Budgeted amount per unit ($)	Static budget 10,000 units ($)	Actual activity (B) 16,000 units ($)	Flexed budget (A) 16,000 units (Standard costs)($)	Flexed budget variance (A -B) ($)
Revenue	40	400,000	670,000	(16,000 x40)= 640,000	30,000
V. costs:					
Materials	15	150,000	230,000	(16,000 x 15)=240,000	
					10,000
Labour	10	100,000	167,000	(16,000 x10)=160,000	
					(7,000)
V.overheads	5	50,000	84,000	(16,000x5) =80,000	
					(4,000)
Fixed costs		150,000	154,000	(No flexing)150,000	(4,000)
Operating income		(50,000)	35,000	10,000	25,000

Clearly, production was more than planned and therefore the costs would have increased. However, only variable costs are flexed to reflect the actual activity. Fixed costs remain the same.

Exercise 16.7
Hannah currently uses a fixed budget. The details for the next trading period are as follows.

Output in units	10 000	12 000
	$	$
Direct materials	10 000	10 000
Direct labour	4 000	4 000
Semi variable overheads	3 000	3 000
Fixed overheads	2 000	2 000
TOTAL	19 000	19 000

Hannah wishes to switch to a flexible budget.
Semi variable overheads are 50 % variable.
Required:
Calculate the total flexible budgeted cost for 12 000 units.

Q. Define:

a. Total sales variance

b. Sales volume -(sub)variance

c. Sales price- (sub)variance

Ans. a. The total sales variance: measures the difference between budgeted and actual revenue and is the result of an actual change in price and/or the quantity sold.

b. Sales volume variance: The sales volume variance is the difference between the actual and expected (standard or budgeted) number of units sold, multiplied by the budgeted price per unit.

c. Sales price variance: is the difference between the actual and expected revenue that is caused by a change in the price of a product or service.

EXHIBIT

A company has given you the following information:

Budgeted sales: 12,000 units; Selling price per unit: $5

Actual sales: 10,500 units; Selling price $5.50 per unit

Required:

Calculate:

   a.   The sales volume variance
   b.   The sales price variance
   c.   The total sales variance

Solution:

SQ x SP = 12,000 x 5 = $60,000

SP(AQ – SQ)

52,500 – 60,000 =   ($7,500): Adverse volume variance

AQ x SP = 10,500 x 5 = $52,500

AQ (AP-SP) = 57,750 – 52,500 = $5,250:

Favourable price variance

AQ x AP = 10,500 x 5 = $57,750

Total sales variance (AQ x AP) – (SQ x SP) = ($2,250) - Adverse: overall adverse impact on profit.

Ans: a. $2,250 (adverse)

  b. $5,250 (favourable)

  c. $2,250 (adverse)

Exercise 16.8

A company has given you the following information:

Budgeted sales: 10,000 units; Selling price per unit: $4

Actual sales: 10,500 units; Selling price $5.00 per unit

Required:

Calculate:

  a. **The sales volume variance**
  b. **The sales price variance**
  c. **The total sales variance**

Q. Discuss the reasons for a favourable and adverse sales price variances.

Ans. A Favourable sales price variance suggests a higher selling price realized during the period than anticipated in the standard. Reasons for favourable sales price variance may include:

- A decrease in the number of competitors in the market.
- Improved product differentiation and market segmentation.
- Better promotion and an aggressive sales campaign.

An adverse sales price variance indicates that sales were made at a lower average price than the standard. The causes for an adverse sales price variance may include:

- An increase in competition in the market.
- A decrease in demand for the products.
- A reduction in price enforced by regulatory authorities.

Exercise16.9

Ruby manufacturing has a standard selling price of $12 per unit. Its budgeted sales is 80,000 units and actual sales 82,000 units. Actual sales revenue was $955,300.

Required:

Calculate the sales price variance.

Q. Explain:

a. Total fixed overhead variance.

b. Fixed overhead expenditure (spending) variance

c. Fixed overhead volume variance

Ans. **Total fixed overhead variance:** is the difference between the actual and absorbed fixed production overheads (flexed) during a period. It explains why there is a difference between the actual fixed overhead incurred and that which is charged to production through the overhead absorption rates.

Fixed Overhead Total Variance = Actual Fixed Overheads - Absorbed Fixed Overheads

EXHIBIT

Semolina PLC is a manufacturing company involved in the production of pasta. Information from its last budget period is as follows:

Actual Production   275,000 units

Budgeted Production   250,000 units

Actual Fixed Production Overheads $526,000,000

Budgeted Fixed Production Overheads $500,000,000

Required:

Calculate the fixed overhead total variance.

Solution:

Standard overhead absorption rate = budgeted fixed overheads

                                                Budgeted output

                                        = $50,000   =$2,000 per unit

                                                250,000

Fixed overhead total variance = actual fixed overheads – absorbed fixed overheads

                                        = $526,000,000 – (275,000 x 2,000)

                                        = $24,000,000 (F)

Note: The variance is favourable because the actual expense is lower than the fixed overheads absorbed during the period.

Q. Name the Fixed overhead sub – variances.

Ans. In case of **absorption costing**, the fixed overhead total variance comprises the following sub-variance:

a. **Fixed overhead expenditure variance** which is the difference between the actual and budgeted fixed production overheads.
b. **Fixed overhead volume variance** which is the difference between the fixed production overheads absorbed (flexed cost) and the budgeted overheads. It is also called the production volume variance as it is a function of the production volume.

In the case of **marginal costing**, the fixed production overheads are not absorbed in the cost of the output. The fixed overhead total variance will therefore equal the fixed overhead expenditure variance because the budgeted and flexed overhead cost will be the same.

Q. Discuss the reasons for:

a. A favourable fixed overhead expenditure variance

b. An adverse fixed overhead expenditure variance

Ans.a. A Favourable fixed overhead expenditure variance suggests that actual fixed costs incurred during the period have been lower than budgeted cost. Reasons for a favourable variance may include:

- Planned business expansion, which was anticipated, to cause a stepped increase in fixed overheads not being undertaken during the period.
- Cost rationalization measures carried out during the period aimed at reducing fixed overheads by elimination of inefficiencies (e.g. through process re-engineering and optimization of the usage of shared resources and facilities).
- Planning inaccuracies (e.g. actual salary raise being lower than anticipated in budget).

b. An adverse fixed overhead expenditure variance indicates that higher fixed costs were incurred during the period than planned in the budget. An adverse variance may be caused by the following:

- Expansion of business undertaken during the period, which was not taken into consideration in the budget setting process, causing a stepped increase in fixed overheads.
- Inefficient fixed overheads management (e.g. due to empire building pursuits of senior management).
- Planning errors (e.g. increase in insurance premium being higher than budget due to changes in the risk profile of business).

EXHIBIT

You are given the following information:
Semolina PLC is a manufacturing company involved in the production of pasta. Information from its last budget period is as follows:

Actual Production	275,000 units
Budgeted Production	250,000 units
Actual Fixed Production Overheads	$526,000,000

Budgeted Fixed Production Overheads $500,000,000

Required:

Calculate:

    a. **The fixed overhead volume variance**
    b. **The fixed overhead expenditure variance**

Solution:

    a. Fixed overhead expenditure variance = budgeted fixed overheads - actual production

$$= 500,000,000 - 526,000,000$$

$$= \$ 26,000,000(A)$$

    b. Fixed overhead volume variance = absorbed fixed overheads - budgeted production

$$= 550,000,000 - 500,000,000 = \$50,000,000 \ (F)$$

√ *Check: Adding the two sub-variance, we get $24,000,000(F) which was the Total fixed overhead variance.*

Q. Explain:

a. Fixed overhead capacity variance

b. Fixed overhead volume efficiency variance

Ans. Fixed overhead capacity variance is the difference between the actual number of hours worked and the budgeted number of hours. This figure is then multiplied by the standard overhead absorption rate per hour of labour.

Fixed overhead volume efficiency variance is the difference between the number of hours that actual production should have taken, and the number of hours actually taken, multiplied by the standard overhead absorption rate per hour.

EXHIBIT
Overheads and activity levels for June for Somner manufacturing Ltd. are as follows:

	Actual	Budgeted
Fixed overheads	$68,600	$70,340
Variable overheads	$23,100	$24,340
Labour hours	*2,800	2,780
Standard hours of production (SHP)	*2,800	2,840

These would be the same for budget purposes.

Required:

Calculate:

    a. **Fixed overhead capacity variance**
    b. **Fixed overhead efficiency variance**

Solution:

Fixed overhead absorption rate (FOAR) = $\dfrac{\$68,600}{2,800}$ = $24.50

    a. **Fixed overhead capacity variance =** (actual labour hours x Fixed overhead

                                        absorption rate) - budgeted

                                        expenditure

                               = (2780 x 24.50) - 68,600

                               = $490(A)

    b. **Fixed overhead efficiency variance** = FOAR (standard hours of production - actual

                                    labour hours)

                               = 24.50 (2840 - 2780)

                               = $1,470 (F)

Exercise 16.10

Karmen PLC manufactures tractors. Their budgeted fixed overhead was $500m while their actual fixed overheads for the period was $538m.

Required:

Calculate the fixed overhead expenditure variance.

Exercise 16.11

Hemmingway Ltd is a manufacturing company and during their last production period they produced 280,000 units. Their budgeted production for that period was 260,000 units. Their standard fixed overhead absorption rate was $1000 per unit.

Required:

Calculate the fixed overhead volume variance.

Exercise 16.12

Use the data from Exercise 16.10.

Additional information:

Standard machine hours per unit   10 hrs

Actual machine hours   3,100,000

Calculate:

    a.   **The fixed overhead capacity variance**
    b.   **The fixed overhead efficiency variance**

Exercise 16.13

Daria budgeted to sell 20,000 units of a new product at a budgeted selling price of $8 per unit. The actual sales volumes during the period were as budgeted at 20,000 units but, due to a competitor's launch of a similar product, the actual sales price achieved was $6 per unit. If Daria was aware of the impending competition, she would have revised her expected selling price to $5.50 per unit which was the price of the competitor's product.

Calculate: The sales price planning variance.

Exercise 16.14

Lim Ltd manufactures plastic storage boxes. The materials are purchased as large sheets of plastic ready for pressing into shape.

Actual results for the year ended 31 March 2009 were as follows:

                   $ $

Sales   190 000

Less variable costs
Raw materials   89 100
Direct labour   33 000   122 100
Contribution   67 900
Additional information
   1.   There were no opening or closing stocks of boxes.
   2.   The budget and standard cost details for the year ended 31 March 2009 were:
      (i) budgeted sales of boxes would be: 24 000 at $10 each;
      (ii) each box would require 1.4 m2 of plastic at $3.20 per m2;
      (iii) each box would require 10 minutes of direct labour time paid at $8.40 per hour.
   3.   The actual results for the year ended 31 March 2009 showed:
      (i) 20 000 boxes were made and sold;
      (ii) 27 000 m2 of plastic was used;
      (iii) 4000 hours of direct labour time were used.

REQUIRED

(a) Calculate the:
   (i) sales volume variance;
   (ii) sales price variance;
   (iii) total sales variance;
   (iv) raw materials usage variance;
   (v) raw materials price variance;
   (vi) total raw materials variance;
   (vii) direct labour efficiency variance;
   (viii) direct labour rate variance;
   (ix) total direct labour variance.

(b) Using the original budgeted figures, prepare a statement showing the budgeted contribution.

(c) Explain one reason why the following variances calculated in (a) might have arisen:
   (i) sales volume variance;
   (ii) raw materials price variance;
   (iii) direct labour rate variance.

(d) Explain how a raw materials usage variance might be connected to a direct labour efficiency variance

(UCLES, 2009, AS/A Level Accounting, Syllabus 9706/04, May/June)

Exercise 16.15

Louie & Company maintains warehouses that stock items carried by its e-retailer clients. When one of Louie's clients receives an order from an online customer, the order is forwarded to Louie who then pulls the item from the warehouse, packs it and ships it to the customer. The company uses a predetermined variable overhead rate based on direct labour hours. According to the company's records, 0.04 direct labour hours are required to fulfil an order for one item and the variable overhead rate is $6.50 per direct labour hour. During February, Louie shipped 240,000 orders using 9,200 direct labour hours. The company incurred a total of $58,880 in variable overhead costs.

Required:

Calculate the variable overhead efficiency variance during February.

Q. Outline the uses of variances.

Ans. A variance is the difference between an actual result and an expected (standard) result. The process by which the total difference between standard and actual results is analysed is known as variance analysis. When actual results are better than the expected results, we have a favourable variance. If, on the other hand, actual results are worse than expected results, we have an adverse variance. Here are some of the uses of variance analysis:

- Variance analysis is used as a controlling tool. Standard costing is a natural extension of budgetary control which aims to make departments more efficient and hence improve the performance of the business as a whole.
- Once the cause of the variance is known, managers can take suitable remedial action to correct adverse variances.
- It acts like a barometer for measuring business efficiency and therefore, profitability.
- Through regular variance analysis, 'weak spots' can be ascertained and remedial action can be taken.
- Variance analysis aids framing of more accurate budgets in the future.
- Variance analysis can be used for comparing the departmental performance of the organisation.

Q. Why is it important to reconcile standard cost to actual cost?
Ans. Accurate costing enables management to understand product costs, provide for fact-based decision making regarding product profitability, and ultimately reduce expenses, increasing profits. A clear reconciliation of budgeted (standard) and actual costs is important to help focus management attention on variances. This enables managers to take remedial action, if necessary.

Q. Outline the steps taken to reconcile standard costs with actual costs.
Ans. These are the steps:
1. Flex the budgets
2. Summarise the variances
3. Use the total to adjust standard costs for materials, labour and overheads. The actual amount should total the actual costs.
4. If the total of the variances calculated add up to a total favourable variance, this is deducted from the standard costs as favourable variances reduce the amount of expenditure incurred.
5. If the total of the variances calculated add up to a total adverse variance, then this is added to the standard cost as the total represents more expenditure.

Q. Why is it important to reconcile standard profit to actual profit?
Ans. Reconciling the standard profit to actual profit enables managers to identify the reasons why and by how much actual profit differs from standard profit. Adverse variances enable managers to identify areas of business that need investigation to ascertain whether remedial action is necessary. Favourable variances can be used as examples of good practice.

EXHIBIT
Tansen Limited use a standard absorption costing system. They have the following standard costs for the production of 100 units:

		$
Direct materials	500 kg @ $0.80 per kg	400
Direct labour	20 hours @ $1.50 an hour	30
Fixed overheads	20 hours @ $1 per hour	20
		450

Budgeted production is 10,000 units.
Budgeted selling price is $6 per unit.

The actual figures for the month of July were:
Units produced and sold	10,600 units
Sales revenue	$63,000
Direct materials: 53200 kgs	$42,500
Direct labour: 2040 hours	$3,100
Fixed overheads	$2,200

Required:
Prepare a statement reconciling actual profit with budgeted profit.

Solution:

Statement reconciling actual profit with budgeted profit

	F	A	
	$	$	$
Budgeted profit [(10,000 x 6) – (450 x 100)]			15000
Sales variances:			
Sales price: ([(63,000/10) -6] x 10,600		600	
Sales volume(10,600 – 10,000) x [6 – (450/100]	900		300
			15300F
Direct materials usage variance: 0.80 x [53,200 – (10,600x500/100)]		160	
Direct materials price variance: 42500 – (53,200 x $0.80)	60		
Direct labour rate variance: 3,100 – (2,040 x 1.50)		40	
Direct labour efficiency variance:150 x [2,040 – 10600 x (20/100)]	120		
Fixed overhead expenditure variance:[1,0000 x (20/100) – 2,200		200	
Fixed overhead volume: 20/100 x (10600 – 10,000)	120		
Total	300	400	100A
Actual profit: 63,000 – (42,500+3,100+2,200)			15200F

TEST YOURSELF

16.1. MULTIPLE CHOICE QUESTIONS

i. Standards that do not allow for machine breakdowns or other work interruptions and that require peak efficiency at all times are known as:

A. Ideal standard   B. Basic standard   C. Attainable standard   D. Average standard

ii. A company manufacturers a plastic tray. Its standard cost for the direct materials included in one tray is 2 kgs of material at the standard cost of $3 per kg. The company produced 100 trays and used 210 kgs of material. The material's actual cost was $3.10 per kg. The direct materials usage or quantity variance is

A. $21   B. $30   C. $31   D. $51

iii. During a recent accounting period a company produced 1,000 units of Item Q and 400 units of Item R. The standard direct labor is 4 hours for each unit of Item Q and 6 hours for each unit of Item R. The standard cost for one hour of direct labor is $20 per hour. The actual direct labor for the accounting period was 6,500 hours at $19 per hour. The direct labour efficiency variance for the accounting period was

A. $1,900 (F)   B. $1,900 (A)   C. $2,000 (F)   D. $2,000 (A)

iv. Which of the following terms would NOT be considered a *quantity* variance associated with a product's inputs under a standard cost system?

A. Efficiency   B. Usage   C. Price   D. None of these

v. Amberiso Company, a dress manufacturer, uses a standard costing system. Each unit of a finished product contains 3 metres of cloth. However, there is unavoidable waste of 0.5 metres per unit of finished product that occurs when the cloth is cut for assembly. The cost of the cloth is $10 per metre. The standard direct material cost for cloth per unit of finished product is:

A. $5　　　B. $25　　　C. $30　　　D. $35

vi.　A favourable labour variance combined with an adverse wage rate variance could be caused by:
A. **Cheaper raw materials imported due to an exchange rate depreciation**
B. **The introduction of performance – related – pay.**
C. **Cost cutting exercises implemented by the management.**
D. **Higher unemployment in the local economy**

vii.　A favourable materials price variance could be due to:
A. **More wastage of materials**
B. **Exchange rate depreciation when materials are imported**
C. **Higher wage costs**
D. **Inferior quality of raw materials used**

viii.　A favourable total sales variance could result from:
A. **Lower output leading to a favourable total cost variance**
B. **A price cut leading to a proportionally higher increase in the sales volume**
C. **A price cut leading to a proportionally lower increase in sales volume**
D. **A fall in sales volume and a price reduction.**

ix.　Which of the following could cause an adverse total labour variance?
A. **Lower wage rate leading to a significant change in productivity.**
B. **Lower wage rates leading to an insignificant change in productivity.**
C. **Higher wage rates leading to an insignificant change in productivity.**
D. **Higher wage rates leading to a significant change in productivity.**

x.　A favourable labour efficiency variance is likely to have been caused by:
A. **Trade union conflicts.**
B. **Higher wages producing motivational benefits.**
C. **Inferior materials being used.**
D. **Lower skilled labour being used.**

16.2. Alfa manufactures a single product. Its budgeted production and sales in March was 8000 units.
The budgeted data per unit is as follows:
Direct materials 3 kilos at $12 per kilo
Direct labour 4 hours at $20 per hour
Fixed production overhead $8 per direct labour hour
The product will be sold at full production cost plus 75%.
REQUIRED
(a) Prepare the trading section of the budgeted income statement for March.

Additional information
The actual results for March were:
Actual production (units) 7 500
22 850 kilos direct materials $269 000
30 800 direct labour hours $631 000
Fixed production overhead $250 000

REQUIRED
(b) State two reasons why a business will prepare a flexed budget.
(c) Calculate the following variances for March:
    (i) direct materials price
    (ii) direct materials usage
    (iii) fixed overhead expenditure
    (iv) fixed overhead volume.

Additional information
The accountant has also calculated the direct labour variances. They are as follows:
Direct labour rate $15 000 (A)
Direct labour efficiency $16 000 (A)

REQUIRED
(d) (i) Explain the possible reasons why the direct labour adverse variances may have arisen.
(ii) Explain the possible reasons why fixed overhead variances may arise.
(e) Explain how the adverse direct labour efficiency variance can be improved
(UCLES, 2016, AS/A Level Accounting, Syllabus 9706/32, Feb/Mar)

16.3. In April Amit introduced a new standard costing system.
He produces and sells one item. The standard production is 5000 units. Amit does not have any opening inventory. Closing inventory is valued at full standard cost.
The standard costs per unit were as follows:
Direct materials 3 kilos at $5 per kilo
Direct labour 4 hours at $8 per hour
Overheads 2 hours at $3.50 per hour
The selling price will allow Amit a profit on the full standard cost of 17.5%.
REQUIRED
    (a) Calculate the standard selling price per unit.

Additional information
The actual results for April were:
Production 5100 units
Sales 5040 units $65.25 each
Direct materials used 15 450 kilos
Direct material cost $78 795
Direct labour hours 20 250
Direct labour cost $172 125
Overhead variance $300 adverse
REQUIRED
(b) Calculate the following variances for April, clearly identifying which variance you have calculated.
    (i) Sales price
    (ii) Sales volume
    (iii) Total sales
    (iv) Direct material price
    (v) Direct material usage
    (vi) Total material
    (vii) Direct labour rate
    (viii) Direct labour efficiency
    (ix) Total labour

(c) Explain how the direct labour variances may have arisen during April.
(d) Calculate the actual profit for April.
(e) Calculate the budgeted profit for the actual units sold for April.

(f) Prepare a statement reconciling the budgeted profit with actual profit. Start your statement with your answer is part (e).
(UCLES, 2015, AS/A Level Accounting, Syllabus 9706/41, May/June)

16.4. Honeybush Limited operates a standard costing system. Monthly standard data is as follows.

Sales are 6000 units with a selling price of $26 per unit
Each unit requires 2.4 kilos of raw material costing $3 per kilo
Each unit requires 1.5 hours of direct labour time costing $7 an hour
REQUIRED
(a) Calculate the expected monthly contribution per unit and in total.
(b) Calculate the quantity of raw materials in kilos normally purchased each month. Assume inventory levels remain constant.

Early in 2013 a new supplier entered the market, selling the required raw material at $1.80 per kilo. In April Honeybush Limited bought all its raw material from this new supplier.
This raw material was more difficult to work with. Therefore, each unit required 2.6 kilos and labour took 40% longer than usual to produce each unit. Overtime premiums caused the average wage rate to rise to $7.80 an hour.
Honeybush Limited managed to produce and sell the usual 6000 units. The selling price had risen by $0.50 per unit.

REQUIRED
(c) Calculate the following variances for April 2013:
    (i) Sales price
    (ii) Direct materials usage
    (iii) Direct materials price
    (iv) Total direct materials
    (v) Direct labour efficiency
    (vi) Direct labour rate
    (vii) Total direct labour
(d) Starting with the original expected total contribution from (a) use these variances to calculate the actual total contribution.
(e) Calculate the change in contribution for Honeybush Limited arising from its decision to change supplier.
(f) Explain what is meant by the expression 'flexing a budget'.

(UCLES, 2013, AS/A Level Accounting, Syllabus 9706/41, May/June)

CHAPTER 17
BUDGETS AND BUDGETARY CONTROL

Q. What is a budget?

Ans. A budget is a quantitative plan used as a tool for deciding which activities will be chosen for a future time period.

Q. What is a forecast?

Ans. A forecast is a prediction of the result of carrying on business over a future period of time, and of the position of the business at the end of that time if present and, as far as they are known, future conditions and trends are allowed to continue without management intervention.

Q. What is a budget center?

Ans. It is any part of an organisation for which a budget is prepared. What constitutes a budget center depends upon the nature of the business, its operations and functions, and its organisational structure. A budget center must be under the control of a manager who is responsible for its revenue and/or expenditure. Budget canters may be:

Revenue centers (Sales budget is prepared)

Cost centers (production departments)

Profit centers (earning revenue and incurring costs. e.g a department of a store)

Q. What is an operating budget (functional budget)?

Ans. They are budgets prepared for each individual department or function of a business showing the budget-responsibility of each manager.

Q. Define:

a. **Master budget**

b. **Budget periods**

c. **Budgetary control**

d. **Principal budget factor (limiting factor, Key factor)**

e. **Management by exception (Exception reporting)**

Ans a. Master Budget: This takes the form of a financial statements (Income statement and Statement of financial position) based upon the operating budgets. It is often referred to as 'forecast financial statements.

b. A budget period is one for which a budget is prepared. Most commonly it spans a year.

c. Budgetary control is when budgets are used to monitor the performance of managers against their operational budgets. The system allows for the continuous comparison of actual with budgeted results at frequent intervals so that corrective action can be taken when necessary. Budget periods are broken down into control periods of, say, months or quarters.

d. Limiting factor is anything that restricts the budgeted level of activity of a business. It is often the volume of sales which is restricted by demand or a shortage of materials, labour or machine hours.

e. Management by exception (MOE) is the focusing by management upon those items, processes etc. which are deviating from the budget, on principle that matters conforming to the budget need no management intervention. Computers may be programmed to print out 'exception reports' of items deviating from the budget.

Q. Define:
a. Top-down budgeting
b. Bottom-up budgeting
c. Budget committee
d. Flexible budgets
e. Incremental budgets

Ans a. Top-down budgeting is a term used to describe the process when budgets are prepared for lower management by top management with, or without, discussion. Lower management tend to feel little commitment to this type of budget.

b. Bottom-up budgeting is when lower management prepare their own functional budgets and submit them to higher management for approval and incorporation into the master budget. Lower management tends to set its targets low in order to reduce the risk of not meeting the budget, or to merit credit when actual performance is seen to be better than budgeted.

c. A budget committee consists of senior management to co-ordinate the preparation of budgets.

d. A flexible budget is one that recognises the different behaviours of fixed and variable costs at different levels of activity. (See chapter 16 for exercises involving flexing of budgets).

e. Incremental budgeting always begins with the budget from the last period. Once there is an established starting point, if a department needs more money than the previous budget, they have to be able to justify the extra expenses. Also, if you do not use your budget, then the next period's budget will be reduced. This type of budgeting often leads to wasteful spending by employees because they do not want to lose their budget.

Q. What is the difference between a fixed budget and a flexible budget?
Ans. The differences are:
- The figures for a fixed budget are for a single level of activity while those for a flexible budget are for variable levels of activity.
- With fixed budgets, managers are held responsible for variances not under their control (both fixed and variable costs).
- The fixed budget is never able to assess the efficiency and actual performance of a manager.
- The flexible budget allows for a more meaningful comparison as it flexes to the actual volume. It is more realistic.
- The flexible budget has the advantage of assisting the manager to deal with uncertainty by allowing them to see the expected outcomes for a range of activity.

Q. Explain the term 'Zero-based budgeting'.
Ans. Zero-based budgeting, or ZBB, is a rigorous budgeting process that requires every dollar of every expense to be justified even if the expense has been occurring for many years. For example, if a company has been spending $100,000 each year for the rent of

warehouse space, the zero-based budgeting process assumes that nothing was spent previously. As a result, the warehousing activities must be reviewed, justified and documented before any amount can be included in the budget.

Zero-based budgeting is in contrast to more common budgeting practices that focus on the incremental change from the current expenses and current budget. In other words, under a more typical budgeting process, the $100,000 of rent expense is accepted and the focus is on whether the rent for the upcoming budget should assume an inflation adjustment of $3,000 or some other amount.

While zero-based budgeting will be far more time consuming than focusing on the incremental changes for the next budget, it can result in significant cost savings. For instance, the analysis and documentation of the warehousing activities required by zero-based budgeting could lead to a better use of space, better inventory management, etc. If those efficiencies will occur, the budget for the warehousing may need to be only $60,000 (instead of more than $100,000).

Q. List the factors to be considered when budgeting.

Ans. The following factors should be borne in mind when drawing up budgets:
1. The long-term objectives of the business
2. The principal budget or limiting factors
3. Internal factors such as available finance, staff training and morale
4. External factors such as international, political, economic and environmental.

Q. Enumerate the uses and advantages of budgets.

Ans. They key to the success of a budget's success is whether they have been planned with much forethought and sensitivity – in these circumstances they can have many advantages:

• They can aid **planning**, which gives a business direction. A budget takes the organisational plan (goal and objectives) and quantifies this into something tangible to aim for. Such forward planning aids anticipating future business conditions and helps avoid otherwise unforeseen problems.

• Budgets have a role to play in **control** within an organisation. So it can be used to measure **performance** against the targets set in the budget. There are alternative performance measurement tools, as discussed in other chapters – whatever their merits the budget remains the mainstay of performance measurement in many organisations.

• The budgeting process can encourage **communication** between departments/employees and aid in the **coordination** of a firm's activities. The budget can be used to communicate financial plans throughout the different parts of the organisation – thus showing how the different parts fit together to form an integrated plan for the organisation as a whole.

• There is also a **motivational role** ole for the budget – if set at the appropriate level. The argument being that the budget gives managers a target to strive towards. However, there is also an argument that if set at an inappropriate level (too high or too low) it can have the reverse impact and can demotivate.

• Budgets formalise management plans

• They insure that all functions of a business are coordinated

• The preparation of budgets for individual departments, functions etc. is a form of responsibility accounting. The manager in charge of a department or function is responsible for earning the budgeted revenue or keeping within the budgeted expenditure. Budgets should present managers with a challenge to meet them, but should be achievable.

Q. What is a sales budget?

Ans. The Sales budget is the first and basic component of the master budget. The sales budget is based upon forecast demand for goods. Usually this forecast is based upon market research, salesmen's reports and other trade information sources. The budget is usually expressed in sales volumes as a number of units. Once the volumes have been forecast, the volume is multiplied by the price to calculate sales revenue.

Sales are usually the **key factor** in a business and the sales budget will therefore determine the other components of master budget either directly or indirectly. This because the total sales figure provided by sales budget is used as a base figure in other component budgets. As many components of master budget rely on the sales budget, the estimated sales volume and price must be forecasted with sufficient care and only reliable forecast techniques should be employed. Otherwise the master budget would prove ineffective for planning and control.

EXHIBIT

Saleem sells a single product A. You are given the following information for the year ended December 20x5:

	Price	units sold
Quarter 1	$91	1320
Quarter 2	$92	954
Quarter 3	$97	1103
Quarter 4	$112	1766

Required:
Prepare a sales budget for A for the year ended 31 December 20x5

Solution:

Sales budget
For the year ended 31 December 20x5

	Quarter				
	1	2	3	4	Year
Sales Units	1,320	954	1,103	1,766	5,143
× Price per Unit	$91	$92	$97	$112	
Total Sales	$120,120	$87,768	$106,991	$197,792	$512,671

Exercise 17.1

Django sell a product B at a price of $160 each. During the three months to 31 December 20x1, he sold 1500 units of B. The turnover was constant every month. He expects that the volume of sales would remain unchanged for January 20x2, but to increase by 5% in February, and by a further 20% in April. The price of B will be increased by 10% in January and by a further 5% in June.

Required:
Prepare a sales budget for Django for the six months to 30 June 20x2.

Exercise 17.2

Jack sells two products M and N. The sales for product M averaged 1000 per month in 20x3 and in the same year an average of 500 product B's were sold per month. Jack estimates that in 20x4, sales of M will increase by 5% in March and by a further 8% in August. Sales of N will increase by 6% in February and by a further 10% in June. Sales of N will then increase to 600 a month by August with a further increase of 4% by October.

The selling price of M is $100 each and for N $120. However, the price of product M will increase by 10% in March 20x4 and by a further 5% in the following September. The price of N will be increased by 5% in May and again by a further $33^{1}/3\%$ in October.

Required:
Prepare Jack's sales budget for the year ended 31 December 20x4.

Q. What is a production budget?

Ans. A production budget is a schedule showing planned production in units which must be made by a manufacturer during a specific period to meet the expected demand for sales and the planned finished goods inventory. The required production is determined by subtracting the opening inventory from the sum of expected sales and closing inventory of the period.
Planned Production in Units = Expected Sales (Units) + Planned closing Inventory (Units) – opening Inventory (Units).
The Production budget is prepared after the sales budget as it needs the expected sales provided by the sales budget. It is important to note that only a manufacturing business needs to prepare the production budget.

Exhibit (using the even production method):
Male Ltd. Manufactures a product A of which it produces 750 units a month. Sales for the 4 months May to August are expected to be as follows:
May 600 units, June 800 units, July 1000 units, August 600 units. At April 30 there were 800 units of product A in stock.
Required:
Prepare Male Ltd.'s production budget for the 4 months May to August.

Solution:

Male Ltd
Production budget for 4 months to 31 August

	May	June	July	August
Opening inventory	800	950	900	650
Production	750	750	750	750
	1550	1700	1650	1400
Sales	600	800	1000	600
Closing inventory	950	900	650	800

Exercise 17.3
Absolute Ltd. Manufactures a product B and has a fixed production of 15,000 units a month. The opening inventory at January 1 20x2 was 16,000. Budgeted sales for 20x2 were as follows:

Quarter 1	42000 units
2	52000 units
3	55000 units
4	32000 units

Required:
Prepare Absolute Ltd.'s production budget for the year ended 31 December 20x2.

Exercise 17.4
Ninja Ltd. manufactures a product C with regular monthly production of 1000 units. Sales for the year 20x1 are expected to be as follows:

September	900 units
October	1000 units
November	1300 units
December	900 units

The company maintains a buffer (minimum) inventory of 600 units every month.

Required:
Prepare the production budget for the four months ending 31 December 20x1.

Note: no opening inventory is given. Begin by preparing the budget inserting monthly opening and closing inventory in pencil. (Insert negative balances at this stage). Find the month which has the biggest shortfall compared with minimum inventory; the shortfall will be the required opening inventory. November has the greatest shortfall from minimum stock: 600+200 = 800.
Enter 800 as the opening inventory in September and substitute new balances for the ones penciled in for opening and closing inventory for the other months.

Exhibit (uneven production):
Bygone Ltd. produces a product D. They have 1200kgs of inventory at January 1, 20x1. Quarterly sales and closing inventory are budgeted as follows:

	Sales	Closing inventory
1st Quarter	3000kgs	1500kgs
2nd Quarter	5000kgs	1800kgs
3rd Quarter	7000kgs	1600kgs
4th Quarter	4000kgs	1300kgs

Required:
Bygone Ltd.'s quarterly production budget for the year to 31 December 20x1

Solution:

Bygone Ltd.
Production budget for the year ended 31 December 20x1

	1st quarter Kgs	2nd quarter kgs	3rd quarter kgs	4th quarter kgs
Opening inventory	(1200)	(1500)	(1800)	(1600)
Sales	3000	5000	7000	4000
Closing inventory	1500	1800	1600	1300
Production	3300	5300	6800	3700

Exercise 17.5
Budgeted sales and closing inventory of a company are given below:

	Sales (units)	Closing inventory (units)
January	7000	1000
February	6000	2000
March	8000	4000
April	7000	5000
May	8000	4000

Required:
Draw up the production budget for the four months to May 20x5

Q. Write a short note on 'Materials purchasing budget'.
Ans. The material purchases budget is a component of the master budget and is based on the following formula:
Budgeted material purchases in units= Budgeted opening material in units + material in units needed for Production − Budgeted closing material in units
In the above formula, the material that is needed for production is calculated as follows:
Budgeted production during the period × Units of material required per unit of product = material in units needed for production

Since the budgeted production figure is provided by the production budget, the material purchases budget can be prepared only after the preparation of production budget.

Exhibit:

ABC Company plans to produce a variety of plastic goods, and 98 percent of its raw materials involve plastic resin. Thus, there is only one key commodity to be concerned with. Its production needs are outlined as follows:

ABC Company
Direct Materials Budget For the Year Ended December 31, 20XX

	Quarter 1	Quarter 2	Quarter 3	Quarter 4
Product A (units)	5000	6000	7000	8000
X resin/unit (kgs)	2	2	2	2
Total resin needed (kgs)	10000	12000	14000	16000

Additional information:

The planned closing inventory at the end of each quarter is 20% of the amount of resin used during that month. Opening inventory for the first quarter is 1600 kgs

The purchasing department expects that global demand will drive up the price of resin, hence it has budgeted price increases as follows:

	Quarter 1	Quarter 2	Quarter 3	Quarter 4
Price(kg)	$0,50	$0.50	$0.55	$0.55

Required:

The raw material purchasing budget for ABC for the four quarters to December 31 20xx.

Solution: ABC's materials purchasing budget for the year ended December 31 20xx

	Quarter 1	Quarter 2	Quarter 3	Quarter 4
Total resin needed (kgs)	10000	12000	14000	16000
Closing inventory	2000	2400	2800	3200
Total required	12000	14400	16800	19200
Less opening inventory	(1600)	(2000)	(2400)	(2800)
Resin to be purchased	10400	12400	14400	16400
Price (kg)	$0.50	$0.50	$0.55	$0.55
Cost of resin purchased	$5200	$6200	$7920	$9020

Exercise 17.6

Norma plastics Ltd. Requires 2 kgs of material to produce one product. Production for the months of September 20x6 to January 20x7 is budgeted as follows:

20x6	Number of units produced
September	1000
October	3000
November	4000
December	2000
20x7	
January	3000

Material inventory at 1 September 20x6 is 2000kgs. It is expected that this material will become difficult to obtain in 20x7 and that the price will increase. It has therefore been decided that the stock of this material will be increased by 1000 kgs each month to the end of 20x6. The material costs $2 per kilo at present but the price is expected to rise to $3 in November.

Required:

The raw materials purchasing budget for Norma Plastics Ltd. For the four months to 31 December 20x6.

Exercise 17.7

Magnum Ltd. manufacture product E. Each unit of the product requires 3kilos of raw materials. The product is made in the month prior to sale and the raw materials are purchased one month before production. Since 1 January 20x1, the raw material had cost $1.50/kg but the price was increased to $2 from June 20x1. The FIFO basis is used for charging the raw material to production. Budgeted sales for product E are as follows:

20x1	units
March	500
April	600
May	800
June	1000
July	900
August	600

The inventory or raw materials at 28 February 20x1 was equal to the production requirements for March.

Required:

The budget for the purchase of raw materials by Magnum Ltd. for the period March to June 20x1.

Q. What is a cash budget?

Ans. The cash budget contains an itemization of the projected sources and uses of cash in a future period. This budget is used to ascertain whether company operations and other activities will provide a sufficient amount of cash to meet projected cash requirements. If not, management must find additional funding sources.

The cash budget is comprised of two main areas: sources of cash and uses of cash. The sources of cash section contains the beginning cash balance, as well as cash receipts from cash sales, accounts receivable collections, and the sale of assets. The uses of cash section contains all planned cash expenditures, which comes from the direct materials budget, direct labor budget, manufacturing overhead budget, and selling and administrative expense budget. It may also contain line items for fixed asset purchases and dividends to shareholders.

If there are any unusually large cash balances indicated in the cash budget, these balances are dealt with in the financing budget, where suitable investments are indicated for them. Similarly, if there are any negative balances in the cash budget, the financing budget indicates the timing and amount of any debt or equity needed to offset these balances. The following example illustrates the format of cash budget. Company A maintains a minimum cash balance of $5,000. In case of a deficiency, loan is obtained at 8% annual interest rate on the first day of the period.

Company A
Cash Budget
For the Year Ending December 30, 2010

	Quarter			
	1	2	3	4
	$	$	$	$
Budgeted Cash Receipts:	37,150	54,190	53,730	62,300
Total Cash Available for Use	37,150	54,190	53,730	62,300
Less: Cash Disbursements				
Direct Material	14,960	16,550	16,810	19,410
Direct Labour	8,830	9,610	9,750	11,900
Factory Overhead	10,020	10,400	11,000	11,780
Selling and Admin. Expenses	7,640	8,360	8,500	9,610
Equipment Purchases		6,000		14,000
Total Disbursements	41,450	50,920	46,060	66,700
Cash Surplus/(Deficit)	(4,300)	3,270	7,670	(4,400)
Opening cash balances	5,200	900	4,170	11,840
Closing cash balances	**900**	**4,170**	**11,840**	**7,440**

Note:

1. *Read the question carefully before preparing the outline template, noting the nature of receipts and payments. Enter these in the template, leaving a few lines to allow for the insertion of additional items later which may have been overlooked.*
2. *Sales and purchases on credit: take care to enter receipts and payments in the period in which the money is expected to be received or paid. If some sales are for cash and others on credit, the receipts will be split between cash sales and the balance, received in a later period, as receipts from trades receivables. Credit transactions require information for the period prior to the budget period to be given; do not be confused by this.*
3. *Other expenses may be paid currently or one period later than that in which they are incurred.*
4. *Depreciation is a non-cash item and must be ignored.*
5. *Receipts and expenditure occurring before the period covered by the budget must be adjusted, if necessary, in the opening balance of cash brought forward and not shown as transactions in the first month, week etc.*
6. *Cash budgets are prepared on a cash and not an accruals basis. Any item, revenue or capital in nature, which should appear in the cash book in the period in question should be included in the budget; but all other items should be ignored.*

Exercise 17.8

Leslie sells 10% of his products for cash and the remainder on one month's credit. He receives one month's credit on all purchases. Sales and purchases are as follows:

	Sales	Purchases
	$	$
December 20x1	30,000	16,000
January 20x2	25,000	14,000
February 20x2	18,000	20,000
March 20x2	22,000	25,000
April 20x2	28,000	30,000

Wages are $2,000 per month and rent $10,000 per year. Leslie paid one year's rent in advance on 1 January 20x2. Other expenses of $1,500 per month are paid currently.

On 6 February 20x2, he plans to sell a van for $2,300 and buy a new one for $6,000 on 15 March 20x2. His drawings are $1,000 per month.

At 31 December 20x1, Leslie's bank balance was $7,000. His father will lend the business $4,000 on 1 April 20x2.

Required:

Prepare Leslie's cash budget for the four months to 30 April 20x2.

Exercise 17.9

Molly commenced business on 1 January 20x2. She paid $25,000 into her bank account on 21 December 20x1 and paid the first quarter's rent on 21 December 20x1 of $1,200. The rent was due on 25 December 20x1. In the same month she purchased non-current assets for cash, $8,000 and inventory $20,000 which was bought on one month's credit.

Estimates of other purchases and sales for the year to 31 December 20x2 are forecasted as follows:

3 months to	Purchases	Sales
	$	$
March 31	12,000	15,000
June 30	18,000	24,000
September 30	21,000	30,000

December 31   15,000   36,000

All purchases and sales will be on one month's credit.

Other expenditure expected:

January: Purchase of motor van for cash $5,000; the van is to be depreciated annually at the rate of 20% on cost.

Wages $2,000 per month paid currently.

Molly's drawings will be $500 per month. She plans to sell her private car in June for $3,500 and to pay the proceeds into the business as capital. A friend has promised to lend the business $6,000 in September 20x2.

Molly's bank has agreed to allow overdraft facilities if required with interest at 10% per annum. Interest will be debited on the last day of each half year by the bank and will be calculated on the average overdraft, if any, for the half year. For this purpose, the overdraft on the last day of the immediately preceding quarter is to be taken as the average for the half year.

Required:

Molly's cash budget for the year to 31 December 20x2.

Exercise 17.10

A company makes 80% of its products in the month before the sale. Each product requires 2kgs. of raw material which is purchased one month before it is required for production on one month's credit. 50% of the sales are for cash and the remainder on one month's credit.

Sales for the eight months December 20x6 to July 20x7 are forecast as follows:

		Number of products (units)	Price
			$
20x6	December	2,300	4
20x7	January	2,000	4
	February	2,500	4
	March	3,500	5
	April	5,000	6
	May	7,000	6
	June	9,000	6
	July	8,000	6

The raw material presently costs $1.50/kg, but a 10% price increase is expected in February.

Required:

Prepare the following budgets:
   a. **Sales**
   b. **Production**
   c. **Materials purchase**
   d. **Cash (extract)**

Exercise 17.11

A company sells for cash as follows:

	Units
April	5,000
May	7,000
June	8,000
July	10,000
August	11,000

The price is $2 but is expected to double from June. Each unit requires 5 litres of raw material at the cost of 25c per litre. Raw material is purchased one month before production on one month's credit. The product is manufactured one month before sale. Opening inventory at 1 April is 2,000 units. It has been decided to increase inventory of the product by 800 units each month to meet increasing demand.

Required:

Prepare the following budgets for the months of April, May and June:
  a. **Sales**
  b. **Production**
  c. **Materials purchases**
  d. **Cash (extract)**

Q. What is a master budget?

Ans. The master budget is the aggregation of all lower-level budgets produced by a company's various functional (operational) areas and takes the form of a forecast Income Statement and Statement of financial position.

Exhibit:

The Statement of financial position of a company at 30 June 20x3 is given below:

Non-current Assets	Cost	Depreciation	NBV
	$	$	$
Equipment	5,000	3,000	2,000
Motor vehicles	8,000	5,000	3,000
	13,000	8,000	5,000
Current assets:			
Inventory		4,800	
Trade receivables		6,800	
Cash at bank		10,000	
		21,600	
Less: **Current liabilities:**			
Trade payables		3,100	18,500
			23,500
Represented by:			
Capital at 1 July 20x2		20,000	
Profit for the year		8,500	28,500
Less: Drawings			5,000
			23,500

Additional information:

The company estimates that purchases and sales for the year to 30 June 20x4 will be as follows:

		Purchases	Sales
		$	$
20x3	July – September	18,000	33,000
	October – December	24,000	51,000
20x4	January – March	21,000	42,000
	April – June	24,000	48,000

The company receives one month's credit on purchases and allows one month's credit on sales.

Expenses for the year to 30 June 20x4 are:	$
Rent per quarter payable in advance on 1 January, 1 April, 1 July and 1 October	800
Wages per month payable currently	1,800
Insurance paid on 1 July for period up to 30 September 20x4	1,500
Additional equipment purchased on 1 October 20x3	3,000
Van sold (cost=$4,000, NBV on 30 June 20x3=$1,500) on 1 January	1,100

Van purchased on 1 October 20x3   8,000
Drawings per month   1,000
Inventory at 30 June 20x4   7,300
Motor vans are depreciated by 12.5% p.a. on cost.
Equipment depreciated by 10% p.a. on cost.
Required:
   a. **The cash budget for the year to 30 June 20x4.**
   b. **A forecast income statement for the year to 30 June 20x4 and a statement of financial position as at that date.**
Solution:
   a.   Cash budget for the year to 30 June 20x4

	20x3		20x4	
	July-Sept	Oct-Dec	Jan-Mar	Apr-Jun
	$	$	$	$
Receipts:				
Receipts from trade receivables	28,800	45,000	45,000	46,000
Proceeds from sale of van			1,100	
Total receipts	28,800	45,000	46,100	46,000
Payments:				
Suppliers	15,100	22,000	22,000	23,000
Rent	800	800	800	800
Wages	5,400	5,400	5,400	5,400
Insurance	1,500			
Other expenses	6,000	6,000	6,000	6,000
Purchase of equipment		3,000		
Purchase of motor van		8,000		
Drawings	3,000	3,000	3,000	3,000
Total payments	31,800	48,200	37,200	38,200
Net receipts/(payments)	(3,000)	(3,200)	8,900	7,800
Balance b/f	10,000	7,000	3,800	12,700
Balance c/f	7,000	3,800	12,700	20,500

   b.   Forecast Income statement for the year ended 30 June 20x4

	$	$
Sales		174,000
Less: Cost of sales:		
Inventory	4,800	
Purchases	87,000	
	91,800	
Less: Closing inventory	(7,300)	(84,500)
Gross profit		89,500
Less: Expense:		
Wages	21,600	
Rent	3,200	
Insurance	1,200	
Other expenses	24,000	
Loss on sale of motor van	150	
Depreciation – equipment	725	
Motor vehicles	1,500	(52,375)
Profit for the year		37,125

Forecast statement of financial position as at 30 June 20x4

Non-current assets:	cost	depr	nbv
	$	$	$
Equipment	8,000	3,725	4,275
Motor vehicles	12,000	3,750	8,250
	20,000	7,475	12,525

Current assets:		
Inventory	7,300	
Trade receivables	16,000	
Prepayment (insurance)	300	
Cash at bank	20,500	
	44,100	

Less: Current liabilities:		
Trade payables	(8,000)	36,100
		48,625

Represented by:	
Capital	23,500
Profit for the year	37,125
	60,625
Drawings	(12,000)
	48,625

Notes:

- Receipts in July 20x3 will include trade receivables shown in the statement of financial position at 30 June 20x4
- One third of the sales in each quarter will be received in the following quarter.
- Payments for purchases in July 20x3 will be to trade creditors shown in the statement of financial position at 30 June 20x3.
- One third of purchases in each quarter will be paid for in the following quarter.
- Depreciation on equipment includes depreciation on new equipment for 9 months.
- Loss on sale of motor van: NBV at 30 June 20x3 = $1,500; further depreciation for 6 months = $250 making NBV of $1,250 at the date of the sale.
- Depreciation on motor vehicles includes depreciation on motor van sold as above as well as depreciation on new motor van for 9 months.

Exercise 17.12

Kimberly Ltd.'s statement of financial position at 31 December 20x1 is given below:

Non-current assets	Cost	Depr	N.B.V.
	$	$	$
Freehold premises	20,000	4,000	16,000
Plant and machinery	15,000	9,000	6,000
	35,000	13,000	22,000

Current assets:	
Inventory	12,000
Trade receivables	17,000
Cash at bank	9,500

| Administration expenses prepaid | | | 2,400 |
| | | | 40,900 |

Less: Current liabilities:			
Trade payables	9,000		
Selling & distribution expenses accrued	1,200	10,200	30,700
			52,700
Less: Long-term liabilities: 12% debentures			10,000
			42,700

Share capital & reserves:		
Ordinary shares of $1		25,000
General reserve		15,000
Retained profit		2,700
		42,700

Additional information:

1. Sales and purchases for the four months to 30 April 20x2 are as follows:

	Jan	Feb	Mar	Apr
	$	$	$	$
Sales	25,000	28,000	30,000	33,000
Purchases	10,000	8,000	12,000	15,000

It is expected that 40% of sales will be for cash; one month's credit is allowed to debtors. One month's credit is allowed on all purchases.

2. Selling & distribution expenses: 10% of sales, payable in the following month.
3. Administration expenses: $8,000 per month. Prepaid administration expenses at 30 April 20x2: $1,300.
4. Inventory at 30 April 20x2: $9,000.
5. Additional machinery will be purchased on 1 March 20x2 at a cost of $24,000.
6. Provision is made yearly for depreciation as follows: freehold premises- 3% on cost; plant and machinery 20% on cost. 50% of all depreciation is charged to selling & distribution expenses and the balance to administration expenses.
7. Debenture interest is payable on 30 June and 31 December.
8. Payment of an interim dividend of 10c a share will be made in April 20x2.
9. It is planned to transfer a further $10,000 to general reserve at 30 April 20x2.

Required:

a. **A Cash budget for the 4 months to 30 April 20x2.**
b. **A forecast income statement for the four months to 30 April 20x2 and a forecast statement of financial position as at that date.**

Test yourself

17.1. Choose the correct alternative:
   i.   Which of the following is not a function of budgeting:
        a. Controlling   b. Motivating   c. Planning   d. Decision making
   ii.   A fixed budget is:
        a. A budget that ignores inflation
        b. A budget that itemises the fixed costs of a department
        c. A budget that is set for a specified level of activity
        d. A budget that never changes

iii.　A Flexible budget is:
a. **A budget that will be changed at the end of every month in order to reflect the actual costs of a department**
b. **A budget that is adjusted to reflect different costs at different activity levels.**
c. **A budget that is constantly being changed**
d. **A budget that comprises variable costs only**

iv　Ava Ltd. Has sales of 2,600 units. There are 1,400 units of opening stock while the closing stock is planned to be 1,800 units. What production is needed to satisfy sales?
a. **3,000 units**
b. **2,437 units**
c. **2,600 units**
d. **2,200 units**

v　The budgeted sales for the next 4 quarters are:
　Quarter 1　$192,000
　Quarter 2　$288,000
　Quarter 3　$288,000
　Quarter 4　$336,000

It is estimated that sales will be paid for as follows: 75% of the total will be paid in the quarter that the sales were made. Of the balance, 50% will be paid in the quarter after the sale was made. The remaining will be paid in the quarter after this. The amount of cash received in the third quarter will be:
a. **$276,000**
b. **$240,000**
c. **$144,000**
d. **$324,000**

vi. Alice Ltd. is preparing the production budget for the second quarter. Projected sales (units) are:
　April 600
　May　680
　June　750

The company policy is to have finished goods inventory of 20% of the next month's projected sales. Assuming that there was no opening inventory for April, what should the production quota for May be?
a. **694 units**
b. **680 units**
c. **666 units**
d. **830 units**

vii. The master budget will comprise:
a. **The budgeted Income statement and statement of financial position**
b. **The cash budget**
c. **All the production, sales and cost budgets**
d. **The cash budget, the budgeted Income statement and statement of financial position**

viii. A crockery company makes china cups and saucers. How much clay would they need to buy if:
- a cup uses 100g of clay
- a saucer uses 150g of clay
- it plans to make 450,000 cups and 280,000 saucers
- there is no opening inventory
- it would like to have closing inventories of 4,000kg of clay?

a. 83,000 kg
b. 99,500 kg
c. 87,000 kg
d. 91,000 kg

ix. What is meant by an incremental budget?
  a. A budget prepared form first principles
  b. The variable elements of a budget, excluding fixed costs
  c. A budget that is based on the previous year, adjusted for known changes.
  d. A budget that breaks even.

x. Which of the following statements can be considered to be an advantage of a bottom-up budget?
  a.   Uses the knowledge of all staff to build a fair budget
  b.   The cheapest method of producing a budget
  c.   Reduces the level of budget negotiation between staff
  d.   Prevents slack being built into budgets

17.2 Zeresh Limited provides the following information from its sales budget for 2014.

	Units	Sales price per unit
		$
January	10 000	20
February	11 000	20
March	11 000	21
April	12 000	21
May	12 000	21
June	14 000	24

Additional information
  1. Inventory of finished goods at each month end is maintained at 20% of the units expected to be sold in the following month.
  2. Each unit requires 0.5 kilos of raw materials, which costs $3 a kilo.
  3. Half a month's inventory of raw materials is maintained, based on the expected usage in the following month.
  4. The total production cost of each unit is $11 and this is the value used for inventory valuation.

REQUIRED
(a) (i) Prepare the production budget for each of the five months January to May 2014.
  (ii) Prepare the purchases budget for raw materials for each of the four months January to April 2014. Show purchases of raw materials in both kilos and dollars.
(b) Calculate the value of finished goods and raw materials inventory at both 1 January 2014 and 30 April 2014.
(c) (i) Prepare a summarised manufacturing account for the four-month period ending 30 April 2014.
  (ii) Prepare the trading account section of the income statement for the same period.
(d) State two advantages and two disadvantages to a company of using a budgetary control system.
(UCLES, 2013, AS/A Level Accounting, Syllabus 9706/13, May/June)

17.3 Echoes plc has the following statement of financial position (statement of financial position) at 30 April 2011.

	$000 Cost	$000 Depreciation	$000 N B V
Non-current assets			
Land and buildings	1200	50	1150
Equipment	230	90	140
Motor vehicles	210	115	95
	1640	255	1385
Current assets			
Inventory		150	
Trade receivables		122	
Prepaid rates and insurance		8	
		280	
Current liabilities			
Trade payables	75		
Tax	30		
Cash and cash equivalents	15	(120)	160
			1545
Equity			
Ordinary shares of $0.50 each		800	
Share premium		100	
Retained earnings		645	
		1545	

Sales and purchases budgets have been produced for Echoes plc for the year ending 30 April 2012 as follows:

	$000 Sales	$000 Purchases
May to February	1060	560
March	100	60
April	100	60
Total	1260	680

Other information is as follows:
1. All sales are on credit.
2. 50% of customers pay in the month after sale and the remaining customers pay in the second month.
3. On 1 May 2011 the company is introducing a 5% cash discount for customers paying in the month after sale, applicable to sales made on or after that date.
4. Discount will only be accounted for when funds are received.
5. Purchases accrue evenly over the month. The company pays its suppliers 1½ months after receipt of goods.
6. The company pays rates six months in advance on 1 June and 1 December each year. Each payment amounts to $9000.
7. The company pays an annual premium for insurance, in advance, on 1 October each year. It is expected that in 2011 the premium will be $30 000.
8. All other selling, distribution and administration payments for the year, including wages and salaries, are expected to amount to $184 000.
9. The company plans to modernise its equipment and upgrade its vehicles during the year.
10. It plans to sell all the vehicles for $80 000 and buy new ones at a total cost of
    d. $400 000.
11. It also plans to sell half the equipment for $75 000 and replace it with new equipment costing $310 000.
12. The cost of land and buildings is split $800 000 for the land and $400 000 for the buildings.

13. The company provides a full year's depreciation on non-current assets purchased during the year but none in the year of disposal. Annual depreciation rates are:
    Buildings 2.5% on cost
    Equipment 20% on cost
    Motor vehicles 30% on net book value
14. The company plans to issue 100 000 new shares at a price of $1.70 on 1 July 2011 to part fund the purchase of the non-current assets.
15. It also plans to issue $300 000 6% debentures, redeemable in 2028, on 1 July 2011. The first interest payment on the debentures will be paid on 30 April 2012.
16. Tax is provided for at 20% of profit after finance charges and is paid ten months after the financial year end.
17. Inventory is expected to increase by 10% over the year.
18. The company intends to pay a dividend of $0.03 per share on 30 June 2011.

REQUIRED

(a) Calculate the bank balance expected on 30 April 2012.

(b) Prepare the forecast income statement (profit and loss account) for the year ending 30 April 2012.

(c) Prepare the statement of financial position (statement of financial position) at 30 April 2012.

(UCLES, 2011, AS/A Level Accounting, Syllabus 9706/41, May/June)

17.5 The trade receivables figure for the year ended 31 December 20x5 was $27 000. There is a collection period of 30 days.

The budget for the year ended 31 December 20x6 provides for an increased turnover of 50 % with the relevant collection period being increased to 60 days.

Required:

What will the year-end trade receivables figure be?

17.6. You are given the following budgeted figures:

	$
Sales	1100 000
Direct materials	150 000
Direct labour	300 000
Fixed overheads	400 000
Profit	250 000

If the volume of sales for the product increased by 20 %, what would be the increase in profit?

CHAPTER 18
INVESTMENT APPRAISAL

Q. Define: Investment

Ans. An investment is the purchase or the creation of non-current assets with the sole objective of making future gains. e.g. purchasing a machine, a plant

Q. What is investment appraisal?

Ans. Investment appraisal is the process of evaluating the attractiveness of an investment proposal. The proposal could be acquiring or replacing a non-current asset, opening a new branch or introducing a new product. It is an integral part of capital budgeting and may be applied to areas other than those mentioned above e.g. marketing, training etc.

Q. What are some of the questions that should be answered when making an investment decision?

Ans. Here are some of the questions that need to be answered:
- What are the expected profits from the investment?
- How much will the investment cost?
- Does the company have the funds to finance the cost?
- How long will it take to pay back the investment?
- When will the investment start to yield returns?
- Could the money being used to finance the investment be used elsewhere to yield higher returns?
- Have social, environmental and political factors been taken into account in addition to the economic factors?

Q. Define:
1. Incremental profits
2. Sunk costs
3. Opportunity costs

Ans.
1. <u>Incremental profits:</u> These are additional profits based on additional benefits and costs incurred as a result of the investing in the project.
2. <u>Sunk costs:</u> These costs are retrospective or past costs that have already been incurred and cannot be recovered. Sunk costs do not have a bearing on future decisions. They are also known as 'stranded costs' e.g. the use of an existing plant required to produce a new product.
3. <u>Opportunity costs:</u> It is the cost of sacrificing the second best choice available to the company who has picked among several mutually exclusive choices. e.g. If a company diverts some resources from what they are being used for now to another project, then the benefits that accrue from the present use of the resources is the opportunity cost.

Q. Name four financial techniques of investment appraisal.

Ans. The four financial techniques of investment appraisal are:
1. Payback period
2. Accounting rate of return
3. Net present value
4. Internal rate of return

Q. Write a short note on: The Payback Period.

Ans. This is the period required for the return (in the form of net cash flow) on an investment to repay the sum of the investment. In other words, it measures how long an investment takes to 'pay for itself'.

It is calculated as:

$$\frac{\text{Cost of the project}}{\text{Annual cash outflow} - \text{annual cash inflow}}$$

The time value of money is not taken into account. All things being equal, a shorter payback period is better than a longer one.

Exhibit

A project costs $120,000. It is expected to return $10,000 net cash flow annually.

Required: Calculate the payback period of the project in years.

Solution:

Payback period = $\frac{\text{Cost of the project}}{\text{Annual cash inflows}}$

$$= \frac{120,000}{10,000}$$

$$= 12 \text{ years}$$

Q. What are the advantages Payback?

Ans. The advantages are:

1. It is easy to calculate
2. It can be used to compare different projects
3. As it uses cash flow, it is less subjective than methods that use profit.
4. Short payback periods allow for increased liquidity thus enabling the business to grow
5. This method underlines the importance of cash flows – their timing and size

Q. What are the disadvantages of Payback?

Ans. The disadvantages are:

1. It ignores the benefits that accrue after the payback period. Hence, it does not measure overall profitability.
2. It ignores the time value of money.
3. Projects with the same payback may have different cash flows. Hence the project with bigger cash flows in the earlier years may be chosen over a more profitable project that had better cash flows in the later years.

Exercise 18.1

You are given the following information regarding projects A and B:

	Project A $	Project B $
Year 0 (initial cost)	(100,000)	(100,000)
Year 1 Net cash flow	20,000	10,000
Year 2	30,000	25,000
Year 3	50,000	30,000
Year 4	15,000	40,000
Year 5	16,000	45,000

Required:

a. Calculate the payback periods for projects A and B

b. State, with reasons which project is more attractive.

Exercise 18.2

You are given the following information regarding Machine 1 and Machine 2:

	Machine 1	Machine 2
	$	$
Year 0 (initial cost)	(90,000)	(90,000)
Year 1 Net cash flow	15,000	20,000
Year 2 Net cash flow	16,000	24,000
Year 3 Net cash flow	25,000	26,000
Year 4 Net cash flow	21,000	30,000

Required:

a. Calculate the payback periods for each machine

b. State, with reasons which machine the company should purchase.

Q. Write a short note on: Accounting Rate of Return

Ans. <u>Accounting Rate of Return:</u> It is the average profit expressed as a percentage of the average investment.

The formula is:

ARR = <u>avg profit (incremental revenues – incremental exps including depreciation) x 100</u>
                                    Average investment

Average here means arithmetic mean. The profit is incremental operating profit and the investment is the net book value (after depreciation and amortisation) of the asset tied up in the project. CIE students will calculate the average investment using the following formula:

Average investment = <u>cost of the assets acquired</u>
                                            2

ARR is often used internally to aid decision making when selecting projects. It can also be used to measure the performance of those projects. It is similar to payback in that it does not take into account the time value of money and does not adjust for greater risk to longer term forecasts. However, payback leads to overly conservative decisions as opposed to ARR that tends to favour higher risk decisions.

The ARR is also known as the Average rate of return or the unadjusted rate of return or the financial statement method.

Q. What are the advantages of ARR?

Ans. The advantages are:
1. It is easy to calculate
2. Expected profitability can be compared with present profitability

Q. What are the disadvantages of ARR?

Ans. The disadvantages are:
1. It does not take into account the time value of money
2. Because it is wholly unadjusted for non-cash items, any method of selecting investments based on it is necessarily seriously flawed.
3. It can be misleading if the alternatives have different cash flow patterns.
4. Many projects do not have constant incremental revenues and expenses over their useful lives causing the ARR to fluctuate from year to year. The project may also appear to be desirable in some years and undesirable in other years.

Exhibit:

A company is contemplating purchasing equipment for an additional processing line. This processing line will increase revenues by $90,000 annually. Incremental cash operating expenses are forecasted at $40,000 p.a. The equipment would cost $180,000 and have a life of nine years with no residual value.

Required:
Calculate the Accounting Rate of Return.

Solution:

ARR = $\dfrac{(\$90,000 \text{ Incremental revenues}) - (\$40,000 \text{ Cash operating expenses} + \$20,000 \text{ Depreciation})}{\$180,000 \text{ (initial investment)}/2} \times 100$

$= \dfrac{\$30,000}{\$90,000} \times 100$

$= 33.3\%$

Exercise 18.3

Taurangi Strawberry Farm, hires people on a part-time basis to pack strawberries. The cost of this labour intensive- process is $30,000 per year. The company is investigating the purchase of an automated system that would cost $90,000 and have a life of 15-years with no scrap value. It would cost $10,000 per year to operate and maintain.

Required:
Calculate the Accounting Rate of Return

Exercise 18.4

A project costing $200,000 is under investigation. The project is estimated to earn a total net profit of $100,000 over five years. This does not include depreciation of $20,000. Further investigation reveals that the company will save $10,000 in costs if the project was used.

Required:
Calculate the Accounting Rate of Return.

Q. Define: Time value of money
Ans. It recognises that the value of money today is worth more than the same amount in the future. e.g. $1 received now, if invested @10% p.a. compound interest will amount to $1.10 in one year's time. Hence if $0.909 were invested now at 10% compound interest, it would amount to $1 in a year's time. Hence the present value of $0.909 is $1 today.

Q. Why is it advisable to discount predicted cash receipts to present day values?
Ans. As with any comparison like should be compared with like. Hence if future cash receipts are to be compared with the present outlay, they should be discounted to present day values.

Q. Define: Net Present Value (NPV)
Ans. The Net Present Value of a project or investment is calculated by discounting cash flows from the project in the future and comparing it with the initial investment in the project. A positive NPV suggests that the project is worthy of further consideration – the larger the value of NPV, the better.

Q. State one advantage of NPV.
Ans. NPV takes into account the time value of money and provides a single number that summarises all of the cash flows over the entire useful life of the project.

Q. State one disadvantage of NPV.

Ans. It is more complicated to calculate than ARR or payback. However, with a suitable computer programme, this problem could be eliminated.

Q. Define: cost of capital

Ans. The cost of capital is the rate of interest to be paid on a loan raised to finance a project or investment. If the finance is being raised out of capital subscribed by ordinary shareholders who expect a dividend of 5% then the cost of capital is 5%. If the capital is raised from the issue of preference shares or debentures, then the rate of interest to be paid would be the cost of capital.

Q. What is a discounting factor?

Ans. This is the value used to discount cash flows. They can be calculated, but are available from tables

Exhibit

Lambert Ltd is considering the purchase of a new machine and must choose between model G and model H costing $100,000 each. The estimated receipts for the two products are:

	Model G	Model H
	$	$
Year 1	30,000	20,000
Year 2	25,000	35,000
Year 3	20,000	40,000
Year 4	15,000	50,000
Year 5	35,000	15,000

Their cost of capital is 10%.

Required:

a. Calculate which of the two models Lambert Ltd should purchase

Solution:

Year	Discounting Factor 10%	G $	NPV $	H $	NPV $
0	1	(100,000)	(100,000)	(100,000)	(100,000)
1	0.909	30,000	27,270	20,000	18,180
2	0.826	25,000	20,650	35,000	28,910
3	0.751	20,000	15,020	40,000	30,040
4	0.683	15,000	10,245	50,000	34,150
5	0.621	35,000	21,735	15,000	9315
			(5,080)		20,595

Model H has a positive NPV of $20,595 indicating that the future net receipts at present day value exceed the initial cost of the investment. Hence Lambert Ltd. should purchase model H and not model G which has a negative NPV.

Exercise 18.5

A company is contemplating buying equipment at a cost of $80,000. This equipment will save the company $40,000 per annum in operating costs over the next three years at the end of which it will have no scrap value. The capital cost is 10%p.a.

Required

Calculate the NPV

Exercise 18.6

Bigbuck Ltd. is considering purchasing a new machine. It has two choices: Bamble and Camble. Bamble has a production capacity of 12,000 units per year and costs $80,000. Camble costs $120,000 and has a production capacity of 14,000 units per year. Both machines have an estimated useful life of 5 years and will be depreciated @ 20% p.a. using the straight line method. Each unit can be sold at $8.

The costs of production are:

Bamble	Camble
$ 6/unit	$5 per unit

Required:

Using a rate of 15%, calculate the NPVs for the two machines. State which of the two machines Bigbuck Ltd. should consider purchasing and why.

Q. What is an Internal Rate of Return?

Ans. The Internal Rate of Return is the discounting rate which equates the discounted net receipts from a project to its cost. It is the rate at which the NPV is zero. It is therefore the rate at which the NPV of costs (negative cash flows) of an investment equals the NPV of the benefits (positive cash flows) of an investment. (See diagram)

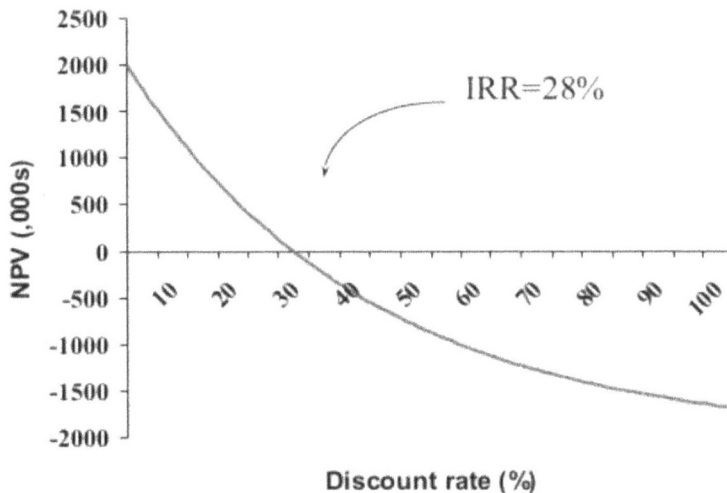

Q. Outline the two steps to be followed to calculate the IRR.

Ans. The steps are:

1. Use two different rates to discount cash flow. The rates have to be sufficiently far apart to give one positive and one negative NPV.

2. Use the formula:

   IRR = X + [pq x ac]
                  ad

Where X = rate giving the positive NPV

pq= difference between the two rates

ac = positive NPV

ad = Positive + negative NPVs (disregard the signs)

Exhibit

A company has $100,000 to invest in a project. The net cash flows for each of the first five years is estimated to be $28,000.

Required:

Calculate the IRR using the rates 10% and 14%.

Solution:

NPV at 10% = 100,000 – [28000 x (0,909+0.826 + 0.751+0.683+0.621)]

=$6,120

NPV at 14% = 100,000 – [28000 – (0.877+0.769+0.675+0.592+0.519)]

= $(3,904)

IRR = 10% +(4%x___6120___) = 12.44%

6120+3904

Exercise 18.7

Kasum Ltd are considering investing in a project which has an initial outlay of $20,000 which they will borrow @14%p.a. If their forecasted cash flow per year is $6,000, calculate the IRR and advise Kasum Ltd. whether or not they should go ahead with the venture.

Q. Outline the advantages and disadvantages of the IRR.

Ans. Advantages

1. The IRR is an indicator of the efficiency and yield of an investment as it is expressed in a percentage. In contrast the NPV is an indicator of the value or magnitude of an investment.

2. An investment is acceptable if the IRR is greater than the cost of capital. If a firm has shareholders, and the IRR exceeds the cost of capital, then the investment will meet with their approval as the investment will economically profitable.

3. The IRR can be used to compare capital projects. The projects with the highest IRR will be the best investment, all things being equal (including risk).

Disadvantages

1. The IRR can be very difficult to calculate as it is dependent on the timing and variances of net cash flow.

2. Without a computer or financial calculator, the IRR can only be computed by trial and error.

3. All cash flows are assumed to be reinvested at the same discount rate, although in reality this will not be the case especially in long term projects.

Exercise 18.8

The directors of Joloss Plc intend to purchase an additional machine to manufacture one of the new products. Two machines are being considered: Milligan and Bentine. The company depreciates its machinery using the straight line method. The company will borrow the money required to purchase the machine and pay interest of 10% per annum on the loan. Estimates for the machine are as follows:

	Milligan	Bentine
	$	$
Cost	100,000	130,000
Receipts: year 1	70,000	72,000
2	80,000	84,000
3	90,000	90,000
4	70,000	80,000

Useful life of the machine: 4 years   4 years

Value at the end of its life   nil   nil

Note: These costs include the charges for depreciation and interest on the loans.

Present value of $1	10%	20%
Year 1	0.909	0.833
Year 2	0.826	0.694
Year 3	0.751	0.579
Year 4	0.683	0.482

Required:

(i)   **Calculate the net present value of each machine. (Base your calculations on the cost of capital)**

(ii)   **State, with your reason, which machine Joloss plc should purchase.**

The directors require the machine to produce a return on outlay of not less than 25%.

REQUIRED

(iii) Calculate the internal rate of return on the machine you have selected in (ii) to see if it meets the required return on outlay.

Q. What is meant by the term: Sensitivity Analysis?

Ans. Sensitivity Analysis is a management accounting tool used to determine how sensitive the outcome of a project is to variations in costs and receipts. It is an important tool as good decisions relating to projects and investments should be based on realistic assessments of costs and receipts. Due to the long time horizon involved in making capital investment decisions, forecasts may be based on unreliable data. The problem is compounded due to the large sums of money involved. Hence the importance of sensitivity analysis to aid decision-making.

Exhibit:

An investment of $1m will generate net receipts of $300,000 over a period of 5 years. The cost of capital is 10%.

The NPV = [(300,000 x 3.792*) – 1,000,000] = $137,300

*3.791 = 0.090 + 0.826 + 0.751 + 0.683 + 0.622

To generate a negative NPV:

NPV @ 18% = [(300,000 x 3.127) – 1,000,000] = $(61,900)

IRR = 10 + (8 x $\underline{137,300)}$ = 15.5%
           137000+61900

This investment should be accepted as the IRR is greater than the cost of capital of 10%. However, the investment should not be considered if the NPV is negative. This situation will result if:

The NPV exceeds the proposed investment by $137,300 i.e. $\underline{137300}$ x 100   = 13.37%
                                          1000000

OR the NPV falls short of the expected $137,300 i.e. $\underline{137300}$ x 100   = 12.07%
                                                1137300

OR the cost of capital increases to 15.5% or above, an increase of 55% on the present cost

$\underline{(15.5 – 10)}$ x 100
   10

Sensitivity analysis is more complex in practice, however, as it is highly likely that several variables could change from the forecasted in a dynamic business environment.

Exercise 18.9

Manchal is considering an investment of $400,000 at the cost of 8%. The net receipts are forecasted to be $110,000 for five years.

Required: Show how the acceptability of the investment is sensitive to changes in the initial investment amount, net receipts and cost of capital.

18.1. Choose the correct alternative:

i.   Investment appraisal is:
   a. **Ensuring that the business has enough assets to operate**
   b. **Ensuring that the business has enough money to purchase assets**
   c. **Ensuring that assets pay for themselves in the shortest possible time**
   d. **Evaluating the costs and benefits of the proposed investment**

ii.   What is NOT relevant when appraising an investment using the payback period method?
   a. **The total cash flows generated by the asset**
   b. **The timing of the first cash flow**
   c. **The cash flows generated by the asset up to the payback period**
   d. **The cost of the asset**

iii.   A capital investment will be given the go-ahead if its NPV is:
   a. **Zero**
   b. **Positive**
   c. **Negative**
   d. **None of the above**

iv.   Davina & Sisters want to make an investment of $120,000. The investment will generate the following net cash

flows:	$
Year 1	30,000
Year 2	40,000
Year 3	15,000
Year 4	40,000
Year 5	25,000
Year 6	35,000

   If the discount rate is 20%, find the payback period.
   a. **5 years**   b. **6 years**   c. **4 years**   d. **None of these**

v. Which of the following is the discount factor used to appraise capital investment a measure of?
   a. **The present rate of inflation**
   b. **The opportunity cost of capital**
   c. **The current commercial bank interest rate**
   d. **The opportunity cost of capital of all businesses in the industry**

18. 2. You are given the following information about a proposed investment in a project whose estimated life is 5 years"
   a. Cost of machine $90 000
   b. Estimated proceeds of disposal of machine after 5 years $10 000
   c. additional working capital required throughout the project $30 000
   d. additional annual revenue (net) $15 000

Required:
Calculate the accounting rate of return on the project.

18.3. The following information relates to a possible capital investment, costing $900 000.

Yr	cash flow($)	discounted cash flow at 6 %($)	discounted cash flow at 8 %($)
0	(900)	(900)	(900)
1	400	377	370
2	600	534	514
	100	11	(16)

The company has a cost of capital of 8 %.

Will the IRR be greater or less than the cost of capital?

18.4. You are given the following information about an investment in a project:

	$
Initial cost of project	20 000
Total net cash flows	35 000
Present value of cash flows	23 465

Would the business accept the project?

18.5. A company can only invest $1 million in the current period. The table shows 5 projects.

Project	capital requirement (current period) ($m)	NPV ($m)
1	1.2	5.0
2	1.0	2.5
3	0.6	1.5
4	0.4	1.2
5	0.4	1.0

Which project(s) should the company undertake to maximise its shareholders' wealth?

18.6 The directors of Relham Ltd plan to introduce a new product.
A new machine costing $125 000 will be required. It will be sold at the end of five years for $30 000. Machinery is depreciated using the straight line method.
The new product will earn $90 000 revenue annually and incur additional expenditure of $60 000 each year.
The purchase of the new machine will be financed by a loan at 8% per annum.
The following discounting factors are given.

	8%	14%
Year 1	0.926	0.877
2	0.857	0.769
3	0.794	0.675
4	0.735	0.592
5	0.681	0.519

REQUIRED
(a) Calculate for the new product
(i) net present value (NPV)
(ii) internal rate of return (IRR)
(iii) accounting rate of return (ARR)
(UCLES, 2004, AS/A Level Accounting, Syllabus 9706/04, Oct/Nov)

18.7. Ghosh Ltd is considering expanding its business and has to decide between taking on Project A or Project B. Both projects have a life of four years. Equipment is expected to have no scrap value. Other information about the projects is as follows:

	Project A	Project B
Initial outlay	$150 000	$140 000
Annual sales	$100 000	$120 000
Annual purchases	$40 000	$65 000
Other costs as a percentage of sales	8%	5%
Increase in working capital	$10 000	$18 000

Ghosh Ltd uses a cost of capital of 10%. Discounting factors at 10% are as follows:
Year 1 0.909
Year 2 0.826
Year 3 0.751
Year 4 0.683
Using a cost of capital of 10% Project B has a net present value of $15 281.

REQUIRED

(a) For each of the two projects calculate the following:
    (i) the annual net cash flow
    (ii) the accounting rate of return
    (iii) the payback period.

(b) Calculate the net present value of Project A only.

(c) State two limitations of each of the following:
    (i) accounting rate of return
    (ii) the payback period
    (iii) the net present value.

(d) State which of the two projects Ghosh Ltd should select. Give reasons for your answer.

(UCLES, 2010, AS/A Level Accounting, Syllabus 9706/41, May/June)

www.ingramcontent.com/pod-product-compliance
Lightning Source LLC
Chambersburg PA
CBHW061105210326
41597CB00022B/3991